GROWING IN FAITH

The Church:
A Living Heritage

Dear Parent,

As your son or daughter begins to study **The Church: A Living Heritage,** we would like to give you a general view of the text, which is a part of our religious education program GROWING IN FAITH.

The Church: A Living Heritage tells the story of Christ's Church, the People of God, through the lives of its heroes and saints. The text shows how the Church has fulfilled its mission in every age — teaching God's word, celebrating the sacred mysteries, and serving God's people. Maps and time lines in the book help students place events and people in their historical context. The last chapter of the book gives students an introduction to the fascinating story of the Church in our own United States.

The seventeen chapters of **The Church: A Living Heritage** are subdivided into lessons. Each lesson concludes with a Recall and Reflect section. The questions in that section afford the students both a checkup on the lesson and an opportunity to reflect on the meaning of the lesson for Catholics today.

Within each chapter, special features add to the insight and depth of the basic text. The feature Words to Live By includes quotations from the Bible and other inspirational sources. The feature Sidelights on Church History adds interesting facets about the Church's long history. Some tell the stories of men and women who lived heroic lives for Christ in many different times and places. Others teach about Church feasts and practices.

At the end of each chapter is a Review and Celebrate page. That page includes the following: (1) a Doctrinal Summary, which points up the religious content of the chapter; (2) a Religious Vocabulary, which lists important religious terms introduced or defined; (3) Review Questions, which help the teacher find out how well the students have grasped the chapter's content; and (4) a Prayer Celebration, or common prayer, which is based upon the lessons in the chapter. This prayer service offers the class an opportunity to celebrate together, giving thanks to God for His blessings to the Church and asking for His help in their own lives.

The content and approach of **The Church: A Living Heritage** and the other texts in the GROWING IN FAITH program are in accordance with *Sharing the Light of Faith: National Catechetical Directory for Catholics of the United States,* published by the United States Catholic Conference, Department of Education, and approved by the National Conference of Catholic Bishops. We would be pleased to have your comments about **The Church: A Living Heritage** and the other books in the GROWING IN FAITH program.

GROWING IN FAITH

Nihil Obstat
Reverend Anselm Murray, O.S.B.
Censor Librorum
July 15, 1980

Imprimatur
✠ Most Reverend Frank J. Rodimer
Bishop of Paterson
July 25, 1980

The *nihil obstat* and *imprimatur* are official declarations that a book or pamphlet is free of doctrinal and moral error. No implication is contained therein that those who have granted the *nihil obstat* and *imprimatur* agree with the contents, opinions, or statements expressed.

The Church: A Living Heritage

Reverend Cyprian Davis, O.S.B.

Professor of Church History at the St. Meinrad
School of Theology, St. Meinrad, Indiana

SILVER BURDETT COMPANY

Morristown, New Jersey
Glenview, Illinois • Palo Alto • Dallas • Atlanta

About the Author

Father Cyprian Davis, O.S.B., is a professor of Church history at the St. Meinrad School of Theology, St. Meinrad, Indiana. A member of the Benedictine community of St. Meinrad Archabbey, Father Davis is the abbey's archivist. He received a bachelor of arts degree from St. Meinrad College and holds graduate degrees from the Catholic University of America and the University of Louvain, Belgium. In 1977, Louvain granted Father Davis the degree of Docteur en Sciences Historiques. Father Davis has authored several articles for the *New Catholic Encyclopedia* and has written for many learned publications. He is a member of the American Catholic Historical Association, the Society of American Archivists, and the Society of Indiana Archivists.

Acknowledgments

Excerpts from *The New American Bible*, © Confraternity of Christian Doctrine 1970, are used by permission of the copyright owner. Excerpts from the English translation of the Roman Missal, © 1973, International Committee on English in the Liturgy, Inc. (ICEL). All rights reserved. Page 35: "Prayer of Self-dedication to Jesus Christ"; page 145, "Canticle of the Sun"; page 195, "Gift," all from *Lord Hear Our Prayer*, compiled by Thomas McNally, C.S.C., and William G. Storey, D.M.S. Copyright © 1978 by Ave Maria Press, Notre Dame, Indiana 46556. Used with permission of publisher.   Page 91: Excerpt from *Decree on the Bishops' Pastoral Office in the Church*, 2, from *The Documents of Vatican II*, Abbot-Gallagher edition. Copyright 1966 America Press, Inc., 106 W. 56 St., New York, New York 10019. Reprinted by permission.   Pages 101, 107: *Declaration on the Relation of the Church to Non-Christian Religions*, 3, 5; page 169, *Decree on Ecumenism*: 3, page 219, *Decree on the Apostolate of the Laity*, 12; page 241, *Pastoral Constitution on the Church in the Modern World*, 42, all published by the United States Catholic Conference, 1312 Massachusetts Avenue, N.W., Washington, D.C. 20005. Page 143: Prayer "For the Needy" by Saint Thomas Aquinas from *PRAYER FOR EACH DAY* by Jose Feder. Copyright © 1974 by the Missionary Society of St. Paul the Apostle in the State of New York. Reprinted by permission of Paulist Press.   Page 221: Mary's Prayer: Magnificat from *Living Water: Prayers of Our Heritage* by Carl J. Pfeifer and Janaan Manternach. Copyright © 1978 by the Missionary Society of St. Paul the Apostle in the State of New York. Reprinted by permission of Paulist Press.   Inside back cover: Morning Offering, Act of Faith, Act of Hope, Act of Love — prayers from *WORSHIP II: A Hymnal for Roman Catholic Parishes*. Copyright © 1975 by G. I. A. Publications, Inc. Reprinted by permission.

CONTENTS

UNIT FOUR: The Church—Needing Reform

UNIT FIVE: The Church—Meeting New Challenges

SPECIAL FEATURES

PRAYER CELEBRATIONS

A Prayer Celebration, or common prayer, based on
the lessons in the chapter, appears on the
Review and Celebrate page at the end of each chapter.
Prayer Celebrations are found on the following pages:

SIDELIGHTS ON CHURCH HISTORY

CHARTS

MAPS

Introduction

WHY WE STUDY CHURCH HISTORY

Jesus in His Church Christians believe that Jesus Christ is the central person in history. We believe this because God sent His Son, Jesus, to become man and dwell among us. We believe Jesus is the bridge between God and ourselves. We believe that Jesus founded His Church to bring us God's own life. It is only through Jesus that the world can find its true meaning and destiny. We believe that we are the Church. We are the continuation of Jesus in time and space. We study history to find out what human beings have done in the past. We study Church history to find out how Jesus, through His Church, has acted and continues to act in our lives.

The Church is like the mustard seed in the Gospel of Matthew (13:31–32). The Church began as a tiny community in Jerusalem. Christ had said to His apostle Simon Peter: "I for my part declare to you, you are 'Rock' [which means 'Peter'], and on this rock I will build my church, and the jaws of death shall not prevail against it" (Matthew 16:18). Peter and the other apostles and their successors carried out Jesus' command to "go . . . and make disciples of all the nations" (Matthew 28:19). The Church grew and became what it is today, a catholic—that is, universal—Church, planted among all peoples and cultures.

To grow is to change. The Church is alive with the life of Jesus. It is always growing, changing, developing. Each generation understands and responds to Jesus and His Church in its own way and according to its own time. The study of Church history tells us how people through the ages have lived lives of faith in times of conflict as well as in times of peace. The more we understand how people have responded to Jesus in the past, the more we become aware of our personal response to Him in the present. In every age the Church continues to witness to the gospel. The Church remains the sign that God is with us.

Time Lines In order to understand Church history, it is important to know when things happened. A time line like the one on page 3 shows when certain things happened in a particular time period. It allows us to see the events in relation to each other. The time line lets us see many years of Church history at a single glance. It helps us to organize and remember information.

A time line is found at the beginning and at the end of each unit in this book. The time line at the beginning of the unit tells us just where we are in time as we begin to study that part of Church history. The time line at the end of the unit gives us the dates of important events that took place within the time span covered by the unit.

UNIT ONE

The Church—Beginning in the Spirit

The Church was born on the first Pentecost, when the Holy Spirit came into an
upstairs room in Jerusalem like a great wind and fire.

1

Early Christian Communities

About 6 B.C.	Birth of Jesus
About A.D. 29	Pentecost: Birth of the Church
A.D. 313	Edict of Milan: End of persecutions
325	Council of Nicaea
800	Pope Leo III crowns Charlemagne emperor
1049	Pope Leo IX elected: Church reform begins
1054	Schism between Rome and Constantinople
1095	Pope Urban II preaches First Crusade
1215	Fourth Lateran Council: Great pastoral council of Middle Ages
1453	Constantinople falls to the Turks
1521	Diet of Worms: Luther breaks with Church
1545	Council of Trent begins
1789	Crisis of the French Revolution
1870	First Vatican Council
1962	Second Vatican Council begins
1978	John Paul II becomes pope

The Church began in an upstairs room in the city of Jerusalem. After Jesus had ascended to His Father, a handful of men and women gathered together for seven weeks in that room to pray for the coming of the Holy Spirit. The twelve apostles were there as well as Mary, the mother of Jesus, and other men and women who were disciples of Jesus. On **Pentecost** (which means "fiftieth day"), the Holy Spirit came into that upstairs room like a great wind and fire. He molded those few people into a community of faith and hope, bound together in love. They became God's people. They became His **Church**, which means a "community called together." This is why we celebrate Pentecost as the birthday of the Church of Jesus.

Filled with the Holy Spirit, this little band of people found the courage to carry out Jesus' command to "go . . . and make disciples of all the nations" (Matthew 28:19).

The first Christian community came into being in Jerusalem that very day. The **Acts of the Apostles** in the New Testament tells us of the wonders that happened when some three thousand people were baptized before nightfall (Acts 2:1–41).

THE EARLY CHURCH

Growth of Christian Communities The Church began in Jerusalem, in the Roman Empire. As early as the middle of the first century A.D., Christian communities were found in many other places. The story of the first groups of followers of Jesus is told in the Acts of the Apostles and in the **epistles**, or letters, of Saint Paul. By A.D. 65 there were Christian communities in many of the cities of Syria, Asia Minor, Greece, and even in the city of Rome, the capital of the Roman Empire. As you can see on the map on the next page, Saint Paul visited many of those communities in his four missionary journeys.

The Roman government quickly became aware that the number of Christian communities was increasing. And it was not long before the Romans began to persecute Christians as enemies of the state. As early as A.D. 67 the apostles Peter and Paul had both been put to death in Rome.

Persecution of the Christians *Persecution* means hurting other people, hunting them down, putting them in prison, or killing them, because they are different. Throughout history, people have been persecuted for many reasons—because of their race, their politics, their religion, and many other things. The Roman state persecuted Christians because of their religion.

This persecution of Christians did not occur every day. Sometimes there were long periods when the Christians were not harmed. They never knew, however, when persecution would begin in a certain place. A person needed a great deal of courage to be a faithful Christian. Not all were faithful. That is why, very early, the Christians remembered those who remained faithful to the death. They honored them as saints.

A Reason for Persecution In the Roman Empire there were many religions. The Romans were very tolerant. People could honor as many gods as they wished. But there was also an official, or state, religion in Rome. The people were expected to make offerings to the state gods of Rome and to the emperor as well, because the Romans thought of their rulers as divine; that is, they honored their rulers as gods. To make an offering, such as incense, to the gods

Saints Peter (left) and Paul both became martyrs. They were put to death in Rome. Peter was crucified; Paul was beheaded.

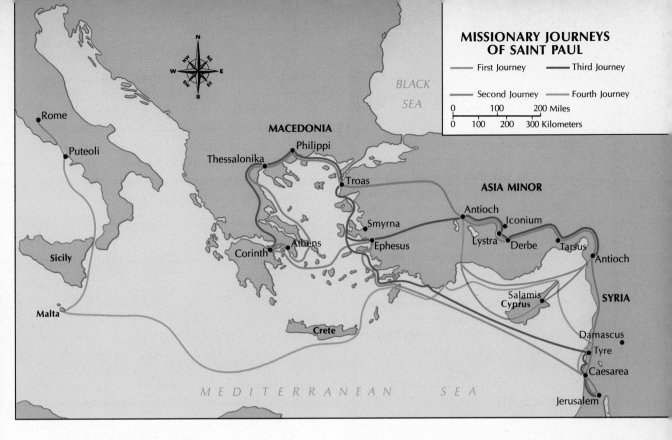

MISSIONARY JOURNEYS OF SAINT PAUL

First Journey   Third Journey

Second Journey   Fourth Journey

0   100   200 Miles

0   100   200   300 Kilometers

BLACK SEA

Rome

Puteoli

MACEDONIA

Philippi

Thessalonika

Troas

ASIA MINOR

Antioch

Iconium

Smyrna

Lystra

Derbe

Tarsus

Ephesus

Antioch

Sicily

Corinth

Athens

Salamis

Cyprus

SYRIA

Malta

Crete

Damascus

Tyre

Caesarea

MEDITERRANEAN SEA

Jerusalem

and to the emperor was a sign of patriotism. And the Roman government was very concerned about people's loyalty. Refusal to worship the emperor branded one as a traitor. But Christians did refuse to offer incense to the emperor and did refuse to worship him as a god. As Christians, they worshiped only Jesus and the One who sent Him. The Roman government, therefore, began to persecute Christians as enemies of the state.

Rome knew about the Jewish religion and had always excused the Jewish people from offering incense to the emperor. But the government did not know much about the Christians and their religion. Because they were being persecuted, the Christians worshiped in secret. They were also a minority in the Roman world. Even today, people in the majority often persecute minorities because they are different.

Martyrs for Jesus From the beginning, Christians were persecuted, even killed, because they believed in Christ. The Acts of the Apostles tells the story of Stephen. This young man so angered people by preaching about Jesus that

> Those who listened to his words were stung to the heart. . . . they rushed at him as one man, dragged him out of the city [Jerusalem] and began to stone him. . . . As Stephen was being stoned he could be heard praying, "Lord Jesus, receive my spirit." He fell to his knees and cried out in a loud voice, "Lord do not hold this sin against them." And with that he died.
>
> —Acts 7:54–60

Thus when the early Christians refused to worship the Roman gods and emperors, they had to be prepared to die for their faith. Those who died became **martyrs** (mär′tərz)* for Jesus. The word *martyr* is a

*Note: The Key to Pronunciation is on the inside back cover.

An Early Christian Secret Sign

During times of persecution, the early Christians used many secret signs and codes to show that they believed in Jesus Christ. One of these signs was the fish. The fish stands for life and happiness in many cultures. In Japan the fish means "long life." Every year flags in the shape of a fish are flown on the Japanese festival of Children's Day, wishing the children long life.

Christians believe Christ has come into the world so that all people may live, and live happily. When early Christians saw a drawing of a fish, they knew other Christians were nearby.

Another reason the early Christians used the fish as a sign is that fish can only be found in fresh, or "living," waters. And Christians are brought to share in Jesus' life through the living water of Baptism.

Finally, in the early Church most people spoke or understood Greek. The Greek word for *fish* is **ICHTHYS** (ik'thəs). In Greek it would look something like this: **I X Ɵ Y C.** To early Christians each letter stood for an important religious word:

I (our J) stood for **JESUS**
X (our CH) stood for **CHRIST**
Ɵ stood for **GOD'S**
Y stood for **SON**
C (our S) stood for **SAVIOR**

"JESUS CHRIST, SON OF GOD, SAVIOR"

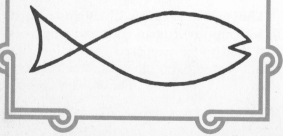

Greek word for "witness." When one speaks up for a friend, one is bearing witness for him or her. When one speaks up for Jesus and says one is a Christian, that person is a witness for Christ. And when one speaks up for Him, knowing that death is the penalty, one is the bravest kind of witness: one is a martyr.

Recall and Reflect

1. When and where can we say that the Church was born?
2. Why were the early Christians persecuted?
3. What was a martyr in the early Church?
4. Individuals and groups today are sometimes persecuted. It may be happening to someone you know right now. What can you do to help a friend deal with persecution and prejudice? How can you deal with them yourself?
5. Have you ever "persecuted" someone because that person was in some way different from you or your friends? Why did you do this? How do you feel about it now?

SAINT IGNATIUS AND SAINT CLEMENT: BISHOPS AND MARTYRS

Prisoner for Christ His name was Ignatius. He was a very important person. But now he was a prisoner. Soldiers were taking him to the distant city of Rome. Along the way, they stopped to rest. One such resting place was a large town called Philadelphia in the country we now call Turkey. At that time, about A.D. 110, Turkey was called Asia Minor and was part of the vast Roman Empire.

Ignatius was a follower of Christ. He was a Christian. He was also the **bishop** of one of the largest cities in the Roman Empire. This was Antioch in Syria; it is now the city of Antakya (ant′ə kyä′), Turkey. *Bishop* means "supervisor." A bishop was the Christian leader of a city. Bishops are the successors of the apostles. Successors are those who take the places of others who will no longer be there to do the job.

Ignatius was a prisoner because he was a Christian. He would not believe in the religion of the Roman Empire. As a Christian he could only worship the true God. So according to Roman law, he had to be punished. He was to be taken to Rome to face death. He was to be torn apart by lions in the Roman games.

The Bishop's Seven Letters When Ignatius was on his way to Rome to be put to death, many Christians in the towns along the way came to see the brave old man. Ignatius was a hero because of his witness to Christ. At two places he wrote letters to Christian communities. He wrote seven letters.

These seven letters are important today. They are some of the oldest Christian writings, and they tell us many things about Christians in the early Church. The letters tell us about their beliefs, the organization of their communities, and their way of worship.

In the early churches the bishop was a sign of unity for the Christian community which he served. Remember, Ignatius was a bishop. In his letters he tells Christians to stay close to their bishops. Ignatius points out that in each church the bishop and his **priests** stand for Jesus and the apostles. Christians are to be united to Jesus by obeying their bishop.

Ignatius also wrote about the **Eucharist** (ü′kər ist). By *Eucharist* he meant the Body and Blood of Christ under the forms of bread and wine. He was also referring to the sacrifice of the Mass. At that time the Christian communities were so small that

The Eucharist is the heart of our Christian life. In receiving Holy Communion we express our oneness with Christ in His Church.

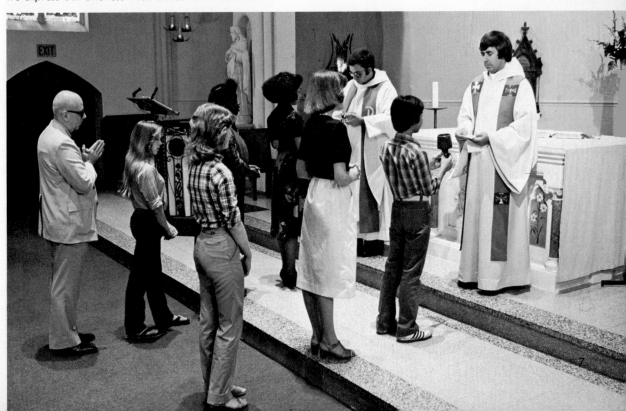

7

each bishop could celebrate the eucharistic liturgy for all his people. Ignatius said that this was a sign of oneness, of unity for the community. He also called the Eucharist a "medicine for the soul." He spoke of Christ as the "physician," or doctor. Ignatius spoke of the bishop as the "father to his people." He spoke of Sunday, the first day of the week, as the "Lord's Day."

Ignatius was one of the first to call the Christian Church **"Catholic."** All the little churches at that time made up the one whole Church and were part of one big community. The big community was universal, or catholic. Today this big community still has the name "Catholic Church."

A Letter to the Church in Rome Ignatius, who was on his way to Rome to die, wanted very much to be a martyr for Christ. He called martyrs "athletes for Christ," because the arenas where they were often put to death were used for athletic contests and games. Just as athletes always had to keep in shape, so Christians always had to be ready to die for Jesus. The apostle Paul had used the same figure of speech about Christians in his first letter to the Corinthian church. Paul said that "athletes deny themselves all sorts of things. They do this to win a crown of leaves that withers, but we [do it to win] a crown that is imperishable" (1 Corinthians 9:25).

Ignatius wanted so much to be a martyr that he wrote a letter to the Roman Christians begging them to do nothing to prevent his death in the arena. In brave words Ignatius said:

> Please let me be thrown to the wild beasts; through them I can reach God. I am God's wheat; I am ground by the teeth of the wild beasts that I may end as the pure bread of Christ.

In another place Ignatius said that he wanted to be ground up by the lions' teeth like grains of wheat are ground up to make the flour that is baked into bread. Ignatius was thinking of the bread that becomes the Body of Christ in Holy Communion. He knew Christians would understand him.

Ignatius' letter to the Christians in Rome is important for another reason. In it Ignatius greeted the Church at Rome as having a most important position. He gives Rome a very special place among the early Christian communities.

Saint Ignatius, bishop and martyr, was taken to Rome as a prisoner for Christ. He was killed by lions in a Roman arena about A.D. 110.

The Bishop as Leader You can see how the letters of Ignatius are important today because of the information they hold about the Church at the beginning of the second century. They are full of information about Christian unity, about the Eucharist, about leadership, and about martyrdom. Ignatius is among the first to tell us that many Christian communities now had one bishop as the leader and that this bishop was helped by priests and **deacons**. Ignatius tells us that the bishop was the leader, the center, and the teacher of the local church. This is the first clear picture of the structure of the Church as we know it today. The Christian writings before Ignatius had not made it clear that there was a difference between bishops and priests. Nor was it clear that one bishop was the head of each church.

Ignatius the Martyr Ignatius had his wish. He became a martyr. This brave man was killed by lions in a Roman arena about A.D. 110. We honor him as a saint today. His feast day is October 17. On that day each year, when we celebrate the Eucharist in memory of Jesus, we remember Jesus' witness, Ignatius. We ask him to help us witness to Jesus in our lives just as he did.

A Letter from the Bishop of Rome Some ten years before Saint Ignatius of Antioch died for Christ, a bishop of Rome wrote a letter to the Church of Corinth. The bishop's name was Clement. He was the third leader of the Church at Rome after Peter. We know very little about him. Clement was probably bishop of Rome from A.D. 92 to 101. He wrote his letter to the Christian community in Corinth around the year 95.

Corinth was a big, busy city in central Greece. (See the map on page 5.) Paul, the great apostle, had started the Church

Pictured above is the Colosseum in Rome. Built for fights of gladiators and wild beasts, it was sometimes the scene of Christian martyrdoms.

there. Two of Paul's letters were written to the Corinthians. But now Paul was gone, and the Christians of Corinth were in trouble.

Their trouble was with each other. They were not practicing Christian love. Instead, they were bitterly arguing with one another. Some were grouped around one leader, others around another.

So Bishop Clement of Rome wrote the Corinthians a letter. He knew the Christians of the world looked to his little Christian community at Rome for leadership. The Christian community in Rome had become very important. So Clement decided to use his influence as bishop of Rome to help the Christians of Corinth. Clement began: "The Church of God which dwells as a pilgrim in Rome, to the Church of God living in pilgrimage at Corinth. . . ." A **pilgrim** is someone on his or her way to visit a holy place—such as Jerusalem or Rome or Lourdes. Clement meant that the Christians at Rome and Corinth were pilgrims on their way to heaven.

Importance of Clement's Letter Remember, in the days of Clement and Ignatius, each Christian community was separated from the others. Each had its own bishop. Communication was not easy. There were no telephones, radios, or quick mail services. You might think the Christians of the different towns would not care much about each other. But Clement's letter shows that they did care. This is the first reason why his letter is so important. Like Saint Ignatius' letters, it shows that Christian unity was very important for the early Church.

Secondly, Clement's letter shows us that in the second century the Church at Rome was the most important local church. That is why Clement, as bishop of Rome, tried to correct the problems at Corinth. Clement's letter says that Rome had a duty to intervene.

Third, like Ignatius' letter, Bishop Clement's letter mentions the ministries of bishops, priests, deacons, and lay people who served the early Church. Today, the Church still has men and women who minister to others through their roles of leadership and service.

Best of all, Clement's letter shows how the first Christians felt about life and faith. It compares the Church of Jesus to an army. But it is an army like the people of

Pope Saint Clement, the third leader of the Church at Rome after Saint Peter, reminds us that we are pilgrims on our way to heaven.

Israel in the desert, in the Old Testament. The Israelites were united as they fled from Egypt and moved toward the Promised Land. The Church's "Egypt" is the sinful world of slavery—slavery to cruel governments like the Roman government, but especially slavery to sin. The "Promised Land" is the Kingdom of God.

Like Ignatius, Clement of Rome is also venerated as a saint. Like many of his early successors as bishop of Rome, Clement died a martyr. It was A.D. 101. Saint Clement died as a slave in the salt mines.

Recall and Reflect

1. Who was Saint Ignatius of Antioch?
2. What do Ignatius' seven letters tell us about the early Church?
3. Why did Bishop Clement of Rome write to the Church at Corinth?
4. Why is Saint Clement's letter important?
5. How can the letters of the early Church leaders be meaningful for us today?

EARLY HEROES FOR JESUS

Acts of the Martyrs Christians of all ages and of every background have suffered as witnesses for Christ. The early Christians wrote down descriptions of the ways many of the martyrs died. These accounts were called the *Acts of the Martyrs*. The word *acta* in Latin means "great deeds." These writings were passed from one community to another throughout the Christian world. They were passed down from parents to children. In this way the Christians inspired courage and faith in one another. The martyrs were examples of how Christians should live and die.

Two Young Women By the beginning of the third century A.D. (the 200s), the Church had spread to all the shores of the Mediterranean Sea. A very famous report of martyrdom comes from North Africa. It is the story of two young women, Perpetua (pər pech′ü ə) and Felicity (fə lis′ə tē), who faced death with other young Christians at the beginning of the third century in Carthage, a city in North Africa.

Perpetua was a young married woman of about twenty. She was from a wealthy family. She became a convert to Christianity. Shortly after Perpetua had given birth to a baby, she was arrested for being a Christian. Her younger brother was arrested also, along with many other young people. Her father, not a Christian, tried to persuade her to give up her religion and return home to her child. She would not.

Felicity was a young slave in the household of Perpetua. She was with child when she was arrested for being a Christian. Felicity wanted to join Perpetua in martyrdom, but it was against Roman law to kill a woman who was with child. But three days before the Christians were to die in the arena of Carthage, Felicity gave birth to a little girl and was able to join the band of martyrs. They were all killed by wild beasts on May 7, 202. We honor the memories of Saints Perpetua and Felicity today when we ask to share in their fellowship in the first eucharistic prayer of the Mass.

Saint Polycarp One of the oldest accounts in the *Acts of the Martyrs* describes the martyrdom of Saint Polycarp. Polycarp was bishop of Smyrna (smər'nə), now called Izmir (iz mir'), in what is today Turkey. He was a friend of Saint Ignatius. In fact, Saint Ignatius visited Polycarp on his way to Rome to be executed and also wrote him one of his seven letters. Saint Polycarp was an old man of eighty-six when he was arrested for being a Christian. Because he was a bishop, the Roman officials wanted to make an example of him. He was dragged into the crowded arena. The mob of people yelled insults at him and shouted that he should be burned alive. This was done. *The Acts of Saint Polycarp the Martyr* describes how the old man told the people not to nail him down to the wood. The same Christ who would give him strength to stand the flames would also give him the grace to stay in the fire without running away. Polycarp prayed aloud. He thanked God for the grace to be among the martyrs. Polycarp knew that by his death he was joined to the suffering and death of Christ. Polycarp died in A.D. 156 in the stadium of Smyrna. His feast day is February 23.

Heroes for Today The people of the ancient world were impressed by the Christians who faced death rather than deny Christ. They were impressed by the faith and love the martyrs showed for Christ.

In every period there have been Christians who were ready to die for Christ. The early martyrs remain heroes for Christians of today. They teach us also that no power on earth can crush the religious faith of people who believe.

Recall and Reflect

1. What were the *Acts of the Martyrs?*
2. Why did Saint Polycarp say he did not need to be nailed to the wood in the fire?
3. How are the early martyrs heroes for us today?
4. We will probably not be asked to give up our lives for what we believe. But often we are called upon to bear witness to our faith in Jesus. Can you give three examples when this might happen?

REVIEW AND CELEBRATE

Doctrinal Summary

Pentecost marks the birthday of the Church. Following this event, Christian communities were established throughout Syria, Asia Minor, Greece, and to the far shores of the Mediterranean Sea. The early Christians used the word *ekklesia* (ə klā′zē ə), which means "assembly," to describe their community. They called themselves "the assembly of God's people."

Religious Vocabulary

Pentecost	epistles	priests	deacons
Church	martyrs	Eucharist	pilgrim
Acts of the Apostles	bishop	Catholic	*Acts of the Martyrs*

Review Questions

Answer the following questions on a separate sheet of paper.

1. Why did the Romans persecute the Christians?
2. Why did Saint Ignatius call martyrs "athletes for Christ"?
3. What did Saint Ignatius write about the Eucharist?
4. What does Saint Clement's letter tell us about the faith of the early Church?
5. Why did Saint Ignatius call the Church "Catholic"?

Prayer Celebration

Leader: We come to pray as God's holy people.

Reader: This is a reading based on Saint Paul's letter to the Ephesians, Chapter 2, verses 20 to 22.
We are part of a building that has the apostles and martyrs for its foundation and Christ Jesus Himself for its main cornerstone. As every structure is founded on Him, we grow into one holy temple in the Lord. We, too, in Him are being built into a house where God lives in the Spirit.
This is the word of the Lord.
All: Thanks be to God.

Leader: Let us give thanks to the Lord with all our hearts.
All: We thank the Lord for His gift of faith.

Leader: God our Father brings all of us together in His name and in the name of Jesus, His Son.
All: We thank the Lord for His gift of faith.

Leader: We ask the Lord our God to make us true witnesses to His Son, Jesus.
All: We thank the Lord for His gift of faith.

Leader: Let us sing together the hymn "Faith of Our Fathers."

In the top panel Constantine dreams of a cross above the sun and the words "in this sign conquer." In the bottom panel he wins the battle of the Milvian Bridge as his vision (with Greek words) appears in the sky.

2

The Church and the Peace of Constantine

In this chapter we will see how the emperor Constantine gave a new kind of life to the Church. We will see how the Church and the Roman Empire were joined together. Finally, we will look at the religious struggles that almost split the Church. We shall also discover how great teachers and leaders, called Church Fathers, helped to pass on Jesus' teachings.

Despite persecution by the Roman government, the Church continued to grow. As the map on page 17 shows, by the year 300, Christian communities were found in all parts of the Roman world.

CONSTANTINE: THE FIRST CHRISTIAN EMPEROR

In This Sign A battle between two Roman armies changed the course of Christian history. The date was October 28, 312. The place was the Tiber River, about eight miles north of Rome, Italy. At this point on the river there was a bridge known as the Milvian (mil′vē ən) Bridge. Thus the battle is called the battle of the Milvian Bridge.

The victorious general was a man in his thirties. His name was Constantine. The son of an emperor, Constantine would soon become the first Christian emperor of the Roman Empire. We call him Constantine the Great. The man he defeated was also the son of a Roman emperor. He was called Maxentius (mak sen′shəs). Constantine and Maxentius were fighting for control of the Roman Empire in the West. Constantine won.

Shortly before the battle of the Milvian Bridge, Constantine had a vision. When he looked toward the sky, he saw a cross above the sun and the words "In this sign conquer." Constantine also dreamed he was to put a sign above his army's standard. The standard was a kind of staff, or pole, decorated with eagles, the sign of Rome. Roman armies always carried such standards into battle.

Constantine's sign was to be made up of two Greek letters: the letter *X* (which has the sound of our letters *CH*) and the letter *P* (which has the sound of our letter *R*). Together they looked something like this: ☧. The sign, the Chi-Rho (kī'rō'), was made up of the first two Greek letters of the name *Christ.*

Constantine put this sign on the shields and helmets of his soldiers. In doing this, he was saying he believed that the God of the Christians would be with him during the battle. After he won the battle of the Milvian Bridge, Constantine recognized the Christian religion, and he ended the persecution of the Church. To understand how and why he did this, we must look at the Roman Empire of the third century A.D. (the 200s).

The Chi-Rho, a Greek monogram for Christ, *is often used in churches. Here it decorates a priest's stole. Can you find this sign used in your church?*

Third Century Roman Empire The Roman Empire was not a country like the United States or Mexico. It was made up of many different nations and peoples. If you look at the map on page 17, you can see that the Roman Empire was very large. It included the lands and peoples around the Mediterranean Sea as well as much of Western Europe. As the map shows, the Empire extended from the Rhine and Danube rivers in Europe to the Sahara in Africa. Its western boundary was the Atlantic Ocean. In the East, all the modern nations of western Asia that border on the Mediterranean Sea were once part of the Roman Empire.

Many of the people in the Empire were Roman citizens. This gave them certain rights and privileges. The apostle Paul had been very proud to be a Roman citizen. But there were many more people in the Empire who were not citizens. By the third century, it was becoming harder and harder to keep all these people loyal to Rome. This was the main reason the Romans wanted everyone to worship the Roman gods and the emperor. It was the chief reason the Roman government persecuted the Christians, who would not do this.

During the third century, the Roman Empire began to fall apart. There were rebellions and civil wars. Roman armies came to have more and more power over the government. Soldiers made and unmade emperors. At the same time, the Roman Empire was also threatened by Germanic peoples outside its borders. These peoples, whom the Romans called barbarians, threatened to invade the Empire. In fact, many of these barbarians were already serving as Roman soldiers.

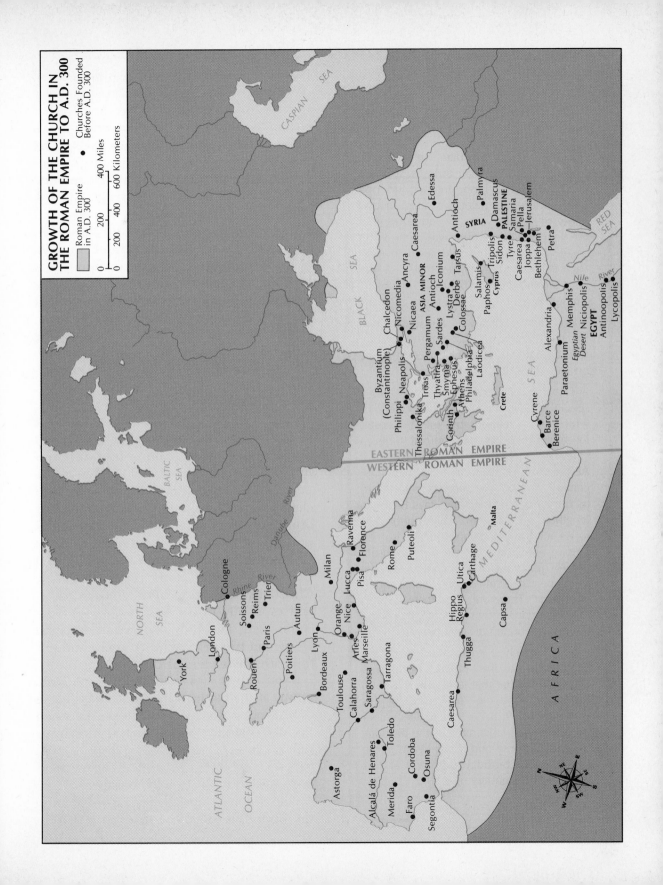

Christmas

December 25 is the date we celebrate Christmas, the birthday of Jesus. It is not the date of His birth. In fact, no one knows the exact date; nor does anyone know the exact year. We do know that the year of Christ's birth was a few years earlier than A.D. 1 would seem to indicate. Scholars today suggest that Jesus was born around the year 6 B.C.

Why, then, the date of December 25? The earliest records we have suggest that by the middle of the fourth century, Christ's birthday was celebrated in Rome on December 25.

The date of December 25 was also a special one in the old Roman calendar, which was revised by Julius Caesar. December 25 was the official time to celebrate the winter solstice (sol'stis). At the time of the winter solstice (December 21–22), the sun begins to return to northern skies and the days begin to lengthen. In the third and fourth centuries A.D., many people in the Roman Empire—including Constantine himself, before his conversion—honored the sun as divine. They called it the "Unconquerable Sun." Therefore, December 25 was also important to those people. It was the time to celebrate the sun's power.

The Church Fathers compared the birth of Jesus to the "rebirth" of the sun. They pointed out that Jesus was the "Sun of Justice," and the "true light" of this world (John 1:9; 8:12; 9:5). So December 25 came to be celebrated as the birthday of Jesus in Rome and in the West. In the East, Christ's birthday was and still is celebrated on January 6.

Diocletian's Reform In A.D. 284, Roman soldiers in the East chose as emperor an officer named Diocletian (dī'ō klē'shən). Diocletian had a plan for reorganizing the Empire. He divided it into two parts—East and West. (See the map on page 17.) Diocletian chose to rule in the East. He selected a fellow soldier to rule in the West. The new ruler in the West, Maximian, was also considered an emperor. Each of those two emperors chose another leader to help him. Constantius Chlorus (kən stan'shəs klōr'əs), the father of Constantine, was one of those leaders. He ruled over lands that are now France and Great Britain. Eventually, Constantius Chlorus became the emperor in the West. When he died in 306, his son Constantine was hailed by the soldiers as the new emperor in the West.

The Edict of Milan As part of his plan for saving the Roman Empire, Diocletian began a widespread persecution of the Christians in 303. This was the last and greatest of the persecutions. It continued even after Diocletian retired in 305. Although all the other emperors agreed to cooperate in the persecution, Constantius Chlorus and later Constantine did little to persecute the Christians in the lands they ruled. But Christians were persecuted in many places, and especially in the East. Churches were confiscated, and holy books were burned. Diocletian tried especially to arrest and put to death the leaders of the Church.

Even before Constantine defeated Maxentius at the battle of the Milvian Bridge in 312, Diocletian's successor in the East had decided that the policy of persecution was a failure. In 311, just before he died, he published an **edict** (ē'dikt) ending the persecution. An edict is a government decree.

The order granting religious freedom to the Church is called the **Edict of Milan.** In the year 313, Constantine met in the city of Milan, in northern Italy, with the new emperor of the East. At this meeting, both men agreed to allow everyone in the Empire to practice their religion freely. The agreement recognized the Christian religion as a legal religion. It granted freedom to all Christians to practice their faith. It allowed them to worship freely and to have churches.

Later, in 324, Constantine defeated the eastern emperor and ruled in both the East and the West. He considered himself a Christian, and became known as the first Christian emperor. However, Constantine was not baptized a Christian until he lay dying in 337.

Recall and Reflect

1. Who won the battle of the Milvian Bridge?
2. Why did Diocletian persecute the Christians?
3. Why did Constantine issue the Edict of Milan?
4. Why was the Roman government afraid of the early Christians? Think about your community and your school. Are people of all religious beliefs and racial and cultural backgrounds made to feel welcome? Can they obtain jobs and take part in community activities?

STRUGGLE WITHIN THE CHURCH

Heresy Christians had now been freed from persecution by people outside the Church. Except for a brief period under the emperor Julian (361–363), no emperor would again persecute the Christians. The next trouble would come from within. It would be Christians against Christians. The problems would come from **heresy**. Heresy means religious belief against the doctrine preached by the apostles and received by the whole Church. Those members of the Church who follow incorrect or untrue religious beliefs are called **heretics**. The problem was that both groups—the Christians who remained faithful and the heretics—turned to the emperor for help.

Split in Church Unity About 317, shortly after Constantine became emperor in the West, a heresy was being taught among some Christians in Egypt. This heresy came to be known as **Arianism** (ãr′ē ə niz′əm), after Arius (ãr′ē əs), the man who first taught it.

Arius was a priest who lived in the city of Alexandria in Egypt. He was a famous preacher and a scholar. Arius was reported to the bishop of Alexandria for teaching untrue doctrines about Jesus. Arius taught that Jesus was in second place, or inferior, to God the Father. He taught that God the

Pictured below are the emperors Diocletian (left) and Maximian. In 303, Diocletian began the last and greatest persecution of the Church.

The Ecumenical Council of Nicaea in 325 was called by Constantine and held in his presence. The council condemned as heretical the teachings of Arius.

Son—Jesus Christ—was not divine like God the Father. In other words, Arius taught that Jesus was not of the same nature as God the Father. According to the teaching of Arius, Jesus was not God.

The bishop of Alexandria called a meeting of all Egyptian bishops to consider the teachings of Arius. In the early Church, bishops often met together to talk about Church problems. The Egyptian bishops judged the teachings of Arius to be heresy.

Arius left Egypt, but his teachings did not die out. Other bishops supported him. Letters were sent back and forth between bishops. Meetings were held. Charges were made. Ordinary people on the streets and in the shops argued about Arius's teachings. Songs were sung for and against his teach-ings. The People of God disagreed about who Jesus was: Was He equal to God or not?

The Christian unity that Constantine wanted was threatened, and the emperor was very upset. He wrote to both Arius and the bishop of Alexandria. For Constantine it was probably only a matter of words. For Christians, however, it was a question that was at the heart of Church belief and practice.

Arius refused to back down. Constantine decided to call together as many of the bishops as possible for a great **council,** or meeting. This was to be the first **ecumenical** (ek′yu̇ men′ə kəl) **council.** *Ecumenical* is an adjective that comes from a Greek word that means "worldwide." This first ecumenical council was held in the city of Nicaea (nī sē′ə), site of the present-day village of Iznik (iz nik′), Turkey. The council was to make clear the Church's teaching that Jesus Christ is the Son of God and equal to the Father.

Arius Before the Council of Nicaea The Council of Nicaea met in 325. Eusebius (yü sē′bē əs) was the first Church writer to give us a picture of the opening of the council. The emperor Constantine, wear-ing beautiful purple robes covered with gold and precious stones, spoke to the bishops. He spoke in Latin, but the bishops' discussions were in Greek. This first world-wide council was an unforgettable event. Thirteen years before, all the Christian bishops had been living in fear of persecution and death. Now they were being given public honor.

We do not know exactly how many bish-ops attended the Council of Nicaea. The traditional number is about three hundred. Most of the bishops came from the eastern part of the Roman Empire. Only a few ar-rived from the West. The bishop of Rome,

THE CREED OF NICAEA

We believe in one God,
 the Father, the Almighty,
 maker of heaven and earth,
 of all that is seen and unseen.
We believe in one Lord, Jesus Christ,
 the only Son of God,
 eternally begotten of the Father,
 God from God, Light from Light,
 true God from true God,
 begotten, not made, one in Being with the
  Father.
 Through him all things were made.
 For us men and for our salvation
  he came down from heaven:
 by the power of the Holy Spirit
  he was born of the Virgin Mary, and
   became man.
 For our sake he was crucified under
  Pontius Pilate;
 he suffered, died, and was buried.
 On the third day he rose again
  in fulfilment of the Scriptures;
 he ascended into heaven
  and is seated at the right hand of the
   Father.
He will come again in glory to judge the
   living and the dead,
 and his kingdom will have no end.
We believe in the Holy Spirit, the Lord,
  the giver of life,
 who proceeds from the Father and the
   Son.
 With the Father and the Son he is
  worshiped and glorified.
 He has spoken through the Prophets.
We believe in one holy catholic and
  apostolic Church.
We acknowledge one baptism for the
  forgiveness of sins.
We look for the resurrection of the
  dead,
 and the life of the world to come.
   Amen.

Pope Saint Sylvester I, was too old to travel. He sent two priests to represent him. Osius (ō′zhē əs), the bishop of Cordoba in Spain, presided. He was the friend and religious adviser of Constantine.

It is interesting to note that today only the pope can call together an ecumenical council. But Nicaea and the other early councils were called not by the popes but by the emperors. As you know, it was Constantine who called the bishops to the Council of Nicaea.

No official records have come down to us from the Council of Nicaea. But we do know what it agreed upon. Arius and his teachings were condemned. He and the bishops who supported him were sent into exile. More than this, the bishops in the council found words to express the Church's teaching about the relationship of Christ the Son to God His Father. The bishops at Nicaea drew up a **creed.** A creed is a summary statement of the main points of belief approved by a church. The council stated that Jesus Christ was "the only Son of God, / eternally begotten of the Father, / God from God, Light from Light, / true God from true God, / begotten, not made, one in Being with the Father. / Through Him all things were made." This is part of the **Nicene Creed**, which we say every Sunday at Mass.

Arius died in 336. He never rejected his heretical teachings. The exiled bishops, however, were allowed to return. Inwardly, many bishops still believed in Arianism in spite of the decision of Nicaea. These people had a great deal of power. Thus it was impossible to prevent a serious disagreement between those who upheld the teaching of the Council of Nicaea and those who followed Arius. An even greater split threatened the Church after the Council of Nicaea.

1. What is the meaning of the word *heresy* as used by the Church?

2. What did Arius teach about Jesus?

3. Why did Constantine call the bishops to the Council of Nicaea?

4. What did the Council of Nicaea decide about the teachings of Arius?

5. Have you ever participated in a group meeting to settle a disagreement? Did the members of the group work well together? How was the disagreement settled?

CHURCH FATHERS PASS ON JESUS' TEACHINGS

A Bishop's Bravery One of the bishops who fought hard for Nicaea and true belief was Saint Athanasius (ath′ə nā′shəs), the bishop of Alexandria in Egypt. As the teachings of Arius continued to spread, bishops who supported Arius fought those who did not. Saint Athanasius was the most famous bishop who upheld the true teaching of the Church, despite persecution, threats to his life, and exile.

As a young deacon, Athanasius had attended the Council of Nicaea. On becoming bishop of Alexandria in 328, Athanasius became the leader of those who accepted the teaching of Nicaea. These people wholeheartedly rejected the teachings of Arius. The Arian bishops charged Athanasius with many crimes, including murder. Finally, Saint Athanasius went to the city of Constantinople, now Istanbul (is′təm bül′), Turkey, to see the emperor Constantine. Constantine had built Constantinople as his new capital.

Athanasius defended himself bravely before Constantine. But Arian bishops told the emperor that Athanasius had threatened to cut off the shipment of Egyptian wheat to Constantinople. The city of Constantinople needed this food supply from Egypt. The charge, of course, was false. But Constantine became very angry. He sent Athanasius into exile in northern Europe, to the city of Trier in what is now West Germany.

This was the first of five exiles that Athanasius endured during his long life. Each exile was imposed because he refused to change his belief that Christ was truly the Son of God, "one in being with the Father." Saint Athanasius died in 373. He was almost eighty years old. The Church celebrates his feast on May 2.

The Church in the Empire It was not until 381, at the First Council of Constantinople, that the heresy of Arianism was finally defeated. This council is known as the Second Ecumenical Council. Again, it was called by the emperor, Theodosius (thē′ō dō′shəs) the Great.

Theodosius the Great was born in Spain in 347. He became ruler in the East in 379 and in the West in 388. A deeply religious man, Theodosius felt that the state should set standards for religious belief. He also felt that the Church should be joined to the state. He published a law in 380 that made the Catholic Church the official church of the Roman Empire. Theodosius ordered all Christians to profess the faith as stated in the Nicene Creed.

When the Catholic Church became the official church of the Empire, people belonging to all other churches or holding other beliefs were persecuted just as the Christians had been. Heretics had no right to have places of worship or the protection of the law. They could be arrested and even be put to death. Theodosius also outlawed all pagan worship, both public and private.

Theodosius would not have understood the idea of religious freedom. He believed that the state had the right to control the Church and to stop the teachings of heretics.

Ambrose and Theodosius The attitude of the emperor Theodosius toward the Church can be seen in the dramatic disagreement that took place between him and Saint Ambrose, the bishop of Milan, Italy. Ambrose, the son of an important Roman family, had been sent to Milan sometime between 368 and 370 to become the governor. Milan was not only the capital of a province in northern Italy but also a place of residence for the emperors when they were in the western part of the Empire.

According to one story, when Ambrose arrived in Milan he had not yet been baptized, even though his family was Christian. It was the custom at the time for young people to put off baptism until later in life. Ambrose was present in the Church of Milan to keep order among the many people who had come together in 374 to elect a new bishop. In the early Church, both the clergy and the people elected their bishops. This time, someone in the crowd shouted, "Ambrose, bishop!" Others took up the cry. More surprised than anyone, Ambrose found himself elected bishop. He was about

Shown below are Saint Ambrose, bishop of Milan, with the emperor Theodosius. In 390, Ambrose made Theodosius do public penance for sin.

forty years old. Within a few weeks he was baptized and ordained. And what a bishop he became! He studied, he read, he learned, and he taught. He became a great preacher, a great pastor, and one of the most famous **Church Fathers** of the fourth century. Church Fathers is the title given to great Christian thinkers and teachers of the third through the sixth century.

In 388, when Theodosius the Great became the ruler in the West, he and Ambrose became close friends. Theodosius was a just ruler, but he had a terrible temper. In 390 there was a riot in the city of Thessalonica (thes′ə lə nī′kə), the present-day Greek city of Salonika (sə lä′ni kə). The riot was caused by a horse race. The great sport in the Roman Empire at that time was chariot racing. Everybody loved the sport, just as Americans love football or baseball. The crowds had their favorite charioteers, or drivers, just as we have our sports heroes today. At Thessalonika one of the most favored charioteers was arrested. In anger, the people killed some government officials. Theodosius, then at Milan, became very angry and sent an order to punish the people. They were to be taken into the stadium, where the soldiers were to put them to death. Saint Ambrose urged the emperor to have mercy. But the order was sent. Shortly after, Theodosius realized that he should have listened to Ambrose, and he sent a second order, canceling the first. Unfortunately, the second order arrived too late. The soldiers had already killed several hundred people.

When Saint Ambrose heard what had happened, he wrote Theodosius that the Eucharist (the Mass) would not be celebrated in the emperor's presence until he had performed public penance. Theodosius at first refused, but he finally did the penance and was readmitted to the Church.

When the emperor Theodosius died in 395, Saint Ambrose preached at his funeral. Referring to the incident at Thessalonica, he said:

> I have loved a man who appreciated the one who rebuked him more than the one who flattered him. . . . He threw aside the . . . [crown] that he used, he wept publicly in the church for his sin. . . . He prayed for forgiveness with tears and sighs. That which ordinary individuals are ashamed to do, the emperor was not ashamed to carry out, namely an act of public penance.

Two years later, in 397, Saint Ambrose also died. He was an example for many bishops in later centuries who would play a part in public life. These bishops would speak out loudly and remind kings and emperors that they also were subject to the Church's law. Saint Ambrose's feast is celebrated on December 7.

Saint Augustine, Church Father One of the greatest Christian teachers and saints of the fourth century was a man from North Africa. His name was Augustine (ô gus′tin). About 384 he went to Milan to teach. There he was influenced by the sermons of Saint Ambrose. Augustine longed to be a Christian. But one thing stopped him. He feared he would not be able to follow Christ's teachings. One day he seemed to hear a child's voice sing out in the garden, "Take up and read." Twice the child sang. Augustine picked up a book. It was the New Testament. He opened it and read:

> Let us live honorably as in daylight; not in carousing and drunkenness, not in sexual excess and lust, not in quarreling and jealousy. Rather, put on the Lord Jesus Christ and make no provision for the desires of the flesh.
> —Romans 13:13–14

Saint Augustine, bishop of Hippo in North Africa, is known as one of the greatest Church Fathers. His writings helped to shape the course of Western history.

Augustine found his answer. He found peace of mind. For he now knew that God would help him.

Augustine was baptized by Saint Ambrose. He returned to North Africa. There he became a priest and then a bishop. Augustine was a brilliant person. He wrote over one hundred books about religion and history. He wrote the story of his life and conversion to Jesus. Over three hundred sermons that Saint Augustine preached to his people and over two hundred of his letters have been preserved. These sermons and letters are studied and referred to by students of Church history.

Saint Augustine's greatest work is called *The City of God.* It is the history of God's work in the world. All religious teachers and thinkers in the Church have been influenced in some way by the ideas and the writings of Saint Augustine. He died in North Africa at the age of seventy-six in the year 430. We celebrate his feast day on August 28.

More Battles Within the Church Once the Arian problem was settled, other misunderstandings arose about Jesus. In 431 the Third Ecumenical Council met at Ephesus (ef′ə səs) in what is now Turkey. This Church council corrected the teaching of Nestorius (nes tôr′ē əs), the bishop of Constantinople. Nestorius had said that there were two persons in Christ: a divine person and a human person. As a result, Mary could be called the Mother of Christ but not the Mother of God! The Council of Ephesus taught that Christ is a divine person who has two natures: human and divine. Mary is the Mother of Jesus, the person; therefore, Mary is the Mother of God.

In 451 the bishops met again in the Fourth Ecumenical Council. It was held at Chalcedon (kal′cə dän′), a town not far from Constantinople. Chalcedon is now called Kadiköy (käd′i koi′). The bishops met to condemn the teaching of an old monk from Constantinople. He had taught that Christ had only one nature, namely the divine nature. The Council of Chalcedon insisted that Christ was truly man as well as truly God. Jesus Christ has two natures: one human, the other divine.

At the time of the Council of Chalcedon, Saint Leo the Great was pope. At the council, Leo's letter setting forth the

Catholic teaching was read aloud to the bishops. This letter stated in strong words: "In the whole and perfect nature of the true man . . . [Jesus] the true God was born, complete in His own nature, complete in ours." The bishops shouted after the reading, "Peter has spoken through Leo!" Like the apostle Peter, the first bishop of Rome, Pope Leo had spoken as head of the whole Church.

The Council of Ephesus declared Mary to be Theotokos—that is, "bearer of God." Since Mary is the Mother of Jesus, the person, she is the Mother of God.

Within a century and a half, the Catholic Church had become the religion of the emperor and the Empire. In a series of ecumenical councils, sometimes stormy and violent, the bishops hammered out the Church's understanding of Christ, His divinity, and His humanity. In the next chapter, we will see that many men and women tried to follow more closely the example Jesus gave during His earthly life.

Recall and Reflect

1. Why was Saint Athanasius persecuted?
2. What did Saint Augustine do to bring the good news of Jesus to the people in North Africa?
3. What did the Council of Ephesus teach about Jesus?
4. Why was the Council of Chalcedon important?
5. One of the things we discover when we study the history of different peoples is that loyalty to one's country was often linked to the acceptance of a religion. Are regular attendance at church and the practice of one's faith signs of good citizenship in our country? Explain.

REVIEW AND CELEBRATE

Doctrinal Summary

"The Word became flesh and made his dwelling among us" (John 1:14). These words sum up for us the doctrine of the Incarnation—Jesus, the Son of God, became man. This doctrine of our faith is found in the Nicene Creed.

Religious Vocabulary

Know

edict	heretics	ecumenical	Nicene Creed
Edict of Milan	Arianism	creed	Church Fathers
heresy	council		

Review Questions

Answer the following questions on a separate sheet of paper.

1. What things did Constantine do to give new life to the Church?
2. Why was the Nicene Creed written? When do we say this prayer?
3. What did the emperor Theodosius believe about the Church?
4. What was Saint Augustine's greatest work? Tell something about it.

Prayer Celebration

Leader: We give thanks to God for the gift of Jesus, His Son.
All: We are the Church, His body on earth.

Leader: Praise God, our loving Father, for sending Jesus to live among us!
All: We are the Church, His body on earth.

Leader: Praise God for the saving death of His Son.
All: We are the Church, His body on earth.

Reader: Let us pray. Lord, many early Christians suffered and died for their faith in You. We honor them today and we ask You to help us live our faith each day of our life.
All: Amen. Alleluia!

Benedictine monks walk and read, or stop to pray in this cloister, or covered walkway, of the abbey of St.-Benôit-du-Lac in Quebec, Canada.

3

The Church and
the Monastic Communities

Egypt, except the land watered by the Nile River, is mostly desert. The desert of Egypt is a hot, dry, and lonely place. It is a place of sand and rocks, sun and open space. It is a difficult place in which to live. Water is scarce. So are trees and vegetation. Even so, the Egyptian desert was chosen by many as a place to be alone with themselves and with God.

In the time of the Roman Empire, people usually fled to the desert for one of two reasons. Either they wanted to get away from high taxes, or they were outlaws and bandits. In the fourth century, Christian men and women retreated to the desert. They wanted to give themselves completely to God—even to die for Him. But the time of persecution had passed. And now the desert offered a place to pray and be alone. It was a quiet place where holy men and women could lift their minds and hearts to God. These men and women were called

monks and nuns. They were unmarried, and they devoted their lives to praising and thanking God for His creation.

This way of life, then as now, is called the monastic life, or monasticism. *Monasticism* comes from a Greek word meaning "to live alone." Since the earliest monks and nuns did just that, they are sometimes called hermits. In the fourth century, a hermit was someone who lived alone in a desert place. (The word *hermit* comes from a Greek word that means "desert.") But many of these monks and nuns soon began living in communities, called monasteries. As a result the monastic way of life also came to mean a "communal" life—that is, a shared life, a life dedicated to God by living in a community. As we shall see in this chapter, the spirit of Christian monasticism reminds us of our need for solitude and our need to be in touch with God by meeting the needs of our neighbors.

THE MONASTIC LIFE

Men and Women of Prayer Monks and nuns, or people like them, are found in nearly all religions. They are people who give up many things—home, family, children—out of love for God. Sometimes they live alone, but very often they live together, in communities. A thousand years before the birth of Jesus there were groups of Hindu monks in India. Hinduism is the religion of most people of India. There are also monks and nuns in the religions of Buddhism (bùd´iz əm) and Islam. At the time of Jesus there was a monastic group, called the Essenes (es´ēnz), who lived among the Jewish people. Even some primitive communities have people, called shamans (shä´mənz), who try to make contact with the divine, and these people, too, are a type of monk or nun.

From the very first days of the Church, there were men and women in the Christian community who followed a strict, self-disciplined way of life. They prayed for the Church and in that way served others. Such people are sometimes called **ascetics** (ə set´iks), and their way of life is called **asceticism** (ə set´ə siz əm). Both these words come from a Greek word that means "exercise," or "training." An ascetic is a kind of spiritual athlete. An athlete goes into training in order to put forth his or her best efforts in a gymnasium or on a playing field. These Christian ascetics went into "training" because they wanted to serve Jesus by living the words of the gospel: "If you seek perfection, go, sell your possessions, and give to the poor" (Matthew 19:21). For that reason, these men and women lived as poor people. They fasted and led lives of prayer and penance. After all, Jesus had also said: "If a man wishes to come after me, he must deny his very self, take up his cross, and follow in my steps" (Mark 8:34).

Saint Anthony of Egypt Most books that reach the best-seller lists today are novels or "how-to" books. There are not too many biographies. This may be so because you really have to know someone in order to write his or her life story. When Saint Athanasius wrote the biography of Saint Anthony of Egypt, he knew his subject well. He had spent time with Anthony and his monks in the desert. Athanasius came to know and understand their way of life. So soon after Anthony died, Athanasius wrote his biography. Today this book might be called a best-seller. It was entitled *Life of Saint Anthony*. People all over the Roman Empire read it. First written in Greek, Athanasius' book was translated into many other languages. Saint Augustine read it in Latin. The *Life of Saint Anthony* gives us our first picture of early Christian monasticism.

Saint Anthony was born in a village in Egypt. When he was a young man of about twenty, his parents died. Anthony and a younger sister were left alone. Anthony placed his sister with a community of nuns. He gave all his property to the poor and went to live as an ascetic near his village. Anthony was soon drawn to go farther into the desert. He wished to be alone with God in order to pray. The desert can be a terrible place, but it can also be a wonderful place to think about God and to feel close to Him.

The Life of the Hermits Anthony became a hermit. Other men heard about Anthony's holy life. They came into the desert to learn from him. Gradually there were hermits living all around Anthony in small huts or cabins. They lived alone in their cabins or huts, but they came together for prayer and

The story of Saint Anthony of Egypt was very popular. This painting from the 1400s shows the saint giving his money to the poor.

Eucharist on Saturdays and Sundays. During the week, they lived by themselves. They prayed and worked, making mats, ropes, and baskets. These things they sold in order to give the money to the poor and to buy food. When strangers came to the desert, Saint Anthony and his fellow hermits would share their food with them. Even on a fast day they would break their fast to be able to share a meal with a traveler.

Anthony lived a very long life. He was over a hundred years old when he died in 356. Although Anthony went farther and farther into the desert to live, he returned from time to time to instruct the other hermits. He was like a father to his fellow hermits. In fact, Anthony was called *abba* meaning "father." From *abba* we get our English word **abbot**, which means "a monk who is in charge of other monks."

Saint Anthony wanted to live alone in order to be close to God. But he also knew that he must be concerned about the needs of others. Many people who were not monks came to see him. They came to ask for his prayers, to seek his advice. They came to find healing of mind and body. "In a word," wrote Saint Athanasius, "it was as though a physician had been given by God to Egypt. For who came to [Anthony] in grief and did not return in joy?" Saint Anthony's feast day is January 17.

Although older, wiser hermits were usually called abba, or father, only a few of them were ordained priests. Most were laymen and laywomen. To the people who lived in the cities of the Empire, the monks

31

Charles de Foucauld (1858–1916) was a French soldier who became a monk. For almost sixteen years he lived as a hermit in the Algerian desert.

and the nuns in the desert were heroes. They were heroes just as the martyrs were heroes. Monks and nuns bore witness to Jesus by putting aside their own needs and wants in order to spend their time praising God and serving others.

The Church is still served by men and women who belong to monastic and religious communities. They serve the needs of the local community and pray for the needs of the whole Church. Some of these communities welcome visitors and provide places for people to make retreats or to

spend shorter periods in prayer. Other religious communities are engaged in education, social work, medicine, family ministry, and almost any work you can think of.

You will find it interesting to investigate some of the religious communities in your area. The members of these groups will be very happy to give you information about their life-styles and their services to the Church.

Saint Moses The hermits were not only Egyptians but Greeks and Romans and also Africans from the region south of Egypt. One of the most famous hermits was Saint Moses who lived in the fifth century. Moses came from Nubia, now known as the Sudan. He was a large, broad-shouldered black man. He was very strong. In his youth he had been a slave. He fled to the desert and became a robber. There he met a community of monks. Moses was so impressed by their way of life that he joined them and became a hermit. He had much to change from his old life. Moses had a violent temper. He worked hard and prayed even harder to bring it under control.

Moses was ordained a priest and became the leader of a large group of hermits. One day the monks in Moses' monastery were called together to judge a monk who had done wrong. All the monks were there except the abbot Moses. They sent for him. Finally they saw Moses coming. But he looked very strange. On his back was a basket filled with sand. But a little sand was running out through a hole in the bottom of the basket. Moses said to the monks, "My sins run behind me like this sand, and I am asked to judge the sins of another?" The story has it that, in shame, the monks agreed to forgive their brother.

Recall and Reflect

1. What is monasticism?
2. What is an ascetic?
3. Describe how Saint Anthony of Egypt lived.
4. What is the lesson in the story of Saint Moses?
5. How could each of the following activities of monks and nuns help you to grow spiritually?
   a. Serving others by using your special gifts
   b. Sharing with others
   c. Being silent and prayerful
   d. Praising God with others in the eucharistic liturgy

THE CENOBITES

Saint Pachomius We have seen that not all monks and nuns were hermits. Many of them lived in communities in the Egyptian desert. They came to be called **cenobites** (sē′nə bīts). *Cenobite* comes from Greek words that mean "common" and "life." It means, therefore, "a member of a group living in common." The founder of this kind of monasticism was Saint Pachomius (pa kō′mē əs).

Pachomius was born in Egypt about 290. He became a Christian as a young man because of the kind example of Christians. Pachomius had been drafted into the Roman army. When he and his fellow soldiers stopped in a Christian village, the people gave them food and drink. Moved by their charity, Pachomius became a Christian.

Pachomius first became a hermit. But he also wanted to serve others. He gradually came to realize that by living in a community, monks would be able to serve each other. And by serving each other, they would be able to serve Jesus. Pachomius, therefore, set up his religious community.

Pachomius's community, or monastery, grew very quickly. Pachomius divided the monks into groups of ten or twenty. Each

Benedictine monks of Weston Priory in Vermont listen to spiritual reading. Saint Benedict said such reading should be done daily.

group had a special task. Some monks were cooks, others were gardeners. There were carpenters, weavers, and basket makers. Some monks were tailors, others were shoemakers. Some took care of the sick and attended to the needs of travelers.

Pachomius even made one group of monks into sailors. The sailor-monks took boats up and down the Nile selling things they had made. Pachomius's monastery was like a village of monks. They came together in the church to pray, to celebrate the Eucharist, and to receive instruction. Pachomius also insisted that all the monks learn how to read.

Manual labor is a part of most monastic rules. Saint Benedict asked that his monks do some manual work every day.

In a short time, other cenobitic monasteries were founded. Pachomius also founded such monasteries for nuns. For all these monks and nuns, Saint Pachomius wrote a rule of life. His rule gave directions to those who wished to live together in communities.

The Nun Egeria If you boarded an airplane today at 2 P.M. in Madrid, Spain, bound for Tel Aviv, Israel, you could arrive at your destination before 10 P.M. Your trip would have taken less than ten hours! At the end of the fourth century, a Spanish nun named Egeria made a pilgrimage to Palestine, or present-day Israel. In those times, such a journey was long and dangerous. It took Egeria months to reach her destination. But Egeria wanted to make a pilgrimage to the holy places connected with the life of Christ. As Egeria traveled, she wrote a long letter to her sisters at home, telling them about the things she was seeing. Most of Egeria's letter remains today, but the first part has been lost.

Thanks to Egeria's letter, we know that in the fourth century there were monks and nuns living in and around Jerusalem as well as in the Egyptian desert. Egeria's letter describes how church services were conducted in Jerusalem at that time. It also describes how the churches and holy places looked. Egeria met many of the monks and nuns who lived in Palestine. She wrote to her sisters about them also. Her letter tells how they made her welcome.

A Grandmother and Her Granddaughter One of the holy women that Egeria might have met in Palestine was Melania the Elder. Melania belonged to one of the oldest and wealthiest families in Rome. She is called "the Elder" because she had a granddaughter who had the same name.

Franciscan Sisters of the Atonement renew their monastic vows in a ceremony at Graymoor Monastery in New York State.

When her husband died, Melania left Rome and went first to Egypt, where she met a group of hermits. Then she went to Palestine and settled in Jerusalem. There she began a monastery for women alongside a monastery for men. The monastery for men was begun by one of the most famous monks and scholars of the fourth century, a man named Rufinus. Melania the Elder and Rufinus worked together. Their two monasteries were located on the Mount of Olives. The monks and nuns prayed, studied, and offered shelter to pilgrims and travelers.

Melania the Elder was a very intelligent woman. She took part in most of the theological discussions of her time. Melania the Elder died in Jerusalem about 409.

Saint Melania the Younger was the granddaughter of Melania the Elder. Well educated and wealthy, young Melania was married in her teens. She and her husband began to live a life of prayer. Both gave up their great wealth to help the poor. They,

WORDS TO LIVE BY

Lord Jesus Christ,
take all my freedom, my memory,
my understanding, and my will.
All that I have and cherish
you have given me.
I surrender it all to be guided by your will.
Your grace and your love
are wealth enough for me.
Give me these, Lord Jesus,
and I ask for nothing more.

PRAYER OF SELF-DEDICATION
TO JESUS CHRIST

too, visited the monks in Egypt and then went to Jerusalem. After her husband died, Saint Melania the Younger lived for many years near Jerusalem as a hermit. Later she founded a monastery for nuns.

Like her grandmother, Melania was interested in the theological discussions of the day. She was a friend of Saint Augustine. Saint Melania the Younger died in Jerusalem on December 31, 439.

Saint Benedict's Rule Monasticism spread from Egypt and Palestine to all parts of the Roman world. Monks and nuns lived not only in the desert but even in large cities, such as Constantinople and Rome. In the sixth century, an Italian monk, Saint Benedict, wrote a rule of life for his monks. His rule is based on an earlier monastic rule. But Saint Benedict added his own spirit.

Saint Benedict's *Rule for Monks* is made up of an introduction and seventy-three short chapters. It gives directions for the government of the monastery. The abbot is to be elected by all the monks. It also tells how young monks are to be educated, and it outlines the daily activities.

At certain hours each day, all the monks are to gather in their monastery church to pray and to sing to God from the Book of Psalms. Saint Benedict called this the "work of God." It was the most important duty

---

SIDELIGHTS ON CHURCH HISTORY

Saint Benedict's *Rule for Monks*

Saint Benedict, a Roman nobleman, lived and worked in central Italy during the first half of the sixth century. Below are some selections from his *Rule for Monks,* one of the most influential books in the history of the West.

"Prologue: . . . we are about to found . . . a school for the Lord's service; in the organization of which we trust that we shall [order] nothing severe and nothing burdensome."

"Chapter 2: What the Abbot should be like. An abbot . . . is believed to be Christ's representative. . . .
 . . . . let him always reflect that he has undertaken to rule souls for which he is to render account [to Christ]."

"Chapter 5: Concerning obedience. [Let monks] . . . consider nothing dearer to them than Christ: so that, as soon as anything is commanded by their superior, they may not . . . delay in doing it, even as if it were a divine command."

"Chapter 16: How Divine Service shall be held through the day. As the prophet says: 'Seven times in the day do I praise Thee.' Which sacred number of seven will thus be fulfilled by us if [we pray] [early in the morning,] at the first, third, sixth, ninth hours, [in the evening,] and at [night]."

"Chapter 48: Concerning the daily manual labor. . . . . at fixed times the [monks] ought to be occupied in manual labour; and again, at fixed times, in sacred reading."

"Chapter 72: Concerning the good zeal which monks ought to have. . . . . There is a good zeal, which separates from [evil] and leads to God and to eternal life. Let the monks therefore exercise this zeal with the most fervent love. . . . Let them love their abbot with a sincere and humble love; let them prefer nothing whatever to Christ, Who leads us alike to eternal life."

Founded in 966 as a Benedictine monastery, Mont-St.-Michel in Normandy, France, is now a museum. Present buildings date from the 1200s.

of his monks. Every day the monks were to spend time in study and in reading holy books. Saint Benedict also asked that his monks work every day with their hands.

Saint Benedict's *Rule* asked his monks to be humble and silent and to obey their abbot. These things would help the monks to grow in God's love.

We know very little about Saint Benedict. He founded and was abbot of a monastery called Monte Cassino, a little to the south of Rome. The story is told that while Benedict was abbot of Monte Cassino barbarian Germanic troops came to visit him in 542. Italy was then being overrun by these Germanic peoples. Their leader, named Totila, tried to trick Saint Benedict by dressing up his swordbearer to look like himself. Benedict was not fooled and he told the real Totila that he would capture the city of Rome. Benedict also predicted that Totila would be dead within ten years. And both these things happened.

Saint Benedict was wise, holy, and firm. But most of all he was fatherly. In the midst of war, Benedict and his monks lived in peace. His *Rule* is one of the great documents of Western civilization. It was eventually followed by all the communities of monks and nuns that were founded in Western Europe after his time. Many monks and nuns still follow this *Rule* today in all parts of the world. Saint Benedict died about 547. We celebrate his feast on July 11.

Benedictine Monasticism Monasticism based on Saint Benedict's *Rule* has been a major force in Church history. Benedictine monasteries offered young men and women an opportunity to seek God in a life of prayer

Following a monastic way of life is one way in which some men and women fill the need that all of us have to be in touch with God.

and service to others. They also played an important role in passing on the learning and culture of ancient Greece and Rome to the peoples of Western Europe. Saint Benedict's monks, like the earlier monks of Egypt and the East, were devoted to learning. If it had not been for the scholarship of these monks and nuns, we would know much less about the ideas and learning of the ancient past.

Recall and Reflect

1. What was the cenobitic style of monastic life?
2. Who founded the first cenobitic monastery?
3. Why was Saint Benedict's *Rule* important?
4. Men and women in religious communities serve the Church in many ways. What could you do to serve the people in your parish? Your school? Your local community?

REVIEW AND CELEBRATE

Doctrinal Summary

The Church is the community of God's people. All members of this community are called to love God and to love their neighbors. All are called to care for the needs of others. The Church's ministry of service is shared by people in every walk of life. Priests and religious, married and single, people are all called to live the command of Jesus, "Love one another as I have loved you" (John 15:12).

Religious Vocabulary

monks	monasticism	ascetics	abbot
nuns	hermits	asceticism	cenobites
monastic life	monasteries		

know

Review Questions

Answer the following questions on a separate sheet of paper.

1. How did the monastic way of life also come to mean a "communal life"?
2. Why have men and women in the Church chosen to live an ascetic life?
3. How was Saint Anthony like a father to his fellow hermits and to others?
4. Give two reasons why Benedictine monasticism has been a major force in Church history.

Prayer Celebration

Leader: Let us pray. Lord Jesus, each of us knows that You love us and that You call us to follow You. Help us to spend this time of prayer quietly remembering Your love and care for each one of us.
All: Amen.

Leader: Thank You, Lord, for reminding us of our call to serve others in Your name.
All: We rejoice in Your love.

Leader: Thank You, Lord, for the example of Saint Benedict and those men and women who live the true spirit of his *Rule* in the Church today.
All: We rejoice in Your love.

Reader: This is a reading from the Gospel of John, Chapter 13, verses 34 and 35.
"I give you a new commandment:
Love one another.
Such as my love has been for you,
so must your love be for each other.
This is how all men will know you
    for my disciples:
your love for one another."
This is the word of the Lord.
All: Thanks be to God.

Leader: God our Father, teach us how to live our lives in service to Your people and in the true spirit of love and faithfulness to Your word.
All: Amen.

This portrait of the emperor Justinian with members of his court is part of a mosaic in the Church of St. Vitale in Ravenna, Italy.

4

Six Centuries of Growth

In its first six hundred years, Christianity grew from a faith believed by a few to one followed by many. The sixth century was a time of continued change and growth for the Church, but it was also a time of pain and unrest. After years of persecution, the Church had become the official church of the Empire. It had splendid buildings and ceremonies of worship. Indeed, by the sixth century the Church had spread far outside the Roman world. In this chapter we will look at some aspects of the Church in the sixth century. We will meet some of the people who contributed to the development of the Church's public forms of worship.

THE AGE OF JUSTINIAN

Justinian and Theodora Two people dominated much of the sixth century. They were the cause of much of the unrest and many of the achievements during that time. They were the emperor Justinian and Theodora, his wife. Justinian was the last Roman emperor to succeed in reuniting both the eastern and western halves of the Empire. Theodora, a beautiful and intelligent woman, both helped and hindered Justinian in his work.

Justinian had married Theodora shortly before he became emperor in 527. Theodora's father had been a circus performer and trainer of bears. She, too, had performed in a circus and had been an actress. Justinian was much taken with Theodora. He not only married her but made her co-ruler. She ruled beside him until her death in 548.

By the sixth century, Roman emperors ruled only in the East. The West was ruled by groups of Germanic peoples. Many of these peoples were still non-Christian.

The empress Theodora, wife of Justinian, with members of her court. Theodora ruled beside her husband from 527 until her death in 548.

Some had been converted to the heretical Arian beliefs. The rulers in Italy were Arian Christians called Ostrogoths. But the Italian people they ruled were Catholics. This sometimes caused problems for the Church leaders.

Even though these Germanic peoples in the West usually honored the Roman emperor in Constantinople, they ran things in their own way. When Justinian became ruler, he had three goals. He wanted to reunite the eastern and western parts of the Empire. He wanted religious unity within the Empire. And he wanted to govern well, according to law.

Justinian sent an army to crush the Ostrogoths in Italy. For seventeen years, war tore up and ruined the country. But the Ostrogoths were finally defeated. Indeed, Justinian succeeded in restoring much of the West to the Roman Empire. The Germanic Visigoths were also pushed back in Spain, and the Germanic Vandals were defeated in North Africa.

Justinian's restored Roman Empire did not last. Justinian died in 565, at the age of eighty-three. In the year 568, Italy was again invaded by another Germanic people, the Lombards. They, too, were Arians. By the end of the sixth century, the Lombards ruled most of Italy. The emperor only ruled the parts around the cities of Rome, Ravenna, Naples, and the island of Sicily.

Justinian and Religious Unity Both Justinian and Theodora were very devout. And both wanted religious unity. Theodora, however, was under the influence of heretical bishops who were called **Monophysites** (mə nof′ə sīts). This word comes from two Greek words meaning "one" and "nature." These people believed there was only one nature in Jesus—the divine nature.

Theodora did all in her power to aid the Monophysites. Secretly, she helped Monophysite bishops to ordain priests who believed as they did. She also protected over three hundred Monophysite monks so that they would not be persecuted by her husband.

Justinian loved **theology**, the study of God and his relation to the world. He would spend many evenings talking about God with monks and priests. He wanted to bring the Monophysites back to the Catholic Church. Justinian wanted the Catholics to meet the Monophysites halfway. He tried to get the pope, Pope Saint Silverius, to change the statements that had been made by the Ecumenical Council of Chalcedon in 451. As we saw in Chapter 2, this council had said that there were two natures in Jesus—human and divine.

Pope Saint Silverius did not do what Justinian wished. In 537, Justinian and Theodora ordered Belisarius (bel ə sār′ē-əs), their general in Italy, to force Pope Saint Silverius out of office. At that time, the clergy and the people of Rome elected the pope. Justinian ordered the Roman clergy and people to elect as pope a man named Vigilius. Vigilius, it seems, had promised to cooperate with Justinian and Theodora.

But after he was elected pope, Vigilius saw that he could not do what Justinian wanted without going against the Catholic faith. When he refused, he was kidnapped by Justinian, taken to Constantinople, and made a prisoner. Vigilius tried both to please the Monophysites and not betray the teachings of the Council of Chalcedon. He wrote a statement in which he tried to please both sides. His statement, however, did not please many bishops in the West. Vigilius was eventually allowed to go back to Rome by Justinian. But the pope died in Sicily on the way back, on June 7, 555.

Justinian and Roman Law Justinian never did bring the Monophysites back to the Catholic Church. One of his lasting works, however, was the ordering of Roman laws into a great collection. This collection of laws is sometimes called the Justinian Code. The work of many scholars, it was finished in 534.

This large collection of Roman law became very important in the later development of Catholic Church law, which is known as **canon law**. Justinian's collection has also served as the basis for the written laws in most European countries down to our own day.

The Spread of the Church By the end of Justinian's reign, Christianity had spread very far outside the lands of the Roman Empire. Christianity had reached as far to the east as Armenia and Georgia, now republics of the Soviet Union. Christian churches were also found in Persia, now called Iran, and in parts of the Arabian Peninsula. There was even a flourishing Christian Church in southern India. Africa north of the Sahara had long been Christian. But Christianity had also spread to parts of black Africa south of the Sahara—the Sudan and Ethiopia. By the end of the sixth century, Christianity was also firmly implanted in Ireland.

One hundred years after the death of Justinian (565), groups of Christians had set up a church in central China. Although

Christianity had spread very far, many of the distant places did not remain Christian. The Church would be reintroduced in those lands many years later.

Pope John Paul II is shown celebrating Mass in Rome. As in the year 500, today's pilgrims to Rome try to attend a papal Mass.

Recall and Reflect

1. What three things did Justinian want to accomplish while he was emperor?

2. What did the Monophysites teach about Jesus?

3. What is the Justinian Code?

4. Name three places, outside the Roman Empire, that had Christian communities in the sixth century.

5. Do you think Justinian and Theodora were fair and just rulers? Give reasons for your answer.

THE LITURGY OF THE CHURCH

Liturgy Is Worship During the early years of the Church's history, different ways of worship developed among Christians living in some of the important cities of the Roman Empire. Rome, Alexandria, Antioch, and Constantinople all developed their own ways of celebrating the **liturgy** (lit′ər jē). Liturgy is the public worship that the Christian community offers to God. In fact, it is the worship that Jesus offers to His Father as head of His Church. Early Christian writers used the word *liturgy* to refer to the Church's official worship, as opposed to private devotions and prayers — even when these were done by groups of people.

Liturgy is public worship. It is done for the good of the whole Church. The heart of the Church's liturgy is the Mass. The conferring of a sacrament is also a liturgical act. The official prayers, said in the Church's name by priests, monks, and nuns, are liturgical prayers called the **Divine Office.**

The different ways of celebrating the liturgy in the early Church often meant using different languages. In Rome, and in the rest of the West after the fourth century, the Mass prayers were usually said in Latin. In Constantinople and in much of the East, the language used was Greek. But the Mass might also be said in the Syrian language or in the Coptic language of Egypt. Even today, there are many different liturgical **rites** — that is, many ways of celebrating the liturgy in the Church.

This has always been the case in Church history. Because the Catholic Church is universal, there has always been much variety in it. There has always been change and development in the way things were done.

The Mass in Sixth-Century Rome Suppose we could go back and visit Rome in the year 500. Like most people, we would attend the pope's Mass on Sunday. This would be the main liturgical celebration. The pope as bishop of Rome would offer Mass together with his priests and deacons. The Mass we would attend would be partly the same as and partly different from the Mass that is offered now on a Sunday morning.

When the pope and those who were to offer Mass with him arrived at the church, the pope would put on special vestments in a room near the door. As the pope entered the church, the people would sing a psalm. He would walk to the altar between two deacons. Seven candles and incense would be carried in front of the pope. These were symbols of respect that were given to high civil authorities within the Roman Empire.

At the altar the pope would stretch out, face downward, in silent prayer, just as priests do today on Good Friday. Then the pope would stand and sing the prayer of the Sunday. He would pray in Latin, the language of the people of Rome in the sixth century. Since this Mass was being offered by the pope, all the people would sing the hymn we call the Gloria. Today we recite or sing this hymn almost every Sunday outside of Lent and Advent. But in the sixth century it was only used on Sundays and great feast days, when the Mass was offered by a pope or bishop.

After the Gloria, lessons from the Bible would be read from a lectern, or reading stand. A deacon would also sing a part of one of the gospels from the stand. After the gospel, the pope would preach. In earlier centuries those who had not yet been baptized were asked to leave the church at this point. Only baptized Catholics could re-main for the rest of the Mass. But this was no longer the case in the sixth century. The kiss of peace would be given after the readings—not before Communion, as it is given today. Pope Saint Gregory the Great, who became pope in 590, moved the kiss of peace to its present spot in the Mass.

The pope would now go to the various parts of the church to receive the people's offerings of bread and wine. People did not sit or stand in church wherever they wished in the year 500. The women were grouped on one side of the church; the men on the other. Some of the wine that was offered was poured into a large two-handled chalice on the altar. The bread that was used was not thin like the bread we use today. It was thick, like the bread we eat at meals.

THE GLORIA

The Gloria is one of the oldest hymns in the Church. It is sung or said at Mass on Sundays outside Advent and Lent, on feasts, and on great occasions.

Glory to God in the highest,
  and peace to his people on earth.

Lord God, heavenly King,
almighty God and Father,
  we worship you, we give you thanks,
  we praise you for your glory.

Lord Jesus Christ, only Son of the Father,
Lord God, Lamb of God,
you take away the sin of the world:
  have mercy on us;
you are seated at the right hand of the Father:
  receive our prayer.

For you alone are the Holy One,
you alone are the Lord,
you alone are the Most High,
  Jesus Christ,
  with the Holy Spirit,
  in the glory of God the Father. Amen.

Not all the bread and wine that was offered was used in the pope's Mass. Much of it was given to the poor.

A very interesting custom was part of the pope's Mass in the sixth century. After the consecration, the pope would break off pieces of the consecrated bread. Those pieces would be sent to priests who might be offering Masses with their people in other Roman churches. In their Masses, those priests would place the bread from the pope in the chalice with the consecrated wine. This was a sign of the unity of the pope and all of his priests in offering the Holy Eucharist.

Because the consecrated bread in the sixth century was like today's ordinary bread, it had to be broken up by priests for the Communion of the Mass. In the sixth century, people received Communion standing. The consecrated bread was placed on their outstretched hands. They would also drink wine from a cup into which had been poured some of the wine consecrated in the Mass. Sometimes people used a straw of gold or silver to receive the consecrated wine. At the end of his Mass, the pope would sing a prayer in blessing. Then the pope and the clergy would walk out in procession.

The Mass and the many other parts of the Church's liturgy have changed much since the sixth century. Some changes have come gradually. Others have been the result of special councils or the decisions of popes. Sometimes changes have brought back the older ways of doing things. In our own time, the Second Vatican Council has made changes in the Mass. For example, its decision to use the languages spoken by the people marks a return to the way Mass was offered in the sixth century.

Recall and Reflect

1. What is the Church's liturgy?
2. What is the heart of the liturgy?
3. What is a liturgical rite?
4. What language was used in the Mass in sixth-century Rome?
5. In what ways does our Mass today differ from Mass in sixth-century Rome?

GROWTH OF THE CHURCH'S LITURGICAL YEAR

The Celebration of Sunday From the earliest days of the Church, Christian communities gathered together to worship on Sundays. Because Jesus had risen from the dead on the first day of the week, Sunday became the "Lord's Day" for Christians. By the beginning of the second century, all Christian communities kept each Sunday as a day for common worship. In 321, Constantine made all Sundays of the year days of rest throughout the Roman Empire. The Jews had always begun their celebration of the Jewish Sabbath at sunset on the evening before. So Christians began their celebration of Sunday at sunset on the evening before, with Bible readings and prayer. Some Christians did not eat from Saturday at sunset until after the celebration of the Eucharist on Sunday. The practice of eating little or no food is known as **fasting**.

WORDS TO LIVE BY

PRIEST: Let us proclaim the mystery of faith.
PEOPLE: When we eat this bread and drink this cup, we proclaim your death, Lord Jesus, until you come in glory.

FROM THE ORDER OF THE MASS

Every Sunday became a feast day for Christians. A feast day is one on which we celebrate the anniversary of an event. Each Sunday of the year Christians celebrated the events of Christ's death and resurrection as well as the mystery of their salvation through Jesus.

Easter Even before the second century, one Sunday stood out before all others for Christians. This was the first Sunday after the full moon of the spring equinox. Although all Sundays celebrated the Lord's rising from the dead, this Sunday was a special remembrance of Jesus' death and resurrection. About the same time each spring, the Jewish feast of **Passover** celebrated the freeing of the Jewish people from slavery in Egypt. As Paul pointed out (1 Corinthians 5:7), Christ became the Christian "Passover" by dying on the cross.

We call this Sunday "Resurrection Sunday," or **Easter**. It is also called the Pasch (pask), or Paschal, Sunday, from the Hebrew word for "Passover." By rising from the dead, Christ, our "Passover," overcame sin and death. In Christ, all Christians have a new life as sons and daughters of God. Easter is the Sunday that, like the sun, shines over the whole Christian year.

The Easter Vigil and Holy Week Just as all Sunday celebrations began at sunset on Saturday, so this Sunday of the resurrection came to have a solemn watch, or vigil. A vigil was a time of prayers and devotions, usually through the night before a feast. During this long vigil before Easter, converts to the Church were baptized. Very soon, the whole Saturday before Easter became a special day of prayer and fasting. People fast in order to pay better attention to what they are doing. This Saturday began to be called **Holy Saturday**.

The blessing of the Paschal candle, the symbol of the risen Lord, is the first part of the Easter Vigil service on Holy Saturday night.

By the year 400, there were special services on the Friday before Easter. These honored Jesus' sacrifice on the cross. This custom began in Jerusalem and gradually spread throughout the Christian world. This Friday became known as **Good Friday**, or the "Pasch of the Crucifixion." Saint Ambrose called it the "Day of Bitterness."

By the fourth century, **Holy Thursday**, the Thursday before Easter, had also become a special day. It was important not only as a celebration of the Last Supper of Jesus but also as a preparation for the Easter Vigil. On Holy Thursday, a bishop blessed the oils that were used in the Church's liturgy. Some of these oils were used in the baptisms that would be performed during the Vigil of Easter. Holy Thursday also became the day on which those Christians who were doing public penance were publicly absolved of their sins by the bishop.

The Sunday before Easter, **Palm Sunday**, was also first kept in Jerusalem as a special Sunday. The people of Jerusalem came together on Palm Sunday afternoon on the Mount of Olives, outside the city. After hearing the gospel, the people walked with their bishop to a church in Jerusalem, carrying palm and olive branches. This custom was soon followed in Spain and other countries. Later it was kept in Rome and in the whole Church.

The period of fasting in preparation for Easter had begun with Holy Saturday. Gradually, however, it came to include the entire week before Easter. Indeed, this week came to be called **Holy Week**.

The Season of Lent The seven days of Holy Week were soon considered not enough preparation for Easter. By the fourth century, a period of forty days was being observed as the period of fasting. It was known as the "Holy Forty Days," or **Lent**.

Because converts to the Church were baptized during the Easter Vigil, Lent was a special time of instruction in the faith and of preparation for Baptism. It was also a time for public penance. By the sixth century, Lent in Rome began on the day we now call **Ash Wednesday**. It began with a public ceremony in which those who were guilty of grave public sins were sprinkled with ashes and began their public penances.

Other Feast Days By the sixth century, many other feasts remembering Jesus were being celebrated throughout the year. From the fourth century, Jesus' birthday was being celebrated—in the West on December 25 and in the East on January 6. From the third century, Pentecost Sunday, recalling the sending of the Holy Spirit, was celebrated fifty days after Easter. Feast days were introduced to celebrate events in the life of Mary, Jesus' mother. There were feasts for the martyrs who had died for the faith and feasts for saints.

Today in the Roman rite, the Church's liturgical year begins with the first Sunday of **Advent**, four weeks before the feast of Christmas. Advent is a time, or season, to

A ceremony of washing feet—here performed in a Greek rite—has long been a part of Holy Thursday liturgy. (See John 13:3–17.)

A popular pilgrim devotion in Jerusalem is the Way of the Cross. On Good Friday, throngs of people follow the route of Christ's journey to Calvary.

prepare for the celebration of Christ's birth. The liturgical year consists of the Christmas Season, the Lenten Season, Holy Week, the Easter Season, and a period after Easter called the Sundays of Ordinary Time. The whole mystery of Christ from his birth to the day of Pentecost and the expectation of His coming again is celebrated by the Church during the course of the liturgical year. The liturgical year also has a Proper of the Saints—that is, a yearly calendar of feasts in honor of Mary, the martyrs, and the other saints and heroes of the Church.

Church Buildings During the centuries of persecution, Christians met in their homes to celebrate the eucharistic liturgy. After the Edict of Milan (313), churches began to be built in large numbers. At times, the homes of wealthy Christians became churches. In Rome such a home was usually built around a courtyard, called an atrium. Many early churches had a courtyard in front, sometimes with a covered walk and columns. In the center of the courtyard there was often a fountain, where those about to enter the church could wash their hands. This was the origin of the holy-water fonts in our churches today.

The Christian church has always been a house for the liturgy. It is a place where the assembly of God's people can gather together to worship. In Rome and in the West in general, the most popular form for the structure was an adaptation of the Roman business hall, called the **basilica**. This was a rectangular building often with a half circle at one end. In the Christian basilica type of church, this half circle came to be called the apse (aps). The bishop's chair stood there, with benches on either side for the priests. The apse ceiling was often decorated with a mosaic (mō zā'ik), a picture formed with small colored stones or glass chips. This picture was usually the figure of Christ or sometimes just His head.

SIDELIGHTS ON CHURCH HISTORY

The Popes: The Bishops of Rome

The name *pope* comes from the Latin word "papa." It was a word that little children used when referring to their fathers. From the third to the sixth centuries, all bishops in the Church were called papa, or pope. In the sixth century, however, the title of pope began to be reserved for the bishops of Rome. And by the eighth century, in the West, only the bishop of Rome, as head of the Church, was called pope.

Between the apse and the body of the church stood the altar. This part of the church was, and still is, called the **sanctuary**. The altar was usually freestanding and could be approached from all sides. A low railing often surrounded the area of the altar. In some Eastern churches, a curtain was hung before the altar during parts of the liturgy. Later in Eastern churches, this curtain would become a partition with three openings between the sanctuary and the rest of the church.

Within the churches there were no permanent pews as there are today in American churches, only a few benches. There were no confessionals. There were two reading stands, where readers or deacons stood to read the lessons of the Mass.

Next to the church there was often a smaller building, usually eight-sided or round. This was called the **baptistry**. Inside, it had steps leading down to a pool. It was here that baptisms took place, especially during the Easter Vigil.

Not all churches were rectangular. Sometimes they were round or octagonal (eight-sided). The round plan was very popular in the East. In the sixth century, the emperor Justinian built a great church in this style in Constantinople. It was known as the Hagia Sophia, or the Church of the Holy Wisdom. One of the great buildings of the world, the Hagia Sophia still stands in Istanbul, the modern name for Constantinople. Today it is a museum.

The early Christian churches were usually quite plain and simple on the outside. But inside they were beautifully decorated with Christian pictures and symbols. A symbol is a sign—something that stands for something else. Pictures of loaves of bread and fishes, for example, were used as symbols of the Eucharist. Water was used as a symbol of Baptism; an anchor, as the sign of

Hagia Sophia, the Church of the Holy Wisdom, in Istanbul (Constantinople) is one of the most important churches to survive from ancient times.

faith. Jesus was often shown as the "Good Shepherd," often with a lamb on his shoulders. Mary, the martyrs, and other saints were also pictured in the churches, as were scenes from the Bible. Stained-glass windows were not yet used. But the many pictures and mosaics on the church walls helped teach the people about their faith.

Recall and Reflect

1. Why do Christians worship on Sundays?
2. Why was Easter such a special feast?
3. What is Holy Week?
4. When does the Church's liturgical year begin today?
5. In what ways does your parish church differ from an early Christian church? In what ways is it similar?

REVIEW AND CELEBRATE

Doctrinal Summary

Throughout its history the Church has encouraged its people
to develop forms of worship that meet their spiritual needs.
The Church teaches that Jesus is especially present in liturgical
celebrations. He is present in the Mass, in the sacraments, in
Holy Scripture, and in the lives of the faithful.

Religious Vocabulary

Monophysites	rites	Good Friday	Ash Wednesday
theology	fasting	Holy Thursday	Advent
canon law	Passover	Palm Sunday	basilica
liturgy	Easter	Holy Week	sanctuary
Divine Office	Holy Saturday	Lent	baptistry

Review Questions

Answer the following questions on a separate sheet of paper.

1. Tell about two or three important achievements of the emperor Justinian and his wife, Theodora.

2. How, do you think, did Christianity become known outside the lands of the Roman Empire?

3. Think about the meaning of the word *liturgy*. Tell about several changes that have taken place in the Church's public forms of worship.

4. Holy Week and Easter are the most solemn times in the Christian Church. People of different countries have special customs for celebrating these days. Choose three countries and describe some of the religious customs the people follow for remembering Jesus, centered around His suffering, death, and resurrection.

5. Describe the architecture of the early Christian churches, and tell how church buildings have changed down through the centuries.

Prayer Celebration

Leader: We come together in the spirit of truth to praise You, Lord God.
All: Alleluia! Alleluia!

Leader: We believe that You are with us as we pray together.
All: Alleluia! Alleluia!

Reader: This is a reading from the Gospel according to Matthew, Chapter 18, verses 19 and 20.

"Again I tell you, if two of you join your voices on earth to pray for anything whatever, it shall be granted you by my Father in heaven. Where two or three are gathered in my name, there am I in their midst."
This is the gospel of the Lord.
All: Praise to You, Lord Jesus Christ.

Leader: Give us a true spirit of prayer as we worship You in common community, O Lord.
All: Amen. Alleluia! Alleluia!

UNIT ONE SUMMARY

In this unit we have seen how the Church of Jesus grew from the small Jerusalem community of A.D. 29 into a truly catholic—that is, universal—religion. Very early in the Church's history it was recognized that union with the bishop of Rome, the successor of the apostle Peter, was a sign of belonging fully to the Church.

Until the beginning of the fourth century, the Church at various times was persecuted by the Roman government. Peter and Paul, martyred in 67, were among the first of many martyrs, witnesses who would give their lives for the faith.

In 313, with the end of the last great persecution, the Church became a legal institution. The Roman emperors themselves became Christians. In 380 the emperor Theodosius the Great declared the Catholic Church to be the official church of the Roman Empire.

Sometimes unity of faith and belief stopped or was hindered because of confusion about what the Church believed. In 325, the Council of Nicaea was called to deal with the heresy of Arianism. It was the first of the long series of ecumenical councils that have dealt with Church problems.

The fourth century of the Church's history saw the development of many forms of Christian asceticism. In the West, Saint Benedict, who died in 547, wrote a monastic rule that became one of the most important tools in spreading the Church among the Germanic peoples of Europe.

Unity of faith, however, has never meant uniformity of practice. The Catholic Church has always contained much variety, both in liturgy and in religious practice and discipline. There has always been change and development in the way things are done in the Church.

We know that every Catholic must work and pray for unity among all Christians. The first step toward union is growth in knowledge and respect for those Christians who are separated from us or who worship differently than we do. That is why the study of Church history is important. History reminds us that to be Catholic is to be universal.

About 6 B.C.	Birth of Jesus
About A.D. 29	Pentecost: Birth of the Church
A.D. 67	Martyrdom of Saints Peter and Paul: Persecutions begin
95	Pope Saint Clement writes letter to Church at Corinth
About 110	Saint Ignatius martyred at Rome
156	Saint Polycarp martyred at Smyrna
202	Saints Perpetua and Felicity martyred at Carthage
284	Diocletian becomes Roman emperor
303	Last Great Persecution of the Church
313	Edict of Milan: End of persecutions
325	Council of Nicaea
337	Death of Constantine
380	Emperor Theodosius the Great makes Catholic Church official church of the Empire
381	First Council of Constantinople
431	Council of Ephesus
451	Council of Chalcedon
500	Most of West ruled by Germanic peoples
527	Justinian becomes Roman emperor
534	Justinian Code published
547	Death of Saint Benedict
565	Death of Emperor Justinian

UNIT TWO

The Church—Growing and Maturing

The cathedral at Mainz, in West Germany, was built between 975 and
1011. Saint Boniface was the first archbishop of Mainz.

5

The Church and the Germanic Peoples

About 6 B.C.	Birth of Jesus
About A.D. 29	Pentecost: Birth of the Church
A.D. 313	Edict of Milan: End of persecutions
325	Council of Nicaea
800	Pope Leo III crowns Charlemagne emperor
1049	Pope Leo IX elected: Church reform begins
1054	Schism between Rome and Constantinople
1095	Pope Urban II preaches First Crusade
1215	Fourth Lateran Council: Great pastoral council of Middle Ages
1453	Constantinople falls to the Turks
1521	Diet of Worms: Luther breaks with Church
1545	Council of Trent begins
1789	Crisis of the French Revolution
1870	First Vatican Council
1962	Second Vatican Council begins
1978	John Paul II becomes pope

In the first unit we saw the Church begin and grow in the lands of the Roman Empire. Now we shall look at how the Church grew among the peoples of Western Europe—both those who had settled within the Empire and those who lived outside it.

Between the fifth and the seventh centuries, the western part of the Roman Empire was torn apart by waves of invading Germanic peoples. Many people felt unsafe and could not find work in the cities. Trade and industry began to decline. People moved to the countryside and city life came to a halt. The Empire continued in the East, but the Western Empire collapsed. In fact, the only institution that survived the collapse of the Empire in the West was the Church.

As we saw in Chapter 4, Justinian had tried in the sixth century to rebuild the Empire in the West. His work did not last,

55

and in the seventh century, the West continued to be a patchwork of kingdoms ruled by Germanic peoples.

Between 600 and 1100 the Church influenced the development of a whole new society. During this period the Church both converted the peoples of Europe and gave them a common culture. Although many non-Christian ideals remained, the culture of the West—of Europe—became more and more Christian. So well did the Church succeed in teaching the gospel to these European peoples that for almost a thousand years Europe would be known as **Christendom** (kris′ən dəm). It was that part of the world where Christianity prevailed and Christian values ruled.

In this chapter we shall look at some of the **missionaries**—that is, the early leaders and teachers who helped spread Christian teaching among the Germanic peoples of Europe. Nearly all of them were monks, or monks who were also bishops. One of these early teachers was Saint Gregory the Great, a monk who became one of the Church's greatest popes.

THE POPES BECOME WESTERN LEADERS

Gregory the Great: Man of Two Worlds Some periods of history are called turning points because of the great changes at those times. The American Revolution, for example, was a turning point for the people who were then living in the English colonies of North America. The colonists lived in two worlds—the world that was passing and the world that was being born. Some among them achieved greatness by bringing about the changes and helping to create the world we know today. These people have taken their places in American history.

And so it has been with other turning points in history. The times offer some strong challenges and urge people toward great achievements. The sixth and seventh centuries marked a turning point in the West and in the Church. This period can be seen through the life of Pope Gregory the Great, a man of two worlds—the old world of the Roman Empire and the new world of the Germanic peoples of Europe. Gregory, in fact, played a key role in bringing this new world into being.

In the West as well as in the East, the Christian Church had developed most in the cities. People in the countryside often continued to worship the old gods. In fact, such people were called **pagans**, from the Latin word *pagus* (pā′gəs), which means "country district." When the population of the cities in the West declined, the Church was hindered in the mission of preaching the gospel until the work was taken up by the communities of monks and nuns. Gregory's greatest work, perhaps, was the establishment of close links between the popes and the monastic missionaries to the peoples of Europe.

Gregory: Roman Leader Gregory was born in the city of Rome around 540. His family was rich and powerful. Many of his ancestors had been senators in the Roman Empire. Two members of his family had been elected popes.

Gregory received a good education. He was trained in Roman law for a career as a public official. Around 570 he became the leader of the Roman people.

When Gregory became leader, it was a time of troubles for Italy and for Rome. The Lombards, a Germanic people, had invaded northern and central Italy, and they threatened Rome itself. It was Gregory's job to defend the Roman people.

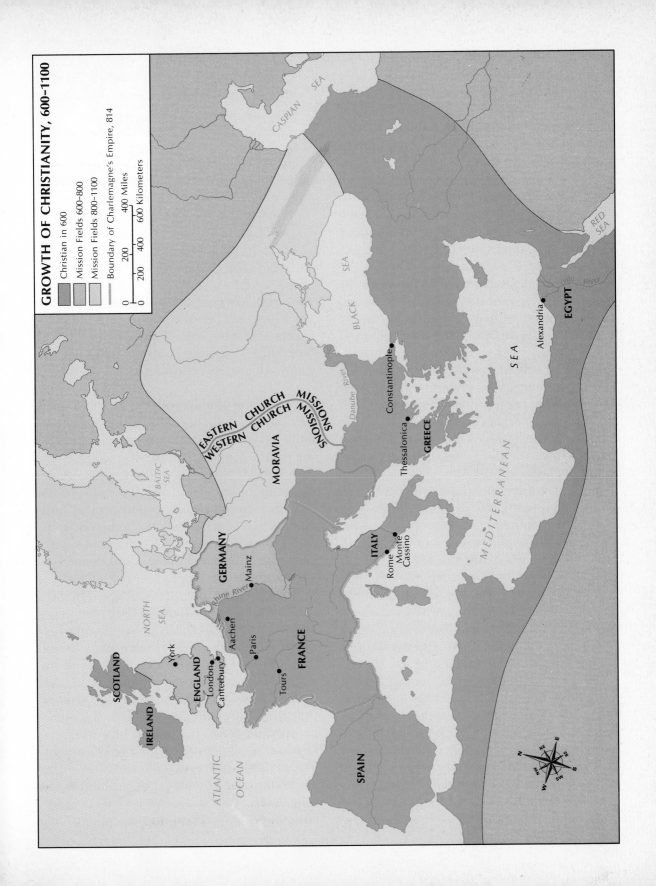

GROWTH OF CHRISTIANITY, 600–1100

Christian in 600

Mission Fields 600–800

Mission Fields 800–1100

Boundary of Charlemagne's Empire, 814

0   200   400 Miles

0   200   400   600 Kilometers

CASPIAN SEA

RED SEA

Nile River

EGYPT

Alexandria

BLACK SEA

Danube River

Constantinople

Thessalonica

GREECE

MEDITERRANEAN SEA

EASTERN CHURCH MISSIONS

WESTERN CHURCH MISSIONS

MORAVIA

GERMANY

Mainz

Rhine River

Aachen

Paris

FRANCE

Tours

ITALY

Rome

Monte Cassino

BALTIC SEA

NORTH SEA

SCOTLAND

IRELAND

ENGLAND

York

London

Canterbury

ATLANTIC OCEAN

SPAIN

N NE E SE S SW W NW

But Gregory wanted to study and pray more. In 575, after his father's death, Gregory surprised everyone by giving his great wealth to the poor. He turned his family's home in Rome into a monastery and began to live there as a monk.

Gregory as Pope This peaceful period in Gregory's life came to an end in 579. Pope Pelagius (pi lā′jē əs) II ordained Gregory as a deacon and sent him to Constantinople. Gregory served there for six years as the pope's personal ambassador to the emperor Tiberius II. Upon his return to Rome, Gregory again took up the life of a monk. Five years later, in 590, Gregory was elected pope by the clergy and people of Rome.

Gregory did not want to be pope. According to one story, when Gregory found out that the people wanted to make him pope, he fled from Rome and hid in the woods. Once elected, however, Gregory became one of the greatest popes in the Church's history.

While Gregory was pope, the Lombards constantly threatened to attack Rome. His appeals for help to the emperor Maurice in Constantinople were not answered. Several times, in order to keep the peace, Pope Gregory paid money to different Lombard armies that were threatening Rome. In fact, Gregory, not the emperor, was the real ruler of Italy, appointing governors of cities, directing generals, and seeing that armies were paid.

As pope, Gregory wrote many letters. Over eight hundred of his letters have come down to us. Pope Gregory wrote to all kinds of people—to bishops, abbots, and monks as well as to German kings and queens and the emperor in Constantinople. Gregory's letters show him to be a good administrator. They show that he upheld the rights of the pope as head of the Church and that he

was also concerned with spreading the teachings of Jesus to all people. In his letters, Gregory often called himself the "servant of the servants of God." Even today, the pope continues to use this title.

Gregory and the Conversion of the English Christianity had been introduced in England by the Romans, perhaps as early as the third century (200s). But during the first half of the fifth century, pagan Germanic peoples whom we call the Anglo-Saxons invaded southern and central England. They pushed back the native Britons, many of whom were Christians. As a result, the Church largely disappeared in what came to be Anglo-Saxon England.

According to one story, Pope Gregory the Great saw some blond young men being offered for sale as slaves in Rome's marketplace. He asked who they were and was told they were Angles from a country far to the north. He is supposed to have said that they should be called "angels." He was sad that they were still pagans. This story may be only a legend. It is a fact, however, that Gregory sent about forty monks from his Roman monastery to convert the Anglo-Saxon people. The leader of the monks was Augustine. He is known to us as Saint Augustine of Canterbury, apostle to the

58

English. In Chapter 2 we read about another Saint Augustine, the great fourth-century Church leader.

Saint Augustine of Canterbury was ordained a bishop, and with his monks, he landed in England in 597. As the map on page 57 shows, Augustine and his monks were able to convert the English. Augustine became the first **archbishop** of Canterbury. An archbishop is head of a district, or territory, of the Church. Later, another archbishop was put farther north in England, in the city of York.

By the end of the seventh century, Anglo-Saxon England was not only Catholic but very closely linked to the **papacy**—as it would be for almost a thousand years. The word *papacy* is used to refer to the office of pope or to the succession of the popes, one after the other.

Pope Gregory: Teacher and Pastor Because of the books he wrote, Gregory is one of the great teachers in the Church. He preached to the people of Rome every Sunday at Mass. These sermons were important; though the news of the day was often very bad, Gregory gave hope to the people. In his later years, declining health prevented him from preaching. Then a deacon would read the sermon Gregory had written. Today we still read the writings of Gregory on various matters, such as how to live a Christian life.

Saint Augustine of Canterbury and his monks are shown preaching the gospel before Ethelbert, one of the Anglo-Saxon kings of England.

Today we still have some of the changes in the Mass that Gregory introduced. He ordered that the **Kyrie Eleison** (kir′ē ē ə lā′ə sən), "Lord have mercy," be said or sung at Mass as it is now. He introduced the Alleluia before the Gospel, and he stressed the importance of the **homily** (hom′ə lē), or sermon explaining the gospel reading during Mass. Pope Gregory is also responsible for the present place of the Our Father, the Lord's Prayer, in the Mass. And as we saw in the last chapter, he ordered that the kiss of peace be given after the Our Father.

Pope Gregory died on March 12, 604. Soon after, he was honored by the Church as a saint. His feast is celebrated on September 3. Gregory's work as pope was so important that people soon began to call him Gregory the Great. Only two other popes in Church history have been given the title of "the Great"—Pope Leo the Great, pope at the time of the Council of Chalcedon in 451, and Pope Nicholas the Great, who died in 867. Both of these popes are also saints.

Recall and Reflect

1. Why is Pope Gregory the Great sometimes called a man of two worlds?
2. Who were the Lombards?
3. What were some of the things Gregory did as pope?
4. The sixth and seventh centuries marked a turning point in the history of the Church. Have you experienced any turning points in your life? How did they change you?

Pope Saint Gregory the Great (590–604), shown here in a tenth-century manuscript, began the work of converting the Germanic peoples of Europe.

MONKS AS MISSIONARIES

Saint Patrick: Apostle to Ireland Even before Pope Gregory the Great set up such strong bonds between missionary monks and the pope, many monastic communities were already working among the peoples of Europe. One of the greatest monk-missionaries was Saint Patrick, the apostle to the Irish people.

Saint Patrick was born about 389 in Roman Britain. At the age of sixteen, he was seized by Irish raiders. Taken to Ireland as a slave, he spent six years working as a shepherd. Patrick escaped, went to southern France, and became a monk. Around the year 432, he asked to be sent on a mission to Ireland. He was ordained as a bishop and began to work among the Irish people. When Patrick died, around 461, most Irish people were Christians.

Irish monks went out as missionaries to other parts of Europe. They set up monasteries and preached the gospel in Scotland and northern England. Some went to France. One Irish monk who went to France was the great saint Columban.

Saint Columban: Monk-Missionary Saint Columban was born in Ireland around 540. In 590, Columban with twelve monks went as a missionary to Europe. He went to work among the Franks, a Germanic people who ruled what had been the old Roman province of Gaul. In fact, the Franks gave their name to the country. We call it France. The Franks and their king, Clovis I, had been converted to the Catholic Church in 496. Saint Columban set up several monasteries in France and wrote a rule for his monks.

When Columban began to work in France, he was about the same age as Pope Gregory the Great. It is interesting to note the differences between Saint Gregory the Great and Saint Columban. Gregory could be firm, but he was always kind. Columban was very outspoken, sharp in his language, and he made many enemies. Columban was even sharp in writing to Pope Gregory the Great.

Many of the Franks did not like Columban. Irish monks had many religious customs that were different from those of the Franks. For example, the Irish used their own method of determining the date of Easter and thus celebrated the feast on a different date than the rest of the Catholic Church. The Frankish bishops, especially, did not like the Irish ways. Columban also spoke out against the kings and queens of the Franks. Finally, Columban was forced to leave the country. He first went to what is now Switzerland and then to northern Italy. In both places Saint Columban did missionary work and founded yet other

While a monk in France, Saint Patrick dreamed he heard the voice of the Irish people calling him back. He returned to Ireland to preach the gospel.

monasteries. He died in Italy in 615. The feast of Saint Columban is celebrated on November 21.

Saint Boniface: Apostle to Germany After the English people had been converted to the Church, they too began to send out monks and nuns as missionaries. A great Anglo-Saxon missionary was Saint Boniface, apostle to the Germans.

Boniface, whose Anglo-Saxon name was Winfrid, was born in England around 673. As a young boy he was educated in a Benedictine monastery. He became a monk and taught in the monastery school. In 716, when Boniface was about forty-three, he decided to become a missionary.

Saint Boniface wanted to preach the faith to the Germanic peoples from whom his ancestors had come. First, however, in 719 Boniface went to Rome to see the pope. The pope, Gregory II, was the one who gave Winfrid the name of Boniface. This new name, which means "one who does good," was to be a sign of Boniface's new life. The pope also told Boniface where to work in Germany.

As a missionary, Boniface always worked closely with the popes. Three times he visited Rome to talk with the pope. On his second visit to Rome, in 722, Pope Gregory II made him a bishop. As leader of the German Church, Boniface became the first archbishop of Mainz (mīnts), today a large city in West Germany. He wrote many letters to the popes, asking their advice. He went from place to place in Germany, preaching and baptizing.

Many other monks left England to help Boniface. And Boniface founded several Benedictine monasteries in Germany to help spread Christianity among the Germanic peoples.

Saint Lioba: Missionary Nun Today in the Church many nuns and other Catholic women work as missionaries. Women also did this kind of work during the period when the Church was converting the peoples of Europe. Nuns acted as missionaries by living in monasteries among those peoples. They prayed for the peoples' conversion, and they taught young girls. The nuns set an example of Christian living for the people among whom they dwelt.

One of the greatest of these missionary nuns, and a co-worker of Saint Boniface's in Germany, was the English nun Lioba (lē ō′bə). Her name, Lioba, is an abbreviation for the Anglo-Saxon name Liobgetha (lē′ob geth′ə) and means "the dear one."

Through her mother, Lioba was related to Saint Boniface.

As a young girl, Lioba was educated in an English monastery, where she developed a great love for learning. When she grew up, she decided to remain in the monastery as a nun.

After Saint Boniface began working as a missionary among the Germans, Lioba wrote to him, promising him her prayers and asking his help in her studies. Lioba and Boniface began to exchange letters.

In 748, Saint Boniface asked Saint Tetta, the **abbess**, or superior, of Lioba's monastery, to send him nuns who could help him in preaching the gospel to the Germans. Saint Tetta sent Boniface thirty nuns, among whom was Saint Lioba.

Saint Boniface built a monastery for these English nuns near Mainz. Lioba became the abbess. Under her wise and gentle rule, this monastery was well-known. So many young German women became nuns that Lioba was able to set up many other monasteries in Germany.

Lioba and her nuns followed the *Rule* of Saint Benedict. Their lives included manual labor as well as prayer and study. Saint Lioba was loved by the German people for her kindness and wisdom. After a very long life, she died in her monastery on September 28, 782.

Saint Boniface: Church Reformer Unlike Saint Columban in the previous century, Saint Boniface had good relations with the rulers of the Franks. At the time of Boniface, the Frankish kings were very weak. The true rulers of the Frankish kingdom, or France, were strong military men who were called mayors of the palace. One such mayor of the palace, Charles Martel, always gave protection to Boniface on his missionary journeys.

With his fellow monks, Saint Boniface worked for the conversion of the Germanic peoples for more than thirty years, until his martyrdom in 754.

After Charles Martel died in 741, his two sons, Carloman and Pepin III (the Short), ruled in the Frankish kingdom. They asked Saint Boniface to come to their lands and reform the Church. The bishops and the other clergy were not living up to their calling as God's ministers. Boniface ordered the bishops to meet from time to time in **synods** (sin′ədz), or Church councils. This old custom of the Church had been allowed to die out in France. Boniface outlawed many pagan practices still used by the Frankish people. He also tried very hard to reform the life-style of the priests.

In Germany, Saint Boniface set up **dioceses** (dī′ə sēz), or Church districts, ruled over by bishops. Here, too, he called synods and corrected the clergy who led evil lives.

Boniface died as he had lived, preaching the gospel. Although he was about eighty, he went with some of his priests to the northern part of what is now Holland to work among the Germanic people called Frisians (frizh′ənz).

Boniface had already baptized many Frisians. While he was preparing to give confirmation to the new converts, the place where Boniface was staying was invaded by a large band of pagan Frisians. In the early morning of June 5, 754, Boniface, his clergy, and all the new converts were killed. When he was attacked, the old bishop held up the gospel book he used at Mass as a shield. The sword of his attacker smashed through the book and split his skull. Thus Saint Boniface died as he had always lived,

holding fast to the gospel. His feast day is June 5.

The Christian religion spread slowly in Europe. At times Christians themselves prevented its spread by their unchristian lives. People like Saint Gregory the Great, Saint Patrick, Saint Columban, Saint Boniface, and Saint Lioba teach us that to spread Christianity requires generosity, love, and courage.

Recall and Reflect

1. Why were monks and nuns important at this time in Church history?

2. Where did Saint Columban set up monasteries?

3. Who were Boniface's chief helpers in preaching to the Germanic peoples?

4. How can you be a missionary and bring Christ to those about you?

This tenth-century illustration shows Saint Boniface blessing a convert at baptism and holding up the gospel book at his martyrdom.

REVIEW AND CELEBRATE

Doctrinal Summary

The Second Vatican Council tells us the Church is missionary by its very nature. The Catholic Church must always preach the gospel everywhere—must seek to win people to Christ. But the council also tells us to respect values found in non-Christian religions. Missionary activity brings to the Church the values and gifts of many different peoples and many different cultures.

Religious Vocabulary

Christendom	pagans	papacy	homily	synods
missionaries	archbishop	Kyrie Eleison	abbess	dioceses

Review Questions

1. Why was Europe known as Christendom for almost a thousand years?
2. Give three reasons why the papacy of Pope Saint Gregory the Great is so important for the history of the Church.
3. Why was the missionary work of Saint Boniface among the Germanic peoples so successful?
4. What important lessons about spreading the faith can we learn from the lives of Saints Gregory, Boniface, and Lioba?

Prayer Celebration

Leader: Come, Holy Spirit, fill the hearts of Your faithful and kindle in them the fire of Your love.
All: Send forth Your Spirit, O Lord, and renew the face of the earth.

Leader: Our prayer is taken from Saint Paul's second letter to the Corinthians, Chapter 4, verses 5 to 6 and 13 to 14. "It is not ourselves we preach but Christ Jesus as Lord. . . ."
All: Come, Holy Spirit, Spirit of Jesus, and fill us with Your power and love.

Leader: "For God, who said, 'Let light shine out of darkness,' has shone in our hearts, that we in turn might make known the glory of God shining on the face of Christ."

All: Come, Holy Spirit, Spirit of Jesus, and fill us with Your power and love.

Leader: ". . . We believe and so we speak, knowing that he who raised up the Lord Jesus will raise us up along with Jesus and place both us and you in his presence."
All: Come, Holy Spirit, Spirit of Jesus, and fill us with Your power and love.

Leader: Holy Spirit of God, we are inspired by people like Gregory, Boniface, and Lioba, and we pray for generosity, love, and courage to spread God's saving love to others.
All: Amen.

Charlemagne ruled the first great empire in Christendom. Out of his reign grew the idea of an empire that was both holy and Roman.

6

Charlemagne and Christendom

The last chapter told how the Church began converting the Germanic peoples of Europe. On becoming Christian, these peoples also became more Roman, for the Church was also a bridge to the culture of the Roman Empire.

One idea that came out of the Roman world was the idea of empire—the idea that all peoples were, or should be, members of one political community, or state. In like manner, out of that same Roman world came the Christian idea that all peoples were called to be members of one church. As the society we have called Christendom continued to grow and develop in Europe, both these ideas—about one empire and one church—would come to be linked in the idea of an empire that was both holy and Roman.

This chapter is about the man who built the first such empire in Christendom. King of the Franks from 768 to 814, he is called Charles the Great, or in Old French, Charlemagne (shär'lə mān). As the map on page 57 shows, Charlemagne conquered a huge empire in Europe. But he tried to do much more; he tried to build a whole new society that would be not only German but Roman and Christian as well. In this chapter also we shall look at the work of two missionaries who were brothers—Saints Cyril and Methodius. In the ninth century, they brought Christianity to the Slavic peoples of Central and Eastern Europe.

CHARLEMAGNE: EMPEROR OF THE ROMANS

Pepin: King of the Franks Charlemagne was born in 742. At that time his father, Pepin the Short, was not yet king of the Franks. As we saw in Chapter 5, Pepin's title was mayor of the palace. But as the strongest military leader, Pepin was the real ruler of the Frankish kingdom.

In the year 749, Pope Zacharias (zak′ə-rī′əs) approved Pepin's desire to be elected king of the Franks. The pope said that the one who held the responsibility and had the power should be king. Thus the Franks' weak king, who was only a young boy, was sent to be a monk. And in 751, Pepin was elected king by the Frankish leaders.

Pepin, the king, was grateful for the support of the papacy. But the popes also needed the help of the Frankish kings. Twice, in 754 and again in 756, Pepin went to Italy to protect the pope against the Lombards. After defeating the Lombards in 756, Pepin gave the country around Rome to the pope. In this way the popes began to rule a part of central Italy that would later be called the **Papal States**. The Papal States would be governed by the popes until 1870.

Charlemagne: King of the Franks When Pepin III died in 768, his two sons, Charlemagne and Carloman, became the rulers of the Franks. After Carloman died in 771, Charlemagne ruled alone. Unlike his father, Charlemagne was over six feet (1.8 m) tall. He had the build of an athlete, and he loved to swim and hunt. Charlemagne was educated at his father's court. He understood Greek and learned to read Latin. But he could not write very well. A strong leader and good soldier, Charlemagne had a powerful personality and made friends easily.

As king, Charlemagne carried on Pepin's policies. He continued to expand the Frankish kingdom. He worked closely with the popes, and he aided Church reform. Like his father, Charlemagne was asked by the pope, now Adrian I, to help defend the papacy against the Lombard

king. This time, in 774, Charlemagne defeated the Lombard king and sent him into exile in the north of Europe. Charlemagne himself took the title "king of the Lombards." At the same time, the pope gave Charlemagne the title "patrician of the Romans." This title meant that, within the Papal States, Charlemagne now had the military power which had been exercised long ago by Roman emperors. In fact, by 774, Charlemagne ruled most of Italy.

During most of his reign, Charlemagne was chiefly concerned with military matters. For almost thirty years, Charlemagne fought against the Germanic Saxon peoples of northern Germany. The Saxons, most of whom were still pagans, resisted bitterly. As part of his efforts to conquer the Saxons, Charlemagne forced them to become Christian under pain of death. Many became Christian, but many more were killed.

By 788 the Germanic Bavarian peoples, who lived in southeast Germany, were also incorporated into the Frankish kingdom. And in 795, Charlemagne conquered the Avars (ā′värz), an Asiatic people who had settled in the lower Danube basin. As the map on page 57 shows, by the year 800, Charlemagne had some kind of authority in most of what we now call Western Europe. He used that authority to appoint leaders called counts and dukes to rule those vast lands in his name.

Charlemagne: Protector of the Pope Pope Adrian I, who was Charlemagne's close friend, died in Rome in 795. His successor was Pope Leo III. Unlike many of the popes before him, Pope Leo did not belong to a powerful, wealthy family. As a result, Pope Leo had little support when important people in Rome began to criticize him. One day in 799, the pope's enemies attacked him as he rode on horseback with his clergy to offer Mass in a Roman church. They knocked Pope Leo from his horse, beat him badly, and shut him up in a monastery. Two of Charlemagne's officers who were in Rome had the pope set free. Pope Leo then fled north to Germany to ask Charlemagne for help. The pope's enemies also went to Charlemagne and accused Pope Leo of many crimes. At the time, Charlemagne was again fighting against the Saxons. He sent Pope Leo back to Rome with a guard of soldiers and promised to go there himself and settle the problems.

When Charlemagne arrived in Rome late in 800, he allowed Pope Leo to publicly clear himself of all charges by taking an oath that he was innocent. Pope Leo's enemies were exiled, and Charlemagne was hailed as the pope's protector.

Charlemagne: Emperor of the Romans On Christmas day in the year 800, Charlemagne went to Pope Leo's Mass in the bascilica of St. Peter in Rome. As Charlemagne knelt before the place where the apostle Peter was buried, the pope put a crown on his head and named him "emperor of the Romans." Then the pope knelt before Charlemagne and bowed down to the ground. The people began to shout, "To Charles crowned by God, the great and peaceful emperor, life and victory!" The crowd chanted this three times.

In this painting Charlemagne is shown three times: being crowned emperor by Pope Leo III, kneeling in prayer, and dressed in armor.

SIDELIGHTS ON CHURCH HISTORY
The Feasts of All Saints and All Souls

In the Roman rite, we celebrate the Feast of All Saints on November 1. The next day, November 2, is All Souls' Day. A special feast in honor of all the saints was celebrated in the West as early as the fourth century. We do not know just when the feast came to be celebrated on November 1. In the eighth century, a Feast of All Saints was celebrated in England on November 1. Alcuin may have brought this English custom to Charlemagne's court. Pope Gregory IV (827–844) asked Charlemagne's son, the emperor Louis the Pious, to extend the November 1 Feast of All Saints throughout the Empire. From the time of Pope Gregory VII (1073–1085), the Feast of All Saints has been kept on November 1 in all of Western Europe.

In England the Feast of All Saints was called Allhallowmas, or All Saints' Mass. October 31, the eve or Vigil of the Feast of All Saints, came to be known as Alla Hallow e'en. We call it Halloween.

The custom of praying for all the faithful departed on November 2, All Souls' Day, is traditionally attributed to Saint Odilo. He was abbot of the Benedictine monastery of Cluny, in what is now east-central France. Odilo's monks were asked again and again by the people to pray for their relatives and friends who had died. About the year 1030, Saint Odilo decided to set aside one day in the year for the monks to pray for all the faithful departed. Soon the custom of the Abbey of Cluny was followed by the entire Church.

This was the same ceremony that was used to crown the Byzantine or Greek emperor in Constantinople. It indicated that Charlemagne, as emperor of the Romans, was the legal successor of the old Roman emperors in the West. (The ceremony also strengthened the strong bonds that already existed between the popes and the Frankish rulers.) In 812, two years before his death, Charlemagne was finally recognized as emperor in the West by the emperor in Constantinople.

Recall and Reflect

1. How did Pope Zacharias help Charlemagne's father become king?

2. Why did the papacy need the support of the Frankish kings?

3. How did Charlemagne carry on his father's policies?

4. Jesus taught that God Himself introduced His reign, or kingship, into history. In one place Jesus said: "The reign of God is like yeast which a woman took and kneaded into three measures of flour. Eventually the whole mass of dough began to rise" (Matthew 13:33). How does this teaching help us to understand the role of the Church in society?

CHARLEMAGNE'S EMPIRE

Charlemagne as Lawgiver Charlemagne governed his Empire firmly. Although military concerns took up most of his time, Charlemagne wanted to set up an orderly government in the lands he ruled. He issued a flood of laws to control society and to keep public order. For Charlemagne there was no difference between civil, or political, matters and religious matters. Many of his laws were concerned with the organization of the Church and the reform of the clergy.

For example, Charlemagne made everyone pay a tax, called a **tithe** (tīтн), to the Church. The tithe was to be paid to the parish church. It was to be used for the upkeep of the church and for charity to the poor in the parish. Charlemagne made all monks and nuns in his kingdom follow the *Rule* of Saint Benedict. He even included those monks and nuns who had followed the *Rule* of the Irish saint Columban. Charlemagne also picked the bishops and abbots in his lands.

Charlemagne used bishops and abbots as public officers. Every part of the Empire was to be visited once each year by two official inspectors, who were to see that Charlemagne's laws were obeyed. One of those inspectors was always a Church official—a bishop or an abbot. The other was a layperson called a duke or a count. The two inspectors always reported to Charlemagne what they had found in each district.

Charlemagne and Feudalism Europe in the time of Charlemagne had few cities. What little trade, or commerce, existed was mostly local. As a result, Charlemagne did not have a very good tax system in his Empire. There was little money to hire either soldiers or civil servants. To govern and defend the Empire, Charlemagne made use of a system of personal ties called feudalism (fyü′də liz əm), or the feudal system.

In feudalism, kings or queens or other powerful leaders bound people to themselves by means of personal oaths, or promises, of loyalty. The powerful persons, known as lords, promised to protect their followers and to keep law and order. Those who put themselves under a king or lord in this way were called the lord's vassals, or followers. In return for the vassals' ser-

vices, the lord gave the vassals farmlands or other means of support. Such lands came to be called fiefs (fēfs).

The chief service that lords required from their vassals was military service. Vassals had to be ready to follow their lords into battle themselves or to provide soldiers to fight for them. Those soldiers, who fought on horseback and wore heavy armor, were called knights.

In feudalism, one could be a vassal of a lord and at the same time have vassals of one's own. Just as Charlemagne, the king, had vassals, so they—his dukes and counts —had their own vassals.

Although Charlemagne used this feudal system as the basis for ruling his Empire, he did not create it. Feudalism already existed in Europe at that time. People were entering into the personal relationships of lords and vassals to find protection when governments were weak or not well or-

Knights, wearing heavy coats of chain mail, fought on horseback. Bishops and abbots as well as kings and nobles had knights to defend them.

ganized. This system worked well as long as kings and lords could hold their vassals' loyalty. Charlemagne was able to do this.

The Church in the Feudal System It is not possible to separate the Church from any society in which it is found. At the time of Charlemagne, the Church became a **feudal Church** and a part of the growing feudal system. Bishops and abbots also became vassals to Charlemagne. They held their lands and offices as fiefs. In turn, the bishops and the abbots had their own vassals; they too became lords. The vassals of bishops and abbots were fighting men, and the bishops and abbots gave Church lands as fiefs to those vassals. Moreover, bishops and abbots, along with their knights, often went into battle with Charlemagne. Sometimes the bishops and abbots fought as well. Popes also became lords and had vassals.

Many bishops and abbots had large territories, with numerous farms and villages under their control. Charlemagne often made these bishops and abbots the princes, or rulers, of these lands. Such bishops and abbots then had to keep public order. They acted as judges and enforced the laws. In this way many Church leaders became temporal, or secular, rulers as well as spiritual leaders. In later times this would sometimes become a serious problem for the Church.

The Manor: A Working Farm The fiefs that Charlemagne granted to his vassals were usually made up of one or more working farms, called manors. A single manor was generally large enough to support one knight's family. A knight had certain rights over the people who lived and worked on the farm. He was called the lord of the manor. The men and women who farmed

A manor might have several villages such as this one, each with its manor house, church, barns, and cottages for serfs who worked the land.

the land were called serfs. The word *serf* means "one who serves."

Serfs lived in villages on the manor. They worked several days each week for the lord of the manor. But they were allowed to grow their own crops on part of the land. Lords of the manors had to protect their workers. Their serfs were not slaves, but neither were they really free. They could not be sold and were said to be "bound to the soil."

Lords of the manors built churches for their serfs. The lords owned these churches and chose their priests. But they also had to keep up the churches and support the priests. Sometimes a lord would pick a serf to become a priest on the manor. The lord was supposed to free the serf beforehand, but this did not always happen.

Monasteries also owned manors. They had serfs who lived in farming villages. A monastery would also own all the churches on its manors. The abbot of the monastery would choose the priests for these churches. This was also the system in monasteries for nuns. The abbess of such a monastery would have charge of the serfs who farmed the monastery land. She owned the churches and picked the priests who served them.

In the feudal system, abbots and abbesses became great and powerful people. Their monasteries also had vassals who were fighting men, or knights. The leaders of the monasteries, then, had a great deal of influence, not only in the Church but in civil, or political, affairs as well.

Bishops and Their Priests In the time of Charlemagne the cities and towns of Europe were not very large. Most wealthy people lived on their manors. Charlemagne himself moved his court from one large estate to another. Only in the last years of

There was always work to be done on the manor: sheep, goats, and other animals to be cared for; fields to be plowed and harvests to be gathered.

his reign did Charlemagne build a palace and cathedral church at Aachen (ăk′ən), in present-day West Germany. Bishops, however, usually lived in the cities. It was there they had their cathedral churches. Priests who lived with the bishop and conducted services in the cathedral were called **canons**. The canons sang the prayers of the Divine Office every day in the church. In addition, some of the canons ran cathedral schools for young boys who were interested in becoming priests.

At this time, a bishop had an important assistant in ruling a diocese. The assistant was called an **archdeacon** and usually was ordained as a deacon or priest. The archdeacon was in charge of all the priests in the diocese. He looked after all church property and took care of the needs of the poor. He also took care of the young men

Schools and colleges continue to be run by monastic communities today, as in the time of Charlemagne.

who wished to become priests. The archdeacon visited every parish to see if everything was in order and to correct what was wrong. Today, however, we do not have the office of archdeacon in the Church.

Charlemagne and Learning Charlemagne ordered that a school be opened in every large monastery and cathedral to train young men who were to become priests. The sons of lords and other wealthy people also went to these schools. Priests in parishes and in churches owned by laypeople or monasteries were also urged to teach the children. One of Charlemagne's laws stated:

> Let there be built schools for young boys to teach them to read. Let there be books with psalms, with notes of music, with numbers and grammar; let the books be corrected. . . . Do not let the boys destroy the books. . . .

There is a story that one day Charlemagne visited a school he had begun for young boys. He wanted to see how well they knew their lessons. He found that the sons of the poorer families were better prepared than those of the rich families. Charlemagne promised the poor boys that if they continued to do well they would become bishops when they were older. He told the wealthy boys that they would receive nothing if they did not study harder.

Charlemagne brought scholars from all over Europe to his court. One of these great teachers was Alcuin (al′kwin), an English scholar. Alcuin wrote books about language, arithmetic, the Bible, and theology. In his old age Alcuin became abbot of a monastery at Tours, in central France. From Tours, he wrote Charlemagne many letters full of good advice. Alcuin died in 804 and is honored in the Church today as "Blessed Alcuin." The title "Blessed" is

THE OUR FATHER

Our Father, who art in heaven,
hallowed be Thy name;
Thy kingdom come;
Thy will be done on earth
    as it is in heaven.
Give us this day our daily bread;
and forgive us our trespasses
as we forgive those who trespass
    against us;
and lead us not into temptation,
but deliver us from evil. Amen.

THE APOSTLES' CREED

I believe in God, the Father Almighty,
Creator of heaven and earth;
and in Jesus Christ, His only Son,
    our Lord,
who was conceived by the Holy Spirit,
born of the Virgin Mary,
suffered under Pontius Pilate,
was crucified, died, and was buried.
He descended into hell;
the third day He arose again
    from the dead.
He ascended into heaven,
sits at the right hand of God,
    the Father Almighty;
from thence He shall come
to judge the living and the dead.
I believe in the Holy Spirit,
the holy Catholic Church,
the communion of saints,
the forgiveness of sins,
the resurrection of the body,
and life everlasting. Amen.

sometimes given by the Church to people who have lived very holy lives.

Charlemagne sincerely tried to spread Christianity. He wanted all the people in his lands to use the same liturgy. He often asked the popes to send him liturgical books. Charlemagne wanted the ceremonies of the Mass, including the music, conducted just the way they were conducted in Rome. He wanted the people to know about their religion. One of Charlemagne's laws required priests in every parish to see to it that everyone knew the Our Father and the Apostles' Creed.

Charlemagne died in 814 and was buried in the church he had built in Aachen. Although his Empire did not last, Charlemagne accomplished three important things. He brought many peoples into the Church. He increased the number of educated people by using the culture of Rome to meet the needs of the Germanic peoples. Finally, Charlemagne permanently linked the Frankish Church—and all of Europe—to the papacy and the Roman Church. Charlemagne's work set the pattern of religious life in Europe for many years to come. He made sure that the Church would have a leading role in building up the new society of Christendom.

Recall and Reflect

1. How did Charlemagne use the feudal system to govern his Empire?

2. What was the chief service that vassals performed for their lords?

3. In what ways did the Church become part of the feudal system?

4. How did Charlemagne encourage learning?

5. What is the relation between the government and the Church in our own country? How does this compare with Charlemagne's attitude toward the Church in his Empire?

THE SLAVIC PEOPLES OF EUROPE

Conversion of the Slavs East of Charlemagne's Empire, in Central and Eastern Europe, lived the Slavs. The word *slava*, means "glory" in the Slavic language. Slavic peoples still live in these parts of Europe.

Like the Germanic peoples before them, the pagan Slavic peoples of Europe encountered Christianity when they came into conflict with peoples of the Roman Empire along the Danube River. By the middle of the sixth century, many Slavic groups had moved south, across the Danube, and were living in the Balkan Peninsula. Many Slavs settled in what is now the northern part of the present-day country of Greece. Slavic people also settled in the lands to the east of the Elbe and Oder rivers.

As the map on page 57 shows, the Church in the Byzantine, or Eastern Roman, Empire had missions among the Slavs and converted many of them. By the time of Charlemagne, German missionaries, many of them monks, had also begun working among the Slavs of Central Europe. Many Slavic peoples of Central Europe, however, resisted the German missionaries, because accepting Christianity from them also meant accepting German political control.

Saints Cyril and Methodius In the ninth century Cyril and Methodius, who were brothers and Greek-speaking monks, began working among the Slavic peoples in Central Europe. They worked in what was then called Moravia, now a part of the country of Czechoslovakia.

Cyril and Methodius were born in Thessalonica, in northern Greece. Their father was an official of that Byzantine province. Cyril, youngest of the seven children in the family, was born in 826 or 827. Methodius was born about 815. Since there were many Slavs living in Thessalonica at that time, both boys grew up speaking the Slavic language as well as their native Greek.

Methodius, the older of the two brothers, had a career in government. Then, after being ruler of a province in the Byzantine Empire for some years, he became a monk. Meanwhile, Cyril at age fourteen was sent to Constantinople to study. A brilliant student, Cyril graduated from the imperial university and became a priest. He was called "The Philosopher" because of his great learning. In 855, Cyril became a

Saints Cyril and Methodius were brothers. In 862 the Byzantine emperor sent them to work among the Slavic peoples of Moravia.

The picture above shows Mass being celebrated in Slavonic.
The Slavonic liturgy is used in Serbian and Russian Catholic Churches.

monk in the monastery where Methodius served.

In 862 the Byzantine emperor sent Cyril and Methodius on a mission to the Slavs in Moravia. The Slavic duke of Moravia, Rastislav, had asked the emperor for missionaries who spoke Slavonic, or the Slavic language. Rastislav did not want the Slavic Church to be under the control of German-speaking bishops and priests.

A Slavonic Liturgy The two brothers arrived in Moravia around 863. Cyril invented an alphabet for writing down the Slavic language, and he began to translate the gospel into Slavonic. Cyril's alphabet is different from the Latin alphabet we use to spell our words. It is also different from

the Greek alphabet. Cyril and Methodius also translated the Mass and other liturgical services into Slavonic.

German-speaking missionaries did not like the work of Cyril and Methodius. By this time in Europe, the only language used for the Mass was Latin. The German missionaries, of course, used the Latin Mass. But the two brothers were successful in Moravia because the Slavs could keep their own language in their liturgy.

In 867, after working four years in Moravia, Cyril and Methodius wanted to return to Constantinople to get a bishop to work among the Slavs. They were invited to go to Rome on their way home. In Rome many people did not like the brothers' use of Slavonic in the liturgy of the

Mass. But Pope Adrian II supported the work of the brothers and gave his permission. He ordained Methodius as a bishop. Cyril, who had become ill, entered a monastery in Rome. He died on February 14, 869, and was buried in Rome.

Pope Adrian made Methodius an archbishop for the Slavs. When Methodius returned to Moravia, however, the German king put him in prison. German bishops falsely accused Methodius of working against them because he preached in the Slavic language. These bishops had no right to judge Archbishop Methodius. And they had no right to keep him from appealing to the pope. After two years, Pope John VIII, who had succeeded Pope Adrian, secured Methodius's freedom. Pope John put the mission to the Slavs directly under the control of the papacy. He allowed Methodius to continue his work among the Slavic peoples. Methodius died on April 6, 884.

All the Slavic-speaking missionaries were driven out of Moravia after Methodius died. They then became missionaries among the Bulgarians and other Slavic peoples of the Balkan Peninsula. As a result of the missionaries' labors, the Slavonic liturgy of Cyril and Methodius is preserved today in the liturgies of the Serbian and Russian Catholic Churches. Saints Cyril and Methodius are the patron saints of the Slavic peoples. We celebrate the feast of these saints on February 14.

In this chapter we have seen that Charlemagne united the Germanic peoples of Europe and linked them to the papacy. We have seen that the Slavic peoples of Central Europe were converted through the work of Saints Cyril and Methodius. And we have noticed that the developing feudal system made bishops and abbots into political leaders as well as Church leaders. As we shall see in the next chapter, feudalism and growing differences between emperors and popes—the leaders of the Empire and the Church—would lead to serious conflicts between church and state.

Recall and Reflect

1. In what parts of Europe do we find Slavic-speaking peoples?

2. How did Saints Cyril and Methodius become missionaries among the Slavic peoples?

3. What greatly helped Saints Cyril and Methodius to preach to the Slavs?

4. Speaking of the Church's missionary activity, the Second Vatican Council states: "The mission of the Church . . . is fulfilled by that activity which makes her fully present to all men and nations" (Decree on the Missionary Activity of the Church, 5). In what ways that you know of does the Church in our country carry out its mission to spread the faith of Christ?

REVIEW AND CELEBRATE

Doctrinal Summary

In our own time, as in ages past, the Church continues the mission of Jesus. It seeks to bring about God's kingdom by preaching the word of God, celebrating the liturgy, and serving the people. Throughout its history the Church has always engaged in these three ministries of word, worship, and service.

Religious Vocabulary

Papal States   canons
tithe   archdeacon
feudal Church

Review Questions

Answer the following questions on a separate sheet of paper.

1. What was the significance of Charlemagne's title "emperor of the Romans"?
2. How would you describe Charlemagne's attitude toward the Church? Toward learning?
3. What were some of the results of the Church's becoming part of the feudal system?
4. How did Charlemagne's work help set the pattern for religious life in Europe after his time?
5. What methods did Saints Cyril and Methodius use to convert the Slavic peoples of Europe?

Prayer Celebration

Leader: Together let us pray that we may be aware of God's presence among us with the words that Jesus, His Son, taught us.
All: Our Father, who art in heaven . . . (continue with the words of the Our Father).

Leader: Deliver us, Lord, from every evil, and grant us peace in our day. In Your mercy keep us free from sin and protect us from all anxiety as we wait in joyful hope for the coming of our Savior, Jesus Christ.
All: For the kingdom, the power, and the glory are Yours, now and forever.

Leader: Together let us express our Faith.
All: I believe in God, the Father almighty . . . (continue with the words of the Apostles' Creed).

Leader: God, our Father, we are grateful for the life You have given us, for the gifts You have given us to keep us alive, and for Your Son, Jesus, whose life and love have given our lives His Holy Spirit of joy and peace.
All: Amen.

Above are three scenes from the life of Pope Gregory VII. At the top, Henry IV
sets up an antipope in Rome as Gregory flees. At the bottom, we see Gregory
in exile with his cardinals and after his death.

7

Struggle Between Pope and Emperor

Imagine this scene. You are before a great castle, massive and still. A young man stands all alone by the closed castle gate. The man is bareheaded and barefoot even though it is midwinter and there is snow on the ground. He is dressed as a penitent, in a coarse white gown. Inside the castle are many people—the great lady to whom it belongs, Matilda, the countess of Tuscany; Hugh, the abbot of Cluny; and the ruling pope, Pope Gregory VII. The lonely young man at the castle gate is Henry IV, king of Germany.

In January 1077, this scene actually took place. For three days King Henry IV of Germany stood before the castle of Canossa (kə näs′ə) in northern Italy. He was begging forgiveness from Pope Gregory VII. The pope had deprived Henry of his rights as a member of the Church. The reasons for this, the events that led up to it, and what happened afterward, will be the subject of

this chapter. Canossa was part of a long struggle between popes and emperors for control of the Church.

THE TENTH CENTURY: A TIME OF CRISIS

Decline of the Carolingian Empire The alliance between the popes and Charlemagne and the rulers who followed him—the Carolingians, as they are called—had united the Church in the West around the popes. Both spiritually and politically, all of Western Europe became identified with Rome. Although Carolingian rulers tried to govern the Church, they also backed papal reforms. Because he had the backing of an emperor, for example, Pope Nicholas the Great (858–867) was able to enforce the rule that no bishop could be chosen or be made to step down if the pope did not agree.

By the end of the ninth century, the Carolingian Empire had fallen apart. As the central government weakened, local feudal lords became more and more powerful. They were more interested in getting the Church's wealth than in aiding good bishops and priests. Adding to the general decline, bands of raiders from Northern Europe invaded the Empire. Called Northmen, the raiders were the ancestors of present-day Swedes, Norwegians, and Danes. The Northmen burned towns, destroyed crops, and looted monasteries. They caused much suffering and upset the Church's government. As the Empire became weaker, the popes no longer could count on the protection of Carolingian rulers. Without that help, the popes also lost both spiritual and political power. Rich and powerful families in Rome fought for control of the papacy. Each wealthy Roman

Below is a portrait of Ramuoldus, a tenth-century abbot. In the feudal system, bishops and abbots were also vassals of kings and other lay lords.

family put forward its own candidate for pope. There was much violence. Some popes ruled for only a few weeks and then —sometimes forcibly—were put out of office. Some popes were even murdered. In the hundred years from the end of the ninth century to the beginning of the eleventh, there were more than thirty-seven popes. Many of the men chosen were not fitted for this office.

One of the worst was Pope John XII, who became pope in 955, before he was twenty years old. Pope John is also remembered for another reason. On becoming pope, he changed his name from Octavian to John. Thus, since Pope John XII, popes have usually changed their names on being elected.

Feudalism Works Havoc in the Church As the papacy lost its power and leadership, the Church came more and more under the power of kings and lay lords. As we saw in Chapter 6, Charlemagne had chosen many bishops and abbots. At that time, this had brought greater peace and order to the Church. By the tenth century, however, many evils had crept in. Bishops and abbots were the vassals of the king or other lords. It became the right of those laypeople to give bishops and abbots not only their lands but their offices as bishops and abbots as well. This practice, called lay investiture (in ves'tə chùr), placed bishops and other members of the clergy under the control of laypeople. It often meant that unworthy people were chosen as Church leaders. Many of those Church leaders became more interested in their political rights than in their spiritual duties.

During the ninth and tenth centuries, two other abuses grew out of the Church's involvement in the feudal system. One abuse was the buying and selling of Church offices, which is called **simony** (sī′mə nē). At that time kings and other lords who had the power to appoint bishops or priests expected to be paid by the people they chose for those offices. Many bishops, in turn, charged money to ordain young men to the priesthood. Priests sometimes asked for money when they gave sacraments to people.

The second abuse was that by the eleventh century many of the clergy in the West were married, or lived with women to whom they were not legally married. From the fifth and sixth centuries, it was the custom for bishops, priests, and deacons in the Western Church not to marry. That custom, or rule, is called the **rule of celibacy** (sel′ə bə sē). A person who is not married is said to live as a celibate (sel′ə bit).

In the early Church, married men could be priests and deacons. Sometimes, though not often, they were even chosen bishops. But many early bishops and priests followed the example of Saint Paul. They did not marry, but remained celibate.

Clerical celibacy, or an unmarried clergy, is a matter of custom and Church law. Today the clergy in the Roman Catholic Church do not marry. Many of the Eastern Catholic Churches do have married priests. But those priests must marry before they become deacons. Bishops in the Eastern Churches are not married. In 1964, the Second Vatican Council revived the office of married deacon in the Roman Catholic Church. But at present married deacons usually do not become priests.

By the end of the ninth century, lay investiture, simony, and the abuse of celibacy by the clergy had become serious problems for the Church in the West. They touched all the members of the Church—popes, bishops, priests, and laypeople. As people abused their power or used Church offices

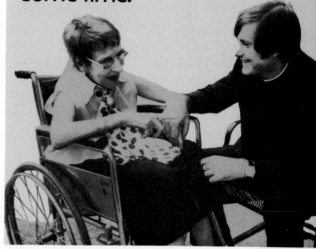

Father Patrick Dunne has had five jobs in the last three years—all at the same time.

Today, as in the past, a priest does many things. Like Father Dunne, he brings people the Mass and sacraments, teaches, counsels, and consoles.

for their own advantage, it became more and more difficult for the Church to preach the gospel. Many people in the Church, however, saw those practices as wrong, and they began to work for Church reform.

Recall and Reflect

1. How did the decline of the Carolingian Empire affect the papacy?

2. What is lay investiture?

3. Name two abuses within the Church between the ninth and eleventh centuries.

4. Monks and nuns in the Church today live celibate lives of poverty. They dedicate themselves to the service of God and His people. Think about the value of this dedication. What good comes to you because these people serve the Church?

REFORM OF THE PAPACY

Revival of Empire In the year 962, Otto I, king of Germany, revived the idea of empire in the West. Otto had become king of Germany in 936. A strong leader, Otto I used his power to appoint bishops to build up support for himself and work against the great feudal lords. Little by little, Otto was able to build up his power in Germany.

In 961, Pope John XII, whom we met earlier in this chapter, asked Otto I for help against people who were attacking the Church. Otto invaded Italy and defeated the pope's enemies. The next year, 962, Pope John crowned Otto as emperor.

Otto I was crowned Roman emperor by Pope John XII in 962. With his reign began an empire that would last for almost 900 years, until 1806.

This second revival of the Roman Empire in the West marks the beginning of what later came to be known as the Holy Roman Empire. This second empire was made up of Germany, the Low Countries, parts of Eastern Europe, and northern and central Italy. Its rulers were both kings of Germany and emperors. This Empire had a very long life, lasting until the year 1806, when it was dissolved by order of the French emperor, Napoleon.

As emperor, Otto I reconfirmed all the gifts of land made to the papacy by Charlemagne and his successors. He also made the Roman people promise never to choose a pope without the emperor's consent. Otto made it clear that he would control the papacy and restore the close cooperation between pope and emperor that had existed in the time of Charlemagne.

In 963, Otto called a synod in Rome to deal with Pope John XII. The pope, charged with murder and other crimes, was made to step down, and a successor was chosen. This synod began a period of almost a hundred years during which the popes were ruled by German emperors. When the emperors were too busy with German affairs, however, the papacy would again fall under the control of local feudal lords. When that happened, unworthy persons often became popes.

Benedict IX, pope from 1032 to 1045, was one such undeserving pope. Benedict's behavior saddened his godfather, John Gratian (grā′shən), a Roman priest interested in reform. In 1045, John persuaded Benedict IX to step down in return for a huge sum of money. Benedict agreed, and on the day he left Rome, John Gratian was chosen pope. He took the name of Gregory VI.

At first the choice of Gregory was hailed by people who wanted Church reform. But the ruling emperor, Henry III (1039–1056), would not agree to Gregory's election without an investigation. A meeting called in 1046 accused Gregory of simony because he had paid money to Benedict IX to give up his office. Pope Gregory was also forced to step down and was sent to Germany.

Henry III, one of the greatest of the German emperors, wanted to reform the Church. He chose the next four popes: Clement II, Damasus (dam′ə səs) II, Leo IX, and Victor II. All four popes were German.

A Papal Reform Program Pope Leo IX (1049–1054) was a relative of Henry III. Chosen pope at a synod in Germany because it was the emperor's wish, Leo IX insisted that his election be agreed to by the people of Rome before he acted as pope. During the five years he was in office, Leo IX spent less than six months in Rome. He traveled all over Europe calling for reform. Pope Leo presided over many synods and published many laws against simony and clerical marriage.

Under Leo IX a papal reform program began to take shape. Many of Leo's helpers were greatly influenced by ideas about reform that had started in Lorraine, a part of the Empire that is now northeastern France. Those reformers wanted a more spiritual Church. To get that kind of Church they needed holier bishops and priests. Therefore they needed to weaken the power of kings and feudal lords to name bishops and priests to Church offices. They believed the clergy must lead better lives, and the popes had to be free to rule the whole Church without interference.

Those three ideas formed the basis of Leo's reforms. From the time of Leo IX, the popes tried to promote papal primacy

The emperor Henry III (1039–1056), shown above on his deathbed, worked hard for Church reform. He chose four popes and used bishops as his helpers.

(prī′mə sē), enforce celibacy, and get rid of lay investiture.

Two of Leo's chief advisers who helped begin those reforms were Humbert (hum′bert) and Hildebrand (hil′də brand), both monks. Humbert, born in Lorraine, had been a helper of Leo IX when the pope had been the bishop of Toul, today a city in West Germany. In 1049, Leo made Humbert archbishop of Sicily, and later a cardinal. Humbert had a clear idea of the problems facing the papacy and worked hard to answer them. Hildebrand, born in Tuscany, Italy, had gone into exile with Pope Gregory VI. Pope Leo appointed Hildebrand archdeacon of the Roman Church. A practical person who could plan very well, Hildebrand could get things done.

In 1053, Pope Leo IX went to war against Norman princes who now ruled southern Italy. Defeated and taken prisoner, Pope Leo was kept in prison in the city of Bari (bär′ē) in southeastern Italy. When he became ill, Pope Leo was allowed to return to Rome. He died there in 1054. Pope Leo IX is honored as a saint. His feast day is April 19.

A Break Between East and West While Leo IX was pope, a **schism** (siz′əm) — that is, a break or separation — took place between the Churches of Rome and Constantinople that has lasted down to our own day. This schism between the Church in the East and the Church in the West has had many harmful results. Today the Roman Catholic and Orthodox Churches are trying, once again, to heal this break.

For many years before the eleventh century, relations between the Churches of Rome and Constantinople had not been friendly. There was a language barrier between the two. The language of the Western Church was Latin. Most Western clergy no longer understood Greek, the language of the Eastern Church. In the East the leader of the Church was the **patriarch** of Constantinople. Patriarch was an old title that was given to the bishops of some important dioceses in the early Church. Liturgical customs were different in the two Churches. Eastern Christians, for example, used ordinary, or leavened, bread in their Liturgy, as the Mass was called in the East. Western, or Latin, Christians used unleavened, or flat, bread. And as we have seen, Eastern priests could be married and have families. In the West, priests were asked not to marry.

Although there had been many breaks between the East and West before the eleventh century, they had been patched up. The Eastern Church, under the leadership of the patriarchs of Constantinople, continued to look upon the pope in Rome as the head of the Church.

Pope Leo IX, shown above blessing a model of the new monastery of Lord Abbot Waranus, began a strong program of papal reform.

The patriarch of Constantinople at the time Leo IX was pope was Michael Cerularius (ser′ü lär′ē əs). Patriarch Michael was a strong-willed, proud person. He came from a powerful family, and he had been a government officer before he became patriarch. Although Michael did not have deep training in theology, he strongly believed that the spiritual power of the patriarch was above the worldly power of the emperor.

Michael began to find fault with many of the liturgical customs of the Western, or Latin, Church. He said they were wrong. Finally, he closed all churches in Constantinople that followed Western practices. Western (Latin) Christians protested this action and told Leo IX.

In 1054, Pope Leo sent three **papal legates** (leg'its), or representatives, to Constantinople to try to work things out. A papal legate is one who acts in the pope's name and with his authority. The leader of the three legates was Cardinal Humbert. Unfortunately, Humbert was much like Michael Cerularius, the patriarch. Humbert, too, was proud and outspoken; he did not have much tact.

Constantine IX, the Byzantine ruler, wanted to restore good relations with the Roman Church. He sought to reach an understanding with Humbert. The people of Constantinople, however, liked their patriarch more than they liked their emperor. They took the side of Michael Cerularius.

When Humbert and Michael met, they did not get along; in fact, the meeting was very unfriendly. Humbert felt that Pope Leo was being insulted by the patriarch. Some days after this meeting, on the morning of July 16, 1054, Humbert and his fellow legates marched into the Church of the Holy Wisdom just as Patriarch Michael was about to celebrate the Liturgy. Cardinal Humbert threw down on the altar a paper excommunicating Michael. **Excommunication** means the taking away from a person all of his or her rights as a member of the Church. Humbert is supposed to have said, "Let God see and judge," and then walked out of the church.

The people of Constantinople became very angry about what had happened. Their patriarch had been insulted. Michael, on his part, excommunicated the papal legates. Humbert and his companions quickly left for Rome. But Cardinal Humbert did not know that Pope Leo IX had

SIDELIGHTS ON CHURCH HISTORY

Conversion of the Russian Peoples

For many centuries, groups of Slavs had settled in Eastern Europe, to the north of the Roman Empire. By the seventh century A.D., Slavs were living throughout the area between the Black Sea in the south and the Baltic Sea in the north. Today much of this land is part of the Union of Soviet Socialist Republics, or the Soviet Union. For hundreds of years, this huge territory was known as Russia.

Beginning in the eighth century, Northmen had begun raiding the lands occupied by the Slavs in Eastern Europe, just as other groups of Northmen had invaded the Carolingian Empire in Western Europe. By the ninth century one group of Northmen had settled in the south of this area, on the Dnieper River. Their settlement on the Dnieper was known as Kiev, and their leaders called themselves the "great princes of Kiev." From Kiev those Northmen began raiding the ports of the Black Sea and sometimes even attacked Constantinople. Byzantine and Slavic writers called them the "Rus." Eventually, the lands they ruled came to be called Russia, and the Slavic people they ruled were called Russians.

Russia became Christian through the efforts of Saint Vladimir, who was the great prince of Kiev from 980 to 1015. In 987, Vladimir married a Byzantine princess, Anna, the sister of the Byzantine emperor. Vladimir became a Christian and brought his people into the Church. The Russian Church thus came under the authority of the patriarch of Constantinople. Its liturgy is that of the Church of Constantinople. Saint Vladimir, the first Christian ruler of Russia, is honored as a saint in the Roman Catholic Church as well as in the Russian Church. In the West his feast day is July 15.

died in April and that the papal legates actually had no power to do anything in the pope's name.

Contemporaries of Humbert and Michael were not aware of any break between the Churches. The excommunication, after all, had been directed only against the patriarch. After 1054, however, the two Churches began to drift apart. Growing misunderstandings in later years widened the break. Today, even though the schism exists, there is better understanding and acceptance between the Churches.

Election Law of 1059 Reforms did not stop with the death of Leo IX. The people whom Leo had brought to Rome continued their work. Under Nicholas II, who became pope in 1058, a very important reform took place. This was the change in the way the pope was elected. In April 1059, a Roman synod said that future popes would be chosen by an electoral college — the **Sacred College of Cardinals**. This election law replaced the traditional right of the Roman clergy and people to choose the pope. Now the cardinals would act as representatives of Rome's clergy and people.

Who were the **cardinals**? Cardinals were important members of the Roman clergy — bishops, priests, and deacons. The name cardinal had been used as early as the sixth century in connection with the Roman Church. It was used to describe the members of the clergy in Rome or neighboring dioceses who not only performed duties in their own dioceses, or parishes, but also did special work for the popes. For example, many bishops of the dioceses near Rome were often asked by the popes to do certain things. In time, such bishops came to be called cardinal bishops. Humbert, for example, was called Cardinal Humbert of

Silva Candida (sil′və kan dē′də). On becoming a cardinal, Humbert also became the bishop of Silva Candida, a small diocese near Rome.

Priests who were in charge of important churches in the city of Rome were also given special duties by the popes. They came to be called cardinal priests. And after 1084, there were also cardinal deacons aiding the popes. By the beginning of the eleventh century, most of a pope's chief helpers were cardinals. Together, the cardinals came to be known as the Sacred College of Cardinals. The cardinals were — and still are — an important part of Church government.

The election law of 1059, making cardinals the only electors of the pope, was one

In 1963, Pope Paul VI and Patriarch Athenagoras of Constantinople met in Jerusalem. Since then, leaders of both Churches have met to talk about reunion.

of the most important reforms of the eleventh century. The German emperors had been able to free the popes from the control of the rich and powerful families of Rome. But the emperors themselves then tried to rule over the popes. Reform-minded Church people — Humbert, Hildebrand, and others — wanted total freedom for the Church in electing the pope.

Although many changes have been made in conducting papal elections since 1059, the cardinals still elect the pope today. Since the pope is also the bishop of Rome, when the cardinals elect him, they act in the name of the clergy and people of Rome. Each cardinal is pastor of a Roman church. As early as the end of the eleventh century, popes were naming men from far-off countries as cardinals. Today there are more than 130 cardinals in the Sacred College. And cardinals are chosen from all over the world. Eleven of our American bishops are cardinals.

Recall and Reflect

1. What was the attitude of the rulers of the Holy Roman Empire toward the Church?

2. What three ideas formed the basis of the papal reform program?

3. Who were the two people most responsible for the schism between the Eastern and Western Churches in 1054?

4. How did the election law of 1059 change the election of the pope?

5. In 1978, cardinals twice went to Rome to elect a pope. In the second election they chose a Polish cardinal, Karol Wojtyla, as pope. As Pope John Paul II, he became the first non-Italian pope in 456 years. (a) Why were people so excited over the election of a non-Italian pope? (b) Do you think that American Catholics would be as excited over the election of an American to the papacy as Polish Catholics were over the election of Cardinal Wojtyla?

THE BEGINNING OF A PAPAL MONARCHY

Hildebrand Becomes Gregory VII With the popes as leaders, the reform movement began to make gains in Europe. Many councils spoke out against simony, clerical marriage, and lay investiture. Some bishops, other clergy, and laypeople did not always agree with the reform. Married priests did not want a rule of celibacy. Kings and lay lords did not want to give up their rights to name as bishops and abbots people whom they could trust.

In 1061, Pope Nicholas II died. The cardinals chose an Italian as pope. He took the name of Alexander II. Hildebrand, now a cardinal, had strongly backed the choice of Alexander II, a person who strongly believed in reform.

The election law of 1059 had not ruled out completely a role for the emperor in the choice of a pope. The decree said that the emperor had the right to confirm the cardinals' choice. However, in 1061 the German king had no part in the election of Alexander II. The king of Germany then was Henry IV, a boy of eleven. His father, Henry III, had died in 1056. Henry IV's advisers, however, did speak out on Pope Alexander's election. They claimed that it went against the traditional rights of the emperors to choose the pope. From the time of Otto I, German emperors had chosen popes, just as the Carolingian emperors had.

Pope Alexander II died on April 21, 1073. The next day the cardinals chose Cardinal Hildebrand as pope. He took the name of Gregory VII. Gregory VII told the German king about his election. After the king confirmed the election, Gregory was consecrated, on June 30, 1073. He would lead the Church for the next twelve years.

The picture above shows cardinals gathering at Rome in 1978 to attend a Mass celebrated for the repose of the soul of Pope John Paul I.

The Papacy of Gregory VII Pope Gregory VII was a man of very high ideals. He believed with all his heart in the reform movement. In fact, so important was Gregory's contribution to this work of reform that the entire eleventh-century reform movement is now called the **Gregorian** (grə gôr′ē ən) **Reform**.

Gregory VII was also a very determined man. He believed that, as head of Christ's Church, the pope had authority over all its members. Gregory strengthened the machinery of papal government set up by Pope Leo IX. The popes would rule and guide the Church through legates, synods and councils, and papal letters.

In Pope Gregory's view of the papacy, the pope was the supreme judge in the Church, but the pope himself could be judged by no one. The pope alone could name bishops or ask them to resign. He alone could make new laws, set up new dioceses, and divide old ones. The pope could also make emperors or kings step down. He could absolve subjects from their oaths of allegience. When papal legates were sent into a country—even if the legates were not bishops—they were to be over all bishops in the country. If anyone appealed to the pope, no bishop or lay ruler could interfere in the case. Acting upon ideas such as these, Pope Gregory

VII and his successors began to build a papacy in which the popes had the greatest authority over everyone in Christendom.

Canossa Pope Gregory's desire to do away with lay investiture brought him into conflict with young King Henry IV of Germany. The fight began in 1075 over the diocese of Milan in northern Italy. The archbishop of Milan had died, and the clergy of the city chose a new archbishop who backed reform. Pope Gregory approved their choice. But Henry IV, now twenty-five, named his own archbishop— one who was loyal to him. King Henry also called a synod composed of German bishops who were against reform. The synod said that Gregory VII had acted against the right of the king to name bishops, and that Gregory was not truly pope.

In answer, Pope Gregory VII excommunicated Henry IV and said that he was no longer king of Germany. In the fall of 1076 most of the German princes sided with the pope. They said that they would no longer recognize Henry as king unless the pope forgave him. The princes also asked Pope Gregory to come to Germany and judge the king. In January 1077 the pope set out for Germany.

By this time Henry IV knew that if he did not seek pardon he would lose everything. Nearly all the German nobles and bishops had turned against him. So it was that Henry journeyed south to meet the pope. As we have seen, pope and king met at Canossa in northern Italy. On January 28, 1077, Gregory VII forgave Henry IV. This event was seen as a great moral victory for the Church. A king, the ruler of the Holy Roman Empire, had been forced to submit to a pope.

Canossa was not the end of the fight between Henry IV and Gregory VII. King Henry regained control of Germany and once again fought the pope in the matter of lay investiture. In 1080, Gregory once more excommunicated the king. Then in 1084, Henry IV invaded Rome, appointed an antipope, and was crowned by him as Holy Roman emperor. Pope Gregory fled to Salerno (sə lər′nō) in southern Italy, in the lands ruled by the Normans. In 1085 the pope died in Salerno and was buried in its cathedral. As he lay dying, Pope Gregory VII is reported to have said: "I have loved righteousness and hated iniquity; therefore I die in exile." Pope Gregory VII is venerated as a saint. We celebrate his feast day on May 25.

The fight over lay investiture went on long after Pope Gregory's death. It was finally settled in 1122 by an agreement between Pope Calixtus (Callistus kə lis′təs) II and Emperor Henry V, the son of Henry IV. This settlement is called the **Concordat of Worms** (vôrms). Worms is a city in Germany. A **concordat** is an agreement, or treaty, between the papacy and a country. By the Concordat of Worms, bishops and abbots in the Empire were to be freely chosen by their clergy. The emperor would have no say in the matter.

WORDS TO LIVE BY

In this Church of Christ the Roman Pontiff is the successor of Peter, to whom Christ entrusted the feeding of His sheep and lambs. Hence by divine institution he enjoys supreme, full, immediate, and universal authority over the care of souls. Since he is pastor of all the faithful, his mission is to provide for the common good of the universal Church and for the good of the individual churches.

VATICAN II, *DECREE ON THE BISHOPS' PASTORAL OFFICE IN THE CHURCH, 2*

Parts of the Cathedral of Worms, shown above, date from 1110. The concordat that ended the investiture struggle was signed at Worms in 1122.

Those chosen bishops and abbots would then promise to be subject to the emperor for any lands (fiefs) that they held. As spiritual leaders, bishops and abbots would be subject only to the pope. As temporal leaders, they would answer to the emperor.

Results of the Gregorian Reform The ideals of Pope Gregory VII had continued to motivate his successors. As a result, by the Gregorian Reform the pope's authority over the Church was made stronger, the emperor's power was weakened, and the rule of celibacy for the clergy was enforced.

This was not the end of the Church's fight to reform and to keep high standards for the clergy. Later popes would face even worse opposition from other kings. Still later many members of the clergy would find celibacy too difficult. Then again, the Church would need reform.

In this chapter we have seen how the Church tried to reform itself. In some ways the Church succeeded. The popes gained authority, and more and more people looked to them for guidance and direction. The popes rather than the rulers of the Holy Roman Empire became the strongest leaders in Christendom. At the same time, new problems were made. The Gregorian Reform weakened the influence of laypeople in the Church. Today we have come to understand more fully the role of laypeople in the Church. The Church is made up of all the People of God—clerical and lay. Today the roles of the clergy and the roles of laypeople in the Church are being looked at in new and different ways.

Recall and Reflect

1. Why did the advisers of Henry IV protest the election of Pope Alexander II?

2. What were Gregory VII's views about the office of pope?

3. Why did Pope Gregory VII excommunicate King Henry IV?

4. Today the clergy and laity of the Church must work together, because both are the Church. Mention two or three ways in which you, your family, and others in your community take an active part in the Church's mission of ministry and service.

REVIEW AND CELEBRATE

Doctrinal Summary

The pope, bishops, and priests of the Church are called to serve Jesus in His people. In the *Decree on the Bishop's Pastoral Office in the Church*, issued by Vatican Council II in 1965, we read that "Christ gave the apostles and their successors the command and the power to teach all nations, to hallow [make holy] men in the truth, and to feed them."

Religious Vocabulary

simony	patriarch	Sacred College of Cardinals	Concordat of Worms
rule of celibacy	papal legates	cardinals	concordat
schism	excommunication	Gregorian Reform	

Review Questions

Answer the following questions on a separate sheet of paper.

1. Why was the tenth century a time of crisis for the Church?
2. How did Otto I's revival of the Roman Empire in 962 affect the papacy?
3. What were the three basic ideas in the papal reform program?
4. What were some of the reasons that led to the schism between the Eastern and Western Churches?
5. Why was the papal election decree of 1059 an important reform?

Prayer Celebration

Leader: We raise our voices in praise to God.
All: Holy God, Holy Mighty One,
   Holy Immortal One,
   Have mercy on us.

Reader: This is a reading from the Gospel of Matthew, Chapter 16, verses 13 to 20.
"When Jesus came to the neighborhood of Caesarea Philippi, he asked his disciples this question: 'Who do people say that the Son of Man is?' They replied, 'Some say John the Baptizer, others Elijah, still others Jeremiah or one of the prophets.' 'And you,' he said to them, 'Who do you say that I am?' 'You are the Messiah,' Simon Peter answered, 'the Son of the Living God!' Jesus replied, 'Blest are you, Simon son of Jonah! No mere man has revealed this to you, but my heavenly Father. I for my part declare to you, you are "Rock," and on this rock I will build my Church, and the jaws of death shall not prevail against it. I will entrust to you the keys of the kingdom of heaven. Whatever you declare bound on earth shall be bound in heaven; whatever you declare loosed on earth shall be loosed in heaven.' Then he strictly ordered his disciples not to tell anyone that he was the Messiah."

All: Jesus, help us to remember that we are Your Church.

Leader: We pray for John Paul, our pope.
All: Give him Your peace, O Lord!
Leader: We pray for our bishops and priests.
All: Give them Your kindness, O Lord!
Leader: We pray for one another.
All: Give us Your understanding, O Lord!

Easter ceremonies are held in the Church of the Holy Sepulcher in Jerusalem. The Holy Land with its shrines was the crusaders' goal.

8

The Church and the Crusades

It was a November day in the year 1095. Pope Urban II stood before a huge crowd outside the town of Clermont (kler mōn′) in central France. For nine days Pope Urban had been meeting in council with the bishops, abbots, and great nobles of France and the Empire. Now he was to speak to all the people. The crowd fell silent as the pope began to speak. Pope Urban told the people that non-Christians had captured the **Holy Sepulcher** (sep′ əl kər), the tomb in Jerusalem where Christ's body had lain for three days before He arose from the dead. It was time, said the pope, for Christians to stop fighting among themselves and fight instead to free the tomb of Christ from the hands of unbelievers. The pope called for an army to free Jerusalem and the Holy Land—today's Israel—where Jesus had lived and died. Urban called for volunteers, reminding those who listened to him of Jesus' words:

"If a man wishes to come after me, he must deny his very self, take up his cross, and begin to follow in my footsteps" (Matthew 16:24). Those who fell in battle, said the pope, would be martyrs for Christ.

When the pope finished speaking, all the people began to shout, "God wills it!" They took strips of red cloth and sewed them in the form of a cross to pin upon their shoulders. This cross became the badge, or sign, of all those who promised to go and fight that "holy war" against the enemies of Christ and His Church.

Thus began the **crusades**. The name comes from *crux*, the Latin word for "cross." For over two hundred years European peoples would give their lives and spend their money on military campaigns to the Holy Land. They would fight under the leadership of the Church in answer to repeated calls of the popes. The crusades, in fact, marked the first time European peoples worked together for a common cause outside of Europe.

This chapter is about those wars of religion, the society out of which they came, and the peoples, the culture, and the religion against whom they were fought. Like the reform of the papacy under Pope Gregory VII, the crusades were part of a great wave of religious fervor that swept across Europe in the eleventh century. It might seem strange to you that religious feelings should lead to war and bloodshed. For an understanding of how this happened, let us look again at European society in the eleventh century.

CHURCH AND SOCIETY IN THE ELEVENTH CENTURY

A Warlike Society From the time of Charlemagne, European society rested upon the personal relationships of lords and vassals —the feudal system. In the last two chapters, we read of some of the troubles the Church faced as part of that society. When Pope Urban II introduced the idea of a crusade at Clermont, he spoke to a society made up of three classes, or groups, of people. There were those who fought and ruled, those who prayed, and those who worked. Each of those groups had its own rights as well as its own duties. At the top were the soldiers, the nobles—lords, vassals, knights—whose duty it was to protect society. The clergy were those who prayed. Those who worked were the peasant-farmers and serfs on the manors and the merchants and craftworkers in the towns.

War and fighting were part of the daily life in feudal Europe. Kings could not always be sure of the loyalty of lords and princes. There were civil wars and wars of rebellion. Feudal nobles also had the right to begin personal or private wars whenever their rights were violated. Even bishops and popes went to war to defend the lands or rights of the Church. As we saw in Chapter 7, Pope Leo IX was taken prisoner while fighting against Norman princes in the south of Italy.

War was also a matter of business in the feudal society. It was not only a means of defending one's rights or lands but also a means of profiting. According to feudal custom, a knight taken in battle could be held for ransom. It made little difference to many nobles that their personal wars threatened the lives and property of innocent people.

The Peace and Truce of God From the tenth century, the Church had tried to control the feudal nobles' appetite for fighting and war. Local councils proclaimed the **Peace of God**. By the Peace of God, the Church tried to protect certain members of society at all times from the violence of feudal warfare. Women, peasant-farmers and serfs, merchants, and all clergy were always to be protected from violence. Any knight or soldier who attacked such a person acted against this Peace of God and was excommunicated.

By the early eleventh century, the Church added a new idea, the **Truce of God**. This was an attempt to cut down the periods, or times, during which nobles could use their right to wage private wars. Under the penalty of excommunication, fighting was not allowed on any Sunday or holy day. Soon the whole weekend was to be free of war. Friday was kept free because it was the day on which Jesus had died for all. Saturday was free because it was the day on which He was buried, and it was special to Mary, His mother. Sunday was kept free because it honored His resurrection. Lent and Advent, times of penance, were then added to the list of war-free days. Little by little, some 240 days of the year came under the Truce of God.

Many Church councils in the eleventh and twelfth centuries called for the Peace and Truce of God. This fact suggests that the private wars continued to be matters of concern in feudal Europe. Even the Council of Clermont, at which Pope Urban II preached the first crusade, called for the Peace of God and the Truce of God. It is against this background that we should look at the crusades of Christian Europe.

Recall and Reflect

1. What were the crusades?

2. What three groups existed in feudal society?

3. What were the Peace of God and the Truce of God?

4. How does the Church in our time care for people who suffer from the effects of war— refugees, oppressed peoples, prisoners of war?

ISLAM AND THE MOSLEMS

The Religion of Islam The peoples against whom the crusaders fought in the Holy Land were not Christian. They believed in the religion of **Islam** (is′ləm). Islam is an Arabic word that means "surrender." Those who believe in Islam are known as **Moslems** (moz′ləmz), which means "those who surrender to the will of God" in the Arabic language. Islam is one of the world's great religions. It began over twelve hundred years ago among the peoples of the Arabian Peninsula, the huge desert land to the south and east of present-day Israel. Today over 400 million people are Moslems.

Because of oil beneath the desert, the peoples of the Arabian Peninsula today are very rich. In the sixth and seventh centuries, however, most Arab peoples were nomadic, moving from place to place with their sheep and goats in search of food and water. Before they were converted to Islam, most Arabs were pagans. They believed in many gods and spirits.

In the sixth century there were few cities in the Arabian Peninsula. Most of them were found in its western part, on or near the coast of the Red Sea. **Mohammed** (mō ham′əd), the founder of Islam, was born in the Arabian city of Mecca (mek′ə) about the year 570. Mecca is about 50 miles (80 km) inland from the Red Sea, in what

Mohammed (570–632), founder of Islam, preached faith in the one God and surrender to His will. God was to be worshiped by prayers, almsgiving, and fasting.

is now the country of Saudi Arabia. At the time of Mohammed, Mecca was a rich trading city. When Mohammed was about twenty-five, he married the widow of a wealthy merchant and became a rich trader in Mecca.

About the age of forty, Mohammed had an extraordinary religious experience. He began to receive what he believed to be revelations from God, or **Allah** (al'ə) in Arabic. The bearer of those messages from Allah, he felt, was the angel Gabriel. For Mohammed, Allah was the God of the Hebrew Bible—the God of Abraham, Ismael (is'mä el), Isaac (ī'zək), and Jacob. Those revelations were eventually written down in a book called the **Koran** (kô rän'), from an Arabic word that means "a recitation." The Koran became the holy book of Islam.

Mohammed began to teach his new religion to the people of Mecca. He taught that there was only one God, Allah, and that he, Mohammed, was the last and greatest of God's prophets, or messengers. Mohammed's task was to preach the final revelations of Allah. It was the duty of his hearers to worship Allah and to accept Mohammed as His prophet.

Only a few people in Mecca were converted to Islam. Mecca had long been a holy place for many pagan gods. Most Meccans did not accept Mohammed's teachings. They began to persecute him, and in 622 Mohammed and his followers were forced to leave Mecca. They fled to the town of Yathrib (yath'rəb), north of Mecca. Mohammed and his followers were welcomed there, and the city was renamed Medina (mə dē'nə), which means "the city of the prophet." The year 622 became the year one for the Moslems. Mohammed began to make many converts among the Arab peoples. He also preached a "holy war" against any unbelievers who actively fought against the spread of Islam. Mecca itself was captured in 630, and Mohammed made it the holy city of Islam. Mohammed died in the year 632. By that time many Arabs had become Moslems.

The Spread of Islam In the hundred years after Mohammed's death, his followers conquered a huge empire. All of present-day Israel and Syria were taken over from the Byzantine Empire before 650. The Persian Empire fell, and Egypt was overrun. By the year 711, all of North Africa and most of Spain had been conquered by Moslems. In fact, all of Western Europe was threatened by the Moslem advance.

Large numbers of non-Arab peoples were converted to Islam. Within a century after Mohammed's death, Islam had become not only a world religion but a huge empire made up of many races, countries, and cultures. This Islamic empire was larger than Charlemagne's empire and the Byzantine Empire together. Damascus, in Syria, became the first capital. In 750 the

This page of the Koran was written between the eighth and tenth centuries. It is in Kufic, a form of the Arabic alphabet.

The Great Mosque at Mecca is the most sacred shrine in Islam. The Kaaba, the square building in the courtyard, contains the sacred Black Stone that Moslems believe was given to Abraham by the angel Gabriel.

capital was moved to the city of Baghdad, on the Tigris River in present-day Iraq. The administrative language of the empire was Arabic. Its official religion was Islam.

Mohammed himself did not name someone to take his place. After his death, his followers named one of his first converts, abu-Bakr (ə bü′bak′ər), as caliph (kā′lif), which means "successor." The caliphs continued Mohammed's "holy war" against all worshipers of idols. Such pagans were to be killed if they did not accept Islam. But Jews and Christians—the "people of the Book" as the Koran calls them—were not to be persecuted. Although Mohammed did not accept Christ as God, he called Christ one of Allah's great prophets. In Islamic lands, Christians and Jews ranked lower than Moslems, and had to pay heavy taxes But they were free to follow their religions. Christian pilgrims continued to visit the shrines in the Holy Land, and the Moslems were happy to trade with Christians and Jews.

The New Moslems At the beginning of the eleventh century, there was a change in Moslem-Christian relations. The Seljuk (sel′jük′) Turks, an Asiatic people, were converted to Islam. Their homeland in central Asia is now part of the countries of the Soviet Union and Mongolia. In the eleventh century they began expanding to the south and west. In 1051 the Seljuk Turks reached Baghdad. The ruling caliph proclaimed their leader a sultan, or ruler. The Turks were sent to fight against the Byzantine Empire. By 1071, Seljuk Turks had conquered all of Asia Minor and had settled there. They have given their name to this land; we know it today as Turkey. Very quickly the Turks were threatening the city of Constantinople.

You can see on the map on page 105, that the Turks also governed all of Syria and the Holy Land. Christian pilgrims now had to deal with Turkish rulers. Unlike earlier Moslem rulers, the Turks often attacked Christians or held them for ransom. Visitors to the Holy Land began to take back to Europe many stories of Turkish persecution.

Because of Turkish pressure against the Byzantine Empire, the Greek emperor Alexius I (1081–1118) wrote to Pope Urban II and asked for soldiers to help fight the Turks. Pope Urban viewed the call for help from the Greek emperor as a chance to bring all Christians back together. He would call for a great war to get back the Holy Land. Pope Urban hoped that this war would not only help Emperor Alexius recover his lost lands but would heal the break between the Eastern and Western Churches. It would also lessen the feudal violence and warfare in Europe. And all this would be done under the leadership of the papacy. Thus in November 1095, at the Council of Clermont, Pope Urban II called for this war. We know it as the First Crusade.

Recall and Reflect

1. When and where was Mohammed born?

2. What is the Koran?

3. What did Pope Urban II hope to do in calling for the First Crusade?

4. Vatican Council II points out that the Church, when examining its relationship to non-Christian religions, "considers above all what men have in common, and what draws them to fellowship." What can we learn from people who have religious beliefs different from ours? What can they learn from us?

THE CRUSADES

A People's Crusade Pope Urban's call for a crusade was addressed to knights and soldiers. But enthusiasm for the cause was so great that thousands of people from every background were eager to take the cross. Before the First Crusade was planned and under way, crowds of people without weapons set out for the Holy Land. They were led by popular preachers—for example, Peter the Hermit (1050–1115)—who believed that God would work miracles for the crusaders.

Without discipline, training, and money, this People's Crusade quickly broke up into disorganized bands of looters and robbers. As these mobs of people moved across Europe toward Constantinople and the East, they often attacked and murdered the Jews who lived in cities along their way. In the minds of those simple people, Jews were the enemies of Christ.

The crusades, in fact, deepened the **anti-Semitism**, or hatred and distrust of Jews, that existed within the Christian world. Though they were not liked, the Jews had always been a recognized group within the Christian community. They did not have equal rights with Christians, but they were under the protection of local princes and bishops. The Justinian law had ordered the toleration of Jews. Pope Saint Gregory the Great said that Jews should not be given any new liberties but any rights they had should not be taken away. After the eleventh century, however, Jews were subject to increasing persecution by both Church and state. One Church council ordered them to wear special badges. Another made them live in a special part of the town.

Large numbers of people who made up the People's Crusade actually reached Constantinople in 1096 and 1097. The emperor Alexius I quickly sent them into lands ruled by the Moslem Turks, where nearly all of them were killed.

The First Crusade It took almost two years to plan the First Crusade. The whole enterprise was under the direction of the Church. Those who went on crusade received a special blessing. If soldiers died in battle, they were to be honored as martyrs. The families and property of crusaders were to be guarded by the Church. Any debts that crusaders might have could not be collected until they returned home from the crusade.

Most of the knights who fought in the First Crusade came from what is now France, Belgium, and the Netherlands. Although Pope Urban had forbidden the taking of the cross for mere glory or temporal gain, the crusaders fought for many different reasons. Besides being motivated by faith and the love of Christ, many people went out of love for adventure—to prove themselves as knights—or out of a desire for land. Many townspeople, especially those of the Italian towns of Venice and Genoa, took part in the crusades because of the money to be made—either by taking crusading armies to the Holy Land or by selling them food, weapons, and other supplies.

In May 1097, an army of about 24,000, including about 10,000 knights, appeared before the walls of Constantinople. Although the emperor Alexius had asked for soldiers, he was not too happy with this large army that sought to pass through his lands to go to Jerusalem. The emperor made the crusaders take an oath of loyalty to him for all the lands they might conquer. Alexius then gave the crusaders help and supplies, and the army moved into Asia Minor. See the map on page 105.

The crusaders recaptured the city of Nicaea from the Turks and returned it to the emperor. The army then moved to attack the city of Antioch, in Syria. But the

Pope Urban II (1088–1099) blesses the knights who took the cross and promised to go to the Holy Land to fight the enemies of Christ and His Church.

Monks Who Were Knights

In the Church the crusades resulted in the creation of a new kind of religious order, the military order. At least twelve such military orders came into being between 1100 and 1300. Members of military orders combined the life of a monk with that of a knight. They promised not only to live lives of poverty, obedience, and chastity but also to defend the Church by force of arms. The members of military orders tried to put into practice the ideas of Christian chivalry, showing in their own lives that knightly service should be used only in the cause of justice.

The three most famous military orders were the Knights of the Hospital of Saint John in Jerusalem, the Knights Templar, and the Teutonic Knights. All three of these orders were founded to meet the needs of pilgrims in the Holy Land. The Knights of Saint John, for example, were also called Knights Hospitaller; they ran a hospital and hotel for pilgrims in Jerusalem even before the First Crusade. After the First Crusade, the Knights of Saint John and the other military orders added the duty of protecting the Kingdom of Jerusalem and the other crusader lands from the attacks of the Moslems.

The military orders declined after the crusades, but the orders of the Knights of Saint John of Jerusalem and the Teutonic Knights still exist in the Church. Because the headquarters of the Knights of Saint John moved to the island of Malta in the sixteenth century, that order is usually known today as the Knights of Malta. The order of the Knights Templar was dissolved by the papacy in the year 1312.

emperor Alexius withdrew his own soldiers, and the crusaders could not capture the city. It was only after an Italian fleet arrived with needed supplies, almost a year later, that the crusaders were able to surround Antioch. The city was taken on June 28, 1098. The battle for Antioch opened a lasting breach between the Greeks and the Latins. The crusaders felt they had been betrayed by the Greek emperor. From that time on, the crusades became more and more a European enterprise.

On June 7, 1099, almost a year after the fall of Antioch, the crusading army, now only a force of about 12,000, arrived before the walls of Jerusalem. On the night of July 13, the crusaders broke into the city. Two days later, all of Jerusalem was in Christian hands. Sad to say, the crusaders began to massacre nearly all the people who lived in Jerusalem—Moslems, Jews, Christians, men, women, and children were killed. Eyewitnesses said the streets of the city were red with the blood of the victims.

On August 12, the crusaders met and defeated a large Moslem army from Egypt. That victory ensured their hold on the Holy Land. News of the success of the First Crusade greatly excited Europe. Unfortunately, Urban II had died in Rome on July 29, 1099, just before the glad news came.

The Crusaders in Asia The crusaders who stayed in the East were kept close to the coast by the Moslems. They could never take the city of Damascus, Syria, or penetrate far inland. The crusaders set up four states, known as Latin States, along the Mediterranean coast. Those Latin States depended upon a constant flow of military aid from Europe to survive. The crusaders in the Holy Land also fought among themselves as well as against the Moslems.

Ruins of crusader castles, like this one in Lebanon on the Mediterranean, are found in all lands that were once part of the Latin States in Asia.

During the two centuries after 1095, eight important crusades were launched to help the Latin States in Asia and to recover the Holy Land. Not all the crusades went to Asia, however. Two attacked the Moslems in Egypt and northern Africa. Aside from the First Crusade, not one was really successful. In 1187, Jerusalem fell again to the Moslems. It was never recovered. By the end of the thirteenth century, crusaders held only one place in Asia, the port city of Acre (äk′ər), in today's Israel. And when Acre fell to the Moslems in May 1291, the great crusades were in effect ended.

The Fourth Crusade One crusade that went "off course" was the Fourth Crusade. It ended up not in the Holy Land, or even in Africa, but in Constantinople. Pope Innocent III (1198–1216) called for a crusade soon after he was chosen pope. Innocent III was one of the most strong-minded popes in the Church's history. In calling for the Fourth Crusade, he hoped to regain control of the crusading movement for the Church and to bring together once more the Greek and Latin Churches.

In 1201, the Venetians agreed to sell the crusaders the ships they needed to reach the Holy Land. Venice, at the head of the Adriatic Sea, had become a rich city-state through its trade with the East. The Venetians had a strong navy. But when the time came to board the Venetian ships (in 1202), the crusaders did not have enough money to pay for their transportation. The Venetians said they would carry out their part of the contract if the crusaders would help them capture the Christian city of Zara —today Zadar—on the coast of the Adriatic, in what is now the country of Yugoslavia. Zara had once belonged to the Venetians but had become a trading rival. The crusaders agreed, and Zara was captured and looted in 1202. Upon hearing that news, Pope Innocent III excommunicated all the crusaders.

The leaders of the Fourth Crusade then decided to change the destination of the crusade to Constantinople. The emperor in Constantinople in 1202 was Alexius III. He had taken the throne from his own brother, whom he had ordered blinded and put in prison. His brother's son, also named Alexius, was sent to prison as well. But the young Alexius escaped to Venice. There he urged the leaders of the Fourth Crusade to put him on the throne in Constantinople. Alexius promised the crusaders money. He also promised to help them get to the Holy Land once he was emperor.

The Venetians also wanted the crusade to go to Constantinople. They had lost some of their trading privileges in the city, and wanted them back. The young Alexius and his cause were very useful to them. The crusaders set sail for Constantinople.

When the crusaders arrived in Constantinople in the spring of 1203, Emperor Alexius III fled. The blind ex-emperor was released from prison and was made emperor again. His son, now Alexius IV, became co-emperor with his father.

It had been easy for Alexius IV to promise money. But now the young emperor could not raise enough money to satisfy the crusaders. When the crusading army began making threats, the people of Constantinople turned against Alexius IV and his father and killed them both. The crusaders then attacked Constantinople. They took the city in April 1204. For three days, Constantinople was sacked. Many churches were destroyed. People were killed; women were raped. Valuable works of art were stolen. This outcome of the Fourth Crusade shocked Innocent III and all of Christian Europe. It served to discredit even more the whole idea of a crusade.

After the Fourth Crusade a Latin empire was set up in Constantinople; it lasted until 1261. A Latin patriarch took the place of the Greek patriarch as bishop. But the people of Constantinople would not accept any union with the Latin Church. Greek emperors and Greek patriarchs ruled from Nicaea. In 1261 a Greek emperor was able to retake Constantinople.

Greek Christians never forgot what the Latin Christians did in Constantinople in 1204. As a result of the Fourth Crusade, the mutual suspicion between East and West hardened. The Greek Church felt the papacy was behind that cruel war, although as we have seen, it was not. Even today, as the Roman Catholic Church seeks reunion with the Greek Orthodox Church, the memory of the Fourth Crusade remains a difficulty.

Many crusaders went to the Holy Land by ship. Here Godfrey of Bouillon, who became king of Jerusalem in 1099, is shown setting out on the First Crusade.

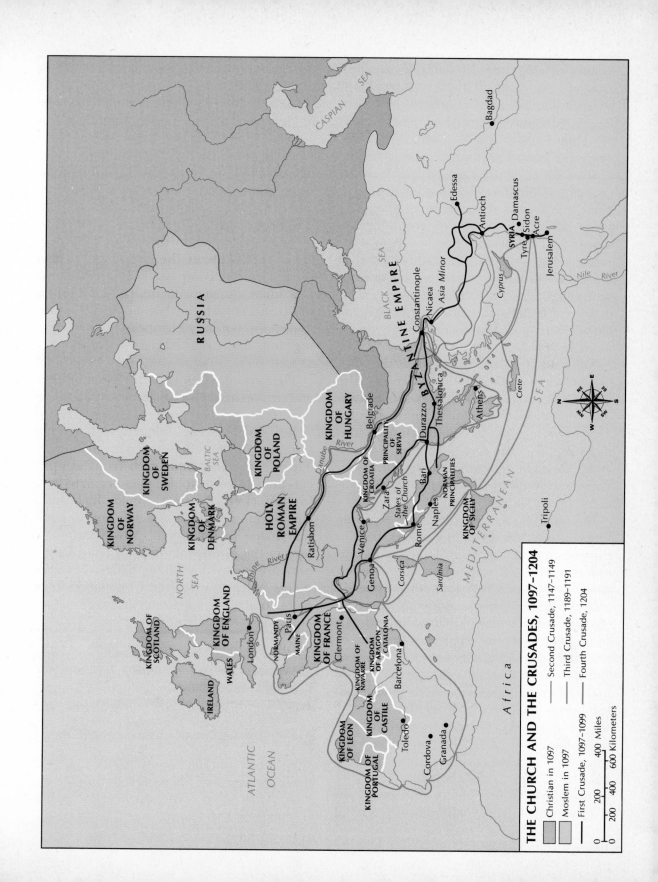

THE CHURCH AND THE CRUSADES, 1097–1204

Christian in 1097
Moslem in 1097

First Crusade, 1097–1099
Second Crusade, 1147–1149
Third Crusade, 1189–1191
Fourth Crusade, 1204

0   200   400 Miles
0   200 400   600 Kilometers

CASPIAN SEA

Bagdad

Edessa

Antioch   Damascus

SYRIA   Tyre Sidon   Acre
                    Jerusalem

Nile River

Constantinople

BYZANTINE EMPIRE

Nicaea   Asia Minor

BLACK SEA

Cyprus

Durazzo   Thessalonica

Athens   Crete

MEDITERRANEAN SEA

Tripoli

RUSSIA

KINGDOM OF HUNGARY

Belgrade

Danube River

PRINCIPALITY OF SERVIA

KINGDOM OF POLAND

KINGDOM OF SWEDEN

BALTIC SEA

KINGDOM OF NORWAY

KINGDOM OF DENMARK

HOLY ROMAN EMPIRE

KINGDOM OF CROATIA

Zara

States of the Church

Bari

Rome   Naples

NORMAN PRINCIPALITIES

KINGDOM OF SICILY

Venice

Genoa

Corsica

Sardinia

Ratisbon

Rhine River

NORTH SEA

KINGDOM OF SCOTLAND

IRELAND   WALES

KINGDOM OF ENGLAND

London

NORMANDY

Paris

MAINE   Clermont

KINGDOM OF FRANCE

KINGDOM OF NAVARRE

KINGDOM OF ARAGON   CATALONIA

Barcelona

KINGDOM OF LEON

KINGDOM OF CASTILE

Toledo

Cordova   Granada

KINGDOM OF PORTUGAL

ATLANTIC OCEAN

Africa

N NE E SE S SW W NW

Results of the Crusades Looked upon as military campaigns, the crusades were failures. They did not do what they set out to do. After the great crusades were over, the Holy Land was still in Moslem hands. And the crusades brought about lasting distrust between the Eastern and Western Catholic Churches. Because of the crusades, the West is still seen as an enemy by many Moslem peoples of the Mediterranean and the Middle East.

Like all wars, the crusades were cruel and caused suffering and death to many innocent people. We must remember, however, that the crusaders thought they were fighting for what was right, even though we see today how narrow their ideals were.

Although the crusades began as the work of the popes, after the First Crusade the popes quickly lost control over them. Raising money, getting soldiers and weapons, and providing ships meant much work and sacrifice. From the very beginning, political and economic rivalries among European kings played an important part in the crusades.

Because of the crusades, more people went on pilgrimages to holy places, both in Europe and in the Holy Land. The crusaders took back to Europe many **relics**. Relics are things connected with the passion and death of Jesus—such as His crown of thorns and the lance that wounded His side—or things connected with the lives of the saints. New churches were built all over Europe to keep those relics. Even though many of the relics were false, they added to the honor given to Christ and His saints by Christian people. The devotion to the passion and death of Christ that we call the "Stations of the Cross" was also brought back to Europe by the crusaders.

The crusades put many Europeans directly in touch with Islamic culture. In the eleventh century, the Islamic world knew much more than Europe did in many fields of knowledge. The crusaders learned a great deal from the Moslems, and this opened the West to many new ideas. Christian scholars began to study the books of Moslem thinkers, and through those writings they were once more brought into touch with the ideas of the Greek thinker Aristotle. Much Arab or Islamic science and technology was better than that of Europe. From the Moslems the crusaders learned how to use the compass. They also learned new ideas about medicine. In fact, crusading contacts with the Islamic world helped to develop not only European higher learning but art, architecture, and literature as well.

The crusades helped improve commerce and trade in European towns. Crusaders took back to Europe a taste for Eastern riches, such as spices, silks, rugs, and metalware. Europeans also learned of sugar cane. They learned to enjoy such fruits as apricots and lemons. Noble ladies began to long for fine cloth of damask (made in Damascus, Syria) and muslin, a soft cotton cloth first made in the city of Mosul (mō sül'), now in the Moslem country of Iraq. In the next unit we shall see how all these developments helped enrich the Christian culture of Europe.

Recall and Reflect

1. What was the People's Crusade?
2. What is anti-Semitism?
3. What were some of the reasons the crusaders fought?
4. Why did the Fourth Crusade go to Constantinople?
5. Jesus teaches us to love our enemies and pray for our persecutors. In the light of that teaching, what can you do when people argue and disagree with you?

REVIEW AND CELEBRATE

Doctrinal Summary

The Church rejects nothing that is true and holy in non-Christian religions, as the Second Vatican Council declares: "[The Moslems] adore the one God. . . . Though they do not acknowledge Jesus as God, they revere Him as a prophet. They also honor Mary, His virgin mother. . . . Finally, they value the moral life and worship God especially through prayer, almsgiving and fasting" (*Declaration on the Relation of the Church to Non-Christian Religions*, 3).

Religious Vocabulary

Holy Sepulcher	Truce of God	Mohammed	anti-Semitism
crusades	Islam	Allah	relics
Peace of God	Moslems	Koran	

know

Review Questions

Answer the following questions on a separate sheet of paper.

1. What aspects of European society in the eleventh century help to explain the crusades?
2. What happened to Moslem-Christian relations in the eleventh century?
3. What was the outcome of the First Crusade?
4. What effect did the Fourth Crusade have on the relationship between the Greek and Latin Christians?
5. Did the crusades accomplish what they set out to do? List four results of the crusades.

Prayer Celebration

Leader: In the Book of Ecclesiastes, Chapter 3, verses 1 and 8, we read:
"There is an appointed time for everything, and a time for every affair under the heavens.
"A time to love, and a time to hate; a time of war, and a time of peace."
All: God's will be done on earth as it is in heaven.

Leader: In the Gospel According to Matthew, Chapter 5, verses 38 and 39 and 43 to 45, we read that Jesus said:

" 'You have heard the commandment, "An eye for an eye, and a tooth for a tooth." But what I say to you is: offer no resistance to injury. When a person strikes you on the right cheek, turn and offer him the other.'
" 'You have heard the commandment, "You shall love your countryman but hate your enemy." My command to you is: love your enemies, pray for your persecutors. This will prove that you are sons of your heavenly Father. . . .' "
All: God's will be done on earth as it is in heaven. Amen.

UNIT TWO SUMMARY

With the collapse of the Roman Empire in the West, the Church, under the leadership of the popes, became the leader of Western civilization. Pope Gregory the Great, who became pope in 590, was a pivotal figure in the great work of converting the Germanic and Slavic peoples of Europe. It was Pope Gregory who sent Saint Augustine of Canterbury and his monks to England.

So well did the Church succeed in preaching the faith to those European peoples that between 600 and 1100 it was able to develop a whole new society in Europe. For almost a thousand years Western Europe would be known as Christendom, a part of the world where Christianity prevailed and Christian values ruled.

In 768, Charlemagne became king of the Franks. Charlemagne—like his father, Pepin—worked closely with the popes and helped the Church in its task of preaching the faith. Charlemagne and his successors became the chief protectors of the papacy. In 800, Pope Leo III crowned Charlemagne emperor of the West. Charlemagne's support of culture led to a revival of learning in the West.

After Charlemagne's death, his Empire began to fall apart. There was no strong central government. Feudalism, a system based upon personal bonds between lords and vassals, grew out of the need for mutual protection and support.

The Church tried to meet the problems of a warlike feudal society by introducing the Peace of God and the Truce of God. When Moslem Seljuk Turks conquered Asia Minor and began attacking pilgrims to the Holy Land, Pope Urban II, in 1095, called for the First Crusade.

Although the crusades were not successful from a military viewpoint, they did introduce Christian Europe to the culture and learning of the Islamic world. The crusades put Christian thinkers in touch once again with the ideas of Aristotle, the ancient Greek philosopher. The crusades also improved the commerce and trade of European towns. In Unit Three we shall see how these developments enriched the Christian culture of Europe.

590	Gregory the Great becomes pope
597	Saint Augustine of Canterbury begins conversion of English
622	Mohammed, founder of Islam, flees Mecca
711	Moslems conquer North Africa and most of Spain
722	Saint Boniface begins conversion of Germans
768	Charlemagne becomes king of Franks
800	Pope Leo III crowns Charlemagne emperor
863	Saints Cyril and Methodius begin conversion of Slavs
962	Otto I, king of Germany, crowned emperor
1049	Pope Leo IX elected: Church reform begins
1054	Schism between Rome and Constantinople
1059	Papal election law: Cardinals elect pope
1073	Hildebrand becomes Pope Gregory VII
1095	Pope Urban II preaches First Crusade
1099	Crusaders capture Jerusalem
1187	Moslems retake Jerusalem
1204	Fourth Crusade captures Constantinople

UNIT THREE

The Church — Realizing Its Mission

A glimpse of green through windows of the bishop's palace at Wells, England, symbolizes the Church's new growth in the twelfth century.

9

A Twelfth-Century Springtime

When birds begin to sing and flowers start to grow, we know it is spring. Spring is the season of new life. The twelfth century was a springtime in the history of the Church. New forms of religious life began to appear. There was an intellectual quickening. New art and architecture developed. All over Europe, forests and swamps were cleared and planted in grain. Population doubled, city life revived, and trade flourished. The Church influenced every aspect of this new life. Twelfth-century European culture was thoroughly Christian.

This chapter begins Unit Three: The Church—Realizing Its Mission. Unit Three looks at four hundred years of the Church's history, from 1100 to 1500. In the fifteenth and sixteenth centuries, writers and historians coined the terms *Middle Ages* and *medieval* (mē′dē ē′vəl). These words are used to describe the way of life created by

About 6 B.C.	Birth of Jesus
About A.D. 29	Pentecost: Birth of the Church
A.D. 313	Edict of Milan: End of persecutions
325	Council of Nicaea
800	Pope Leo III crowns Charlemagne emperor
1049	Pope Leo IX elected: Church reform begins
1054	Schism between Rome and Constantinople
1095	Pope Urban II preaches First Crusade
1215	Fourth Lateran Council: Great pastoral council of Middle Ages
1453	Constantinople falls to the Turks
1521	Diet of Worms: Luther breaks with Church
1545	Council of Trent begins
1789	Crisis of the French Revolution
1870	First Vatican Council
1962	Second Vatican Council begins
1978	John Paul II becomes pope

the peoples of Europe between the collapse of Greco-Roman civilization in the 600s and what people thought was its rebirth, or renaissance, in the 1500s.

In Unit Two we saw the beginnings and growth of this Christian culture in the West. By the twelfth century, Europe had won a political and economic stability that allowed experiments of many kinds. The twelfth century was a seedtime of new ideas. In this chapter we shall see how some of those ideas affected or changed the history of the Church. We shall tell our story through the lives of Bernard of Clairvaux (kler′vō′), Peter Abelard (ab′ə lärd), the monk Gratian (grā′shən), King Henry II of England, and Thomas Becket. All those people helped to make the history of that time through their work, their teaching, the force of their personalities, and their ideas.

SAINT BERNARD OF CLAIRVAUX

A Giant in His Time Some people work so hard and do so much in their lifetime that they seem like giants to those about them. Bernard of Clairvaux—monk, priest, abbot, theologian, and preacher—was such a person. In later times it was said of Bernard that "he carried the twelfth century on his shoulders."

Bernard was born in 1090 in a little village near the town of Dijon (dē zhōN′) in east-central France. His father was a noble who served the duke of Burgundy, the ruler of that part of France. Bernard had five brothers and one sister. Bernard and his brothers were all taught to read and write Latin. His brothers then began training to become knights. But Bernard decided on a life of reading and study.

When Bernard was sixteen, his mother died. Bernard felt her death deeply, and

for some time he could not decide what to do with his life. It was not until four years later, in 1111, that he decided to dedicate his life to God's service as a monk. Bernard joined a new community of monks known as the **Cistercians** (sis tėr′shənz).

As we have seen, monasticism played a very important role in the Church in the earlier Middle Ages. Monks and nuns were missionaries and teachers all over Europe. In the twelfth century, new communities of monks began to appear. One of those new communities began in 1098, in a swampy, wild place near Dijon. The place was called Citeaux (si tō′), and the monks who began to live there soon became known as the monks of Citeaux, or Cistercians.

Saint Bernard greatly influenced people by all that he said and did. When he became a monk, about thirty of his friends and relatives joined him.

White-robed monks at St. Joseph's Abbey, Spencer, Massachusetts, continue to follow the Cistercian way of life.

The Cistercian way of life was based on the *Rule* of Saint Benedict. But it was a simpler, stricter way of life than that followed in other Benedictine monasteries of the twelfth century. Since the new Cistercian monks wore white robes, they came to be known as the "white monks." The Benedictine monks who wore black robes, were called the "black monks."

From the beginning the Cistercians sought out for their monasteries wild places that were not yet cleared for farming. Unlike the monks of older monasteries, the Cistercians at first did not accept any gifts of land or feudal revenues. They supported themselves through the hard work of the monks and lay brothers. As a result, Cistercian monks became pioneers in clearing swamps and turning wasteland all over Europe into productive farmland.

Bernard: Monk and Abbot   Bernard greatly influenced people by what he did and said. Thus when Bernard decided to join the monks at Cîteaux, he did not go alone. He took with him four of his brothers and many of his close friends and relatives — thirty companions in all. Eventually, his youngest brother and his widowed father also became Cistercians.

When he was twenty-five, Bernard, who had been ordained a priest, was chosen by the abbot of Cîteaux to begin another monastery. The new monastery was some distance to the north of Dijon, in a lonely, wild valley that was known as the Valley of Wormwood. After Bernard founded his monastery, however, the valley's name was changed to Clairvaux, which means "clear valley." According to one writer, the place was called Clairvaux because of the sunlight and clarity to be found in Bernard's teachings.

Bernard became abbot of Clairvaux in 1115. He remained there as abbot until his death in 1153. Besides building up Clairvaux, Bernard organized 68 other abbeys. In fact, by the fifteenth century 350 Cistercian abbeys could claim descent from Clairvaux.

Bernard was soon widely known for his holiness. He preached very well, and people came from all over Europe to hear his sermons. Clairvaux became known for its piety and the strict observance of poverty. Under Bernard, Clairvaux gave many leaders to the Church. One of Bernard's monks became Pope Eugene III (1145–1153). Twelve monks of Clairvaux became cardinals, and thirty were made bishops while Bernard was abbot.

Cistercian religious life and Bernard's own teaching stressed devotion to the human person of Jesus and to Mary, His Mother. The beautiful hymn "Salve Regina" ("Hail, Holy Queen"), long attributed to Bernard himself (though it is a much earlier work), sums up Bernard's view about Mary's role in our lives. Mary is our "Mother of Mercy, our life, our sweetness, and our hope."

Bernard became the counselor of many popes and rulers. He traveled all over Europe on Church business. For Pope Eugene III he wrote a book in which he set down spiritual advice for one who was a leader in the Church. Bernard wrote many other books and sermons on religious life and prayer. One of his most famous books, *On the Love of God*, stressed that we must always go to God our Father through His Son, Jesus. So important were Bernard's writings in the history of the Church that in 1830 Pope Pius VIII declared him to be a "Doctor of the Church."

Bernard died on August 20, 1153. Pope Alexander III declared him a saint in 1174. We keep his feast on August 20.

Saint Bernard's writings are perhaps the best examples of what some modern scholars have called **monastic theology**. Bernard believed that Church teaching should present the truths of faith in a clear, orderly way. The purpose was to draw people to God, who is love; who created human beings out of love, and by love redeemed them. For Saint Bernard the sources of theology were the Bible, the writings of the Church Fathers, and the liturgy.

Saint Bernard's great zeal and devotion made him quick to speak up whenever he felt that the Church's teaching was being threatened. This led him to bitterly oppose the teachings and ideas of Peter Abelard. Perhaps the greatest teacher in the twelfth century, Peter Abelard had one of the best minds in human history.

Peter Abelard taught that human reason could be used to build up a science of theology. Such a scientific theology need not go against the traditional theology of Saint Bernard. But Bernard himself could not see the need for such a theology. As a result, he led the fight against Peter Abelard and caused Abelard's teaching to be condemned by the Church.

Recall and Reflect

1. How was life in a Cistercian monastery different from life in other Benedictine monasteries in the twelfth century?

2. What did Saint Bernard believe about Church teaching?

3. What did Saint Bernard say were three sources of theology?

4. Saint Bernard thought about the importance of both Jesus and Mary to the Christian life. Write a prayer that says something about the importance of either Jesus or Mary in your life.

PETER ABELARD

A Man Ahead of His Time   Peter Abelard, whose teaching Bernard of Clairvaux regarded as a grave danger to the Church, was born in 1079 near the city of Nantes (nants´), in the northwestern part of France. He was eleven years older than Bernard.

Although of noble birth, Peter Abelard passed over a knightly career to devote his life to study and scholarship. He went from school to school in search of the best teachers. A very fine student, Abelard often asked deep questions that made his teachers uncomfortable. He learned easily, but he was also quick to disagree and very strong in his criticism. Abelard often made people angry.

In Chapter 6 we learned that Charlemagne had ordered that schools in his Empire be attached to monasteries and cathedrals. In the troubles of the ninth and tenth centuries, many of those schools were destroyed, and a general decline in learning resulted. By the eleventh century in Europe, the greater political stability and improving economy had led to renewed interest in higher learning. Many schools opened once again. But at that time, although some monastery schools continued, the best teachers and the most students went to the cathedral schools that were opening in many towns. Many of those schools became centers of learning, drawing students from near and far. Perhaps the most famous cathedral school in Europe was that in Paris. In the early years of the twelfth century, Abelard went to Paris.

The school of Paris had begun next to the Cathedral of Notre Dame, on an island in the Seine, the river that divides the city into two parts. By the time Abelard went to Paris to study, the school had grown so large that classes were being held in build-

Around the year 1110, Peter Abelard began to teach in Paris. He quickly became one of the most popular teachers in Europe.

ings on the south bank of the river. In fact, so many classes were held in that part of Paris that it was—and still is—called the Latin Quarter. In the Middle Ages, all students used the Latin language in their studies.

Later in the twelfth century, around 1170, the teachers of various subjects in the Paris school banded together to form a corporation, or "guild of teaching masters." The Latin name for such a guild is *universitas*, from which we get our word "university." The guild of teachers in Paris thus became the first institution of higher learning that today we call a university. By the thirteenth century the University of Paris had become the intellectual center of Europe.

The Most Famous Teacher of Europe Around the year 1110, Peter Abelard began to teach in Paris. He drew many students and quickly became the most popular teacher in the school. Abelard had a fine mind, one of the greatest in the intellectual history of Europe. He was sure of the power of the human mind to know truth. He believed that logic, the science of reason, could help human beings fit all experience — including theology — into a rational system of thought.

Abelard's method was to test his sources. He insisted on careful scholarship. In so doing, Abelard laid the foundations of the educational system of the later Middle Ages. Soon Abelard's method — it came to be called the **scholastic method** — was being used in all the schools and in all subjects. In the thirteenth century, Saint Thomas Aquinas, the greatest theologian of the Middle Ages, used Abelard's method to build up a great system of **scholastic theology**.

Around 1121, because of personal problems, Abelard stopped teaching and entered the Benedictine monastery of St.-Denis, just outside Paris. After many years of trouble and suffering, during which Abelard was for a time abbot of a monastery, he began teaching again. In 1136, he was back in Paris.

Abelard and Bernard of Clairvaux Abelard's use of logic and reasoning in talking about questions of faith brought him to the attention of Bernard of Clairvaux. Bernard was a conservative theologian. He was convinced it was unwise to reason about matters of faith. Peter Abelard sincerely believed in all the teachings of the Church. He just pointed out that God had given human beings the power to reason, and expected them to use it. But to Saint Bernard, Abelard was a theologian filled with pride.

Bernard was a great person. Even so, he was sometimes narrow-minded and unbending. Saint Bernard asked some bishops to call Abelard before a council. In 1140, Abelard was asked to appear at a council in the city of Sens (säns´) in northern France. Abelard went, thinking he was going to have a public debate with Bernard. Instead, Bernard read out a list of Abelard's ideas that he and other conservative theologians thought were heretical. When Abelard was asked to admit his error, he said he would appeal to the pope and walked out of the council. The bishops condemned Abelard's teachings.

On his way to Rome to present his case to the pope, Abelard stopped at the great Benedictine abbey of Cluny in east-central France. During the Middle Ages, travelers often received food and shelter in monasteries. The abbot of Cluny at this time, was Peter, a very holy man. He would later be declared a saint, and is known today as Peter the Venerable. Peter knew about Abelard's troubles with Bernard of Clairvaux and tried to help.

Before Abelard could continue his journey, word reached Cluny that the pope had agreed with the Sens council's condem-

WORDS TO LIVE BY

Jesus to me is honey in the mouth, music in the ear, a song in the heart.

SAINT BERNARD OF CLAIRVAUX

nation of Abelard. A kindhearted man, Peter urged Abelard to become a monk at Cluny. Abelard did so, and Peter was able to make peace between Abelard and Saint Bernard. He also persuaded the pope to lift the condemnation of Abelard. Abelard died in a religious house belonging to Cluny on April 21, 1142.

Today we owe much to both Saint Bernard and Abelard. Saint Bernard was a great leader. He preached not only through his sermons and writings but by the holiness of his life. Abelard also gave much to us and to the Church. His love of truth and his sharp mind enabled him to make a great contribution to the way people after him studied theology.

Recall and Reflect

1. What method did Peter Abelard use in his teaching?
2. Why did Saint Bernard object to Peter Abelard's method?
3. How did Peter the Venerable try to help both Peter Abelard and Saint Bernard?
4. Jesus said, "Blest . . . are the peacemakers; they shall be called sons of God" (Matthew 5:9). Sometimes we know two good people who cannot agree with one another. What are some things we might do to serve as peacemakers?

In the Middle Ages this was the Cistercian monastery of Fontfroid in the south of France. The buildings are now privately owned.

TWELFTH-CENTURY CONFLICT BETWEEN CHURCH AND STATE

Church Law All societies—organized groups of people—have laws. Laws are rules that govern how a group's members act. Laws are made for the common good of a society. As we saw in Chapter 4, the Church, the society of all those who are baptized into Jesus, has its code of law, called the Code of Canon Law. The purpose of canon law is to help the Church teach the message of Jesus and administer His sacraments. Though the Church is much more than laws or customs, the laws and legal institutions help the Church live a life of grace.

By the twelfth century, the Church was already over a thousand years old. It had a huge number of laws, rules, and customs. They included laws made by ecumenical councils and local synods as well as laws made by popes and individual bishops. There were many decisions of Church courts and various ideas of Church teachers. All those laws, rules, and customs made up the great body of Church law. Up to the eleventh century, only incomplete collections had been made of all that material.

The development of the Church's body of law was affected by the laws of the many different peoples among whom the Church worked. But Roman law had the greatest influence upon canon law. As you know, in the sixth century the Roman emperor Justinian had made a great collection of all Roman laws—the Justinian Code. (See Chapter 4.) The eleventh century saw a renewal of the study of Roman law, or as it came to be called civil law, in the West. The center of those legal studies was the northern Italian town of Bologna (bə lōn′yə).

The interest in the study of civil law also stimulated scholars to begin studying canon law. One of the legal scholars at Bologna in the early twelfth century was an Italian monk named Gratian. Not much is known about him. We do not know when he was born or when he died. But around 1141, Gratian wrote a very important book, the first scientific collection of canon law.

In his study of Church law, Gratian used the same methods Peter Abelard had used to study theology. Gratian was careful to note the exact meaning of the words used in a law. He tried to figure out when and where the law had been made. He listed how different people had interpreted the law, and he tried to reconcile those interpretations when they seemed to be in conflict.

Gratian's work proved that Church law, like civil law, could be organized into a complete system. His book was a huge success. By 1150 it was being used as a textbook in Bologna and elsewhere. The school—later the University of Bologna—became a center for the study of canon law as well as civil law. Students came to Bologna from all over Europe. Many scholars became learned in both civil and canon law. Lawyers found more and more careers opening up both in the Church and in the service of kings and princes of Europe. And differences soon began to develop between those two great systems of law as both Church and European rulers began to enforce and apply them in the twelfth century.

Henry II of England Because of the differing claims of canon law and the laws of European countries, conflicts often developed between Church and state. Such a conflict took place in England during the reign of King Henry II (1154–1189). Henry II was twenty-one when he became king. He was the great-grandson of William the Conqueror (1027–1087), the duke of Normandy who had conquered all of England in 1066.

William the Conqueror had set up a strong central government in England and Normandy. The Church was allowed to keep its lands. However, William named all bishops and abbots in his kingdom. By order of the king, the bishops of England were given their own courts and the right to try members of the clergy who were accused of crimes. William and his successors usually chose their chief administrators from among the clergy.

Henry II (1154–1189) was not only king of England but ruler of many lands in France. He spent less than half of his reign in England.

Like his great-grandfather, Henry II was a strong ruler who wanted better order for England and more power for the king. He carried out many reforms. Under Henry II, the ideas of the King's Peace and a common law for all England—both enforced by royal courts—were firmly established in the country.

King Henry II expected the help of the Church in his reforms. He also believed that as king he should have more control over the public affairs of the Church. He believed that members of the clergy who were guilty of serious crimes, such as murder, should be judged not in the bishops' courts but in the king's court. That last idea was to lead to a great test of wills when Henry II appointed his friend and chancellor, Thomas Becket, as archbishop of Canterbury and leader of the English clergy.

Thomas Becket of London Thomas Becket was born in London in 1118. His parents were Norman but not of noble birth. They came from the new class of town-dwellers, called burghers, that had appeared in Europe with the rebirth of towns and trade. That new middle class would later be called the bourgeoisie (bùr'zhwä'zē').

Becket's father had been sheriff of London, and Thomas was educated in London schools. He loved riding, hunting, and other field sports. Before he was twenty-one, both of his parents had died. For a while he worked as a clerk in a relative's business. Then, around the age of twenty-four, Thomas became a member of the clergy. He went to live and study in the house of Theobald, the archbishop of Canterbury.

In the Middle Ages there were no seminaries for those who wanted to become parish priests. Young men who wished to

SIDELIGHTS ON CHURCH HISTORY

Romanesque and Gothic Churches

In Western Europe during the Middle Ages, two styles of building churches developed—the Romanesque and the Gothic. The older of the two styles, the Romanesque, is based upon the Roman, or rounded, arch. It developed between 950 and 1150 and is found all over Europe. Since many great abbey churches were built in the Romanesque style, it is sometimes called the monastic style.

The nave, or main body, of a Romanesque church was usually rectangular in shape. Very often the Romanesque church was built in the form of a cross, with two shorter rectangles, called transepts, meeting the longer nave at right angles. To cover, or roof, such spaces, the Romans used two methods. In one they built a barrel vault—which can be thought of as a series of round arches—to cover each rectangular space. In the other method, the Romans divided up a barrel vault into squares, called bays. Each bay was then covered with a vault made up of two barrel vaults that met at right angles. Such a vault was called a cross vault.

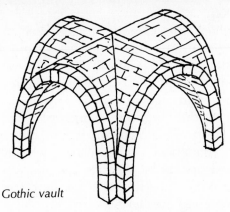

Gothic vault

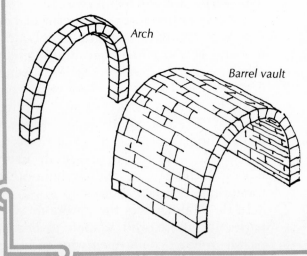

Arch

Barrel vault

Romanesque churches appear very strong and solid. Thick walls were needed to support the heavy stone vaults described above. Only small windows could be put in the upper walls without weakening the walls. As a result, Romanesque churches were usually rather dark inside. Often a tower would be built over the crossing—the place where the nave and transepts met—to bring more light into the church.

With its massive walls, round arches, and strong towers, the Romanesque church has great power and majesty. It reflects both the strong faith of its builders and a world that does not change.

During the twelfth century, a new style of church building, called Gothic, appeared in France and quickly spread all over Europe. One of the first churches built in the Gothic style was the great abbey church of the Benedictine monastery of St.-Denis, just to the north of Paris, France. Suger (syü′zhär′), the abbot of St.-Denis from 1122 to 1151, began rebuilding his church in the Gothic manner around the year 1135. Most of the work was done by midcentury.

Unlike the Romanesque church, whose thick walls are needed to support heavy vaults, the Gothic church does not rely on its walls for stability. The Gothic church is really a skeleton—a framework of stone piers, arches, and columns. It is that framework of stone which supports vault and roof in the Gothic church (much as the framework of steel beams supports the modern skyscraper.)

In the Gothic church the walls could be raised high, since the church did not depend on them alone to stand. If those high walls needed support, as they sometimes did, it could be given by adding flying buttresses, or supports that "flew" over lower roofs or vaults. The space between piers could then be filled with large windows of stained glass. The Gothic church was flooded with colored light. To increase the impression of height, Gothic builders used pointed arches between columns and in church vaults.

If the Romanesque church shows us the stability and serenity of a traditional faith, the Gothic church expresses a faith pulsing with vigor and life. The Gothic church voices in stone the new-found confidence of twelfth-century Christian Europe. With its great height, soaring piers, and lofty vaults, the Gothic church shows us a people who are not only sure of their faith but sure of their power to reason and understand.

Flying buttresses

Cross vault

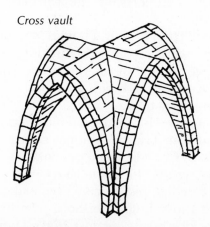

Both Romanesque and Gothic churches were "books in stone." In them, medieval men and women could see the story of redemption—from Adam and Eve to the coming of Christ in glory. The interior walls of the churches were covered with scenes from the Bible and the life of Christ. (Today most of those pictures have faded away, and the interiors of those churches seem gray or white.) Statues of our Lord, our Lady, prophets, and saints were everywhere, inside and outside those churches. Even Satan was carved in stone as a warning. All decorations of those churches—paintings, sculpture, stained glass—were used to teach the truths of faith. And the bells in church towers sounded the good news, the beauty and joy of the Christian life, to town and countryside.

study for the priesthood went to live in the house of a priest or bishop. Joining the group of young men who lived with Archbishop Theobald, Thomas came to know a great deal about how the Church was run in England. He met important people in the Church and government. Thomas was very intelligent. Several times Theobald sent him to Rome on Church business. In 1154, Thomas Becket was ordained a deacon. Archbishop·Theobald thereupon made him archdeacon of Canterbury. That important office gave Thomas great authority. He ran the daily affairs of the diocese for the archbishop.

Thomas also became a close friend of Henry II, the young man who had just become the king of England. Both Henry and Thomas enjoyed hunting and spent much time together. Henry thought so highly of Thomas that in 1155 the king made him chancellor of England, one of the most important positions in his government. A large income went with those high offices, and Thomas lived very well. Many people thought Thomas was very proud. He was also known for his violent temper.

Archbishop Theobald died in 1161. Henry II thought it would be a very good idea to make his friend Thomas archbishop. Thomas did not want the position, but the king insisted. Thomas was elected archbishop in 1162. He was ordained a priest, then a bishop, and was recognized as the archbishop of Canterbury by Pope Alexander III.

Thomas, Archbishop   As soon as Thomas Becket became archbishop of Canterbury, he changed his way of life. He spent longer hours in prayer. He fasted often. Although he had always given aid to the poor, he now took greater care of them, invited them to eat at his table, and served them. Above all,

Thomas no longer always agreed with the king about the power that the king had over the Church.

You can imagine how disappointed King Henry II was. He had thought Thomas would continue to support him and all his plans. As archbishop, however, Thomas saw that his first responsibility was to the Church.

In 1163 an English priest was accused of murder. As a member of the clergy, he had the right to be tried in a bishop's court. Henry II, however, demanded that the priest be tried in the king's court. Archbishop Becket refused. Henry was very angry. In 1164 he called a great meeting and ordered Thomas to appear before his court.

At first, Thomas said he would not go because the king had no right to judge him. Henry fined him a large sum of money. At the last moment, the archbishop did appear before the court, dressed in his vestments and with a tall cross, the sign of his office, carried before him. In a loud voice, Thomas announced that he would appeal to the pope, and left the court. The king ordered Thomas's arrest. The archbishop fled to France, where he lived in exile for six years. King Henry, meanwhile, seized much of the property of the Church of Canterbury.

In 1170, Henry and Thomas met in France and were reconciled. But the king did not give up any of his rights over the Church. And he did not give back the Church property he had taken.

While Henry II remained in the lands that he ruled in France, Thomas returned to England. Crowds came to meet him along the roads to Canterbury. When Thomas reached his diocese, he excommunicated those English bishops who had taken the king's side against him. Those

Thomas Becket was archbishop of Canterbury from 1162 to 1170. The present cathedral, dating from 1170, has been enlarged several times.

bishops then joined Henry in France and complained about Thomas.

Thomas Becket, Martyr It is said that when King Henry heard about the excommunications of the bishops he shouted, "Will no one get rid of this troublesome cleric?" Four of Henry's knights decided to kill the archbishop. They set out for Canterbury and got there on December 29, 1170. Forcing their way into the archbishop's house, the knights demanded that Thomas withdraw the excommunications. Thomas refused, and the knights left.

Thomas's servants urged him to go to the cathedral, where monks attached to Canterbury were singing the evening service, called vespers. Thomas went to the cathedral but would not let the doors be locked. He said that all must be free to enter the house of God. The four knights, now wearing armor and carrying swords, followed Thomas into the church. They beheaded the archbishop before the altar.

Thomas Becket's death sent a shock wave through England and the rest of Europe. The pope excommunicated the four knights. Although King Henry said that he had nothing to do with the murder of the archbishop, he, too, was excommunicated. He did public penance in Canterbury Cathedral. Part of his penance called for the king to be stripped to the waist and whipped.

Thomas Becket was declared a saint in 1173. His body was buried in his cathedral. Canterbury became a popular pilgrimage center in the Middle Ages. We keep the feast of Saint Thomas on December 29, the anniversary of his death.

The twelfth century was indeed a time of great promise in the history of the Church. During those years, there was a revival of learning. The Church created the university, a new theology, and a system of canon law. Great cathedrals began to rise throughout Europe. Before the century was over, new engineering techniques had resulted in a new style of architecture, which we call Gothic. Large windows of stained glass filled the new churches with light. In Chapter 10 we will see the harvest of those advances, as great saints did wonderful things for Christ and his Church.

Recall and Reflect

1. How did the revival of Roman law affect the study of Church, or canon, law?

2. Who put together the first great collection of canon law?

3. Why wasn't King Henry II pleased with Thomas Becket as the archbishop of Canterbury?

4. "Lives of great men all remind us
   We can make our lives sublime,
   And, departing, leave behind us
   Footprints on the sands of time."
   Could those words, from Longfellow's "A Psalm of Life," have been said of Saint Thomas Becket after his death? Why? How can we try to live lives worthy of Jesus?

On December 29, 1170, Thomas Becket was martyred in Canterbury Cathedral. After his death, his tomb in the church became a popular place of pilgrimage.

Henry II lost this fight with the Church. But there were many such battles in the Middle Ages between kings who wished to control the Church and brave leaders who fought for its freedom. As kings gained more power, they were often successful in controlling the Church in their countries.

REVIEW AND CELEBRATE

Doctrinal Summary

In the Middle Ages the Church and the state were often
united. Many bishops were also leaders in the government.
Today that is rarely the case. Indeed, the Second Vatican
Council reminds us that the Church is "not bound to any
political system." It is the duty of Church leaders to point out
what is right and what is wrong, what is just and what is
unjust. It is the duty of Catholic citizens to fulfill their
political obligations and work for good government.

Religious Vocabulary

Cistercians   scholastic method
monastic theology   scholastic theology

Review Questions

Answer the following questions on a separate sheet of paper.

1. What did Saint Bernard do as abbot, theologian, and preacher that led people to say "he
   carried the twelfth century on his shoulders"?

2. What was Peter Abelard's method of learning and teaching? How did that method affect
   the study of theology?

3. What is the purpose of canon law in the Church?

4. How did Henry II think of the Church during his time as king?

5. What three things were done that made it possible to describe the twelfth century as a
   time of great promise in the history of the Church?

Prayer Celebration

Leader: Let us pray together to the Mother of
Jesus and our Mother.
All: Hail, Holy Queen, Mother of Mercy, our
life, our sweetness, and our hope.
To you do we cry, poor banished children of Eve.
To you do we send up our sighs, mourning
and weeping in this valley of tears.
Turn, O most gracious advocate, your
eyes of mercy toward us, and after this our exile
show us the blessed fruit of your womb, Jesus.
O clement, O loving, O sweet Virgin Mary.

Leader: Pray for us, O Holy Mother of God.
All: That we may be worthy of the promises
of Christ.

Leader: Mary, our Mother in heaven,
we have confidence in your love for us.
We hope to respond to that love by
responding to others through the power
of your Son and our Brother, Jesus Christ.
All: Amen.

Dedicated to the Virgin Mary, Chartres Cathedral in France is one of the glories of the Gothic style. Most of the church dates from the 1200s.

10

Thirteenth-Century Greatness

It was the year 1223 in the little town of Greccio (grek´ē ō) in central Italy. A deacon whom the people called Brother Francis of Assisi (ə sē´zē) was preparing to celebrate Christmas. Because of his great love for Jesus, Brother Francis had found much joy and happiness in his life. As he made ready to keep the feast of Christ's birthday, Brother Francis decided he wanted others to see and understand the hardships of the infant Jesus. Francis had a scene built showing Mary and Joseph, and the baby Jesus lying in straw in a manger. Nearby were an ox and a donkey. When the people crowded into the church for midnight Mass, they were astonished to see the figures—Jesus, his mother and Saint Joseph, and the live animals standing by. In that way, Brother Francis began our custom of building manger scenes at Christmastime as a reminder of the meaning of Christ's birth.

In this chapter we shall see how that same Brother Francis and several other great leaders helped the people of the thirteenth century to better understand and love the Church. We shall read about a Spanish priest and preacher, Dominic Guzman; a noble lady, the lady Clare; thinkers and scholars Thomas Aquinas (ə kwī´nəs), Albert the Great, and Bonaventure; and one of the greatest popes of the Middle Ages, Pope Innocent III. All those people had great love for the Church. Through their lives, by their teaching, and in their writing, they helped to make the thirteenth century a time of special greatness in the Church's long history.

For almost eight hundred years the organization of the Church in the West was like the organization of the society it served. Before the 1100s, Western society was mostly agricultural. There was little that ever changed. Most people lived in small

A manger scene at Christmas reminds us of the gospel story of Jesus' birth.
Saint Francis introduced this custom in 1223.

villages that were part of larger working farms, or manors. People who were born peasants or serfs had little chance to change the kind of work they did during their lifetime. The religious orders that served the society—the Benedictine and (later) the Cistercian orders—were also found in the country. Those orders used the *Rule of Saint Benedict*, which we read about in Chapter 3. The monks and nuns lived in abbeys that were also organized on a farming basis.

The new towns, the revival of trade, and the renewal of learning began to change all that. In the eleventh and twelfth centuries, more and more people lived in towns and were busy in trade and industry. Many new and different careers became possible for many more people. Rapid and far-reaching changes began taking place in medieval society and in the Church.

Towns were centers of trade, and many had new universities as well. As we saw in Chapter 9, the townspeople made up a new class, a middle class, in medieval society. They were not nobles with many rights and privileges, but neither were they peasant farmers or serfs tied to the land. Townspeople were free; their liberties were guaranteed by charters that had been granted by kings or great nobles or the Church.

Towns and townspeople, therefore, gave the Church new chances to carry out its mission. But they gave it many new problems as well. Clearly, a new kind of religious leadership was needed to meet the needs of the society, which was becoming more urban. The one person who did more than any other to bring about that leadership was Brother Francis, a young man from the town of Assisi in central Italy. We know him today as Saint Francis of Assisi. Brother Francis founded a new kind of religious order that enabled the Church to serve the new towns and the needs of a changing society.

A NEW RELIGIOUS ORDER

Francis, "Poor Man" of Assisi   The person we know as Saint Francis of Assisi was born about 1182 in the central Italian town of Assisi. His father, Peter Bernardone, a cloth merchant, was a typical representative of the new middle class. By hard work and business skill, he had become very rich. His mother, Pica, was a Frenchwoman. Although Francis had been baptized John, he was usually called "Francesco," or "the Frenchman," by his family and friends. Francis spoke French from childhood, and much of his father's business was in France.

Like other town boys, Francis went to school and learned a little Latin to go along with his French. He was high-spirited and had a great love of life. As a young man, Francis became a leader of Assisi's young people. Wherever Francis was found, there was sure to be much fun and merriment.

Like other young people, Francis had dreams of becoming a hero. He wanted to become a famous soldier. In 1202, when he was about twenty, Francis took part in a war between Assisi and the town of Perugia (pə rü′jē ə). He was captured and kept as a prisoner for almost a year. For some time after his release, Francis was seriously ill. But in 1205 he was preparing to be a soldier again. While on his way to join an army that was fighting for the pope, Francis had a dream. A voice told him to go back to Assisi and serve the Master—that is, Christ —rather than His servant, the pope.

Francis returned to Assisi and began to question the way in which he was living. He prayed hard, becoming convinced that he had something important to do for the Church. While riding one day, Francis met a leper whose face and body were badly disfigured by the disease. When the man asked for money, Francis dismounted, gave

him money, and then kissed him. After that, Francis spent much time visiting hospitals and serving the sick. He gave money, and sometimes even his clothes, to the poor.

One day about that time, Francis was praying in the church of St. Damian (dā′mē ən), outside Assisi. He seemed to hear a voice coming from a crucifix. It said, "Francis, go and repair my house, which you see is falling down." Since the church of St. Damian was indeed old and half in ruins, Francis took the command literally.

Francis went home, took one of his father's horses and a cartload of cloth out of his father's warehouse, and sold everything for money. Francis took the money to the priest in charge of St. Damian's and asked to stay there with him. The priest welcomed Francis but refused to accept the money. Francis left it on a windowsill.

Peter Bernardone became angry at what he thought was his son's lack of common sense. He went to St. Damian's to get Francis and the money. But Francis went into hiding. When he did reappear, some days later, his father took him home, beat him, and locked him up. His mother set Francis free while his father was out of the house. Francis disappeared again.

Francis Chooses God Francis's father now went to the bishop of Assisi and demanded that his son either return home or give up his inheritance and give back the purchase price of the horse and goods he had taken. The bishop ordered Francis to return the money. Francis did as he was told, and even took off his clothes and gave them back to his father. The bishop gave Francis a tunic, a shirtlike garment worn by workingmen. Francis put it on, marked it with a cross, and went out to begin his new life. He began to beg for money for the poor and

Saint Francis of Assisi saw God's love for us in earth and sky and all living creatures. He is often shown praising God in natural settings.

Francis and his father had serious differences over money and about careers. Francis was determined to live exactly like Christ. He did not want to own anything at all. He wanted to serve Jesus in the sick and poor. Francis's father could not understand that point of view. Francis believed God was asking him to lead a life of poverty and service, so he gave up everything he owned. He even gave up family ties. As Francis said to his father, "Before now, I called you father . . . but now I say, 'Our Father, who art in Heaven.'" The Our Father became one of Francis's favorite prayers. Since God was our Father, everything that came from God was good. Francis looked on all creatures as a reflection of the wonderful goodness of God. He wrote a famous hymn in which he called the sun his "brother" and the moon, and even death, his "sister."

The First Franciscans Many people admired Francis, and some men began to join him as companions and followers. Soon a little band was living and working with Francis among the people of the towns and villages of Italy. That little group became known as the first **Franciscans**.

About that time it became clear to Francis what God wanted him to do in the Church. On February 24, 1209, Francis was reading Saint Matthew's gospel. He read how Jesus, after choosing his apostles, sent them on mission with special instructions.

> Provide yourselves with neither gold nor silver nor copper in your belts; no traveling bag, no change of shirt, no sandals, no walking staff. The workman, after all, is worth his keep.
> —Matthew 10:9–10

Francis decided to organize his little group into a new **religious community**, or order, that would own nothing. His fol-

for the repair of St. Damian's. He even carried stones and helped the stonemasons work on the church.

It often happens that young people do not get along with their parents. Sometimes it is a question of a few rules of behavior. Sometimes it goes much deeper. Parents see things one way; a son or daughter sees things in a very different way. Each one's point of view is different, because each is looking at things from a different angle. It is like one person seeing a football game from the end zone and another seeing it from the fifty-yard line. They see the same game but from different points of view.

lowers would beg for everything—food, clothing, even shelter. Like the apostles, they would walk everywhere, doing whatever work came to hand, caring for the people, and preaching to them. The Franciscans became the first of the **mendicant orders** in the Church. A mendicant is a person who lives by begging. Not only would Francis's followers live without money or land, but the Franciscan community, or group, itself would not own property. The Franciscan order would live only on the gifts of the people. Members of older orders also lived lives of poverty, but their monasteries could own land and have money. Indeed, they *had* to own property, because income from their farms was used to build the buildings and

Since the mendicant orders begged for everything, their members lived in towns like this, caring for people and preaching to them.

to support the monks and nuns who lived in the monasteries. Although the earlier monks and nuns lived simple lives, many monasteries could and did become very rich.

Francis called his followers **Friars Minor**, or Little Brothers. They wore simple, coarse robes of gray-brown tied with rope or cord. Clothing like that was worn by pilgrims in the Middle Ages. Because the color of their robes, or habits, was mostly gray, the Little Brothers of Saint Francis, or Franciscans, were also called Gray Friars.

Francis and his followers were not the first people in the Middle Ages to live like that. At the end of the twelfth century and the beginning of the thirteenth, there was a great movement among laypeople, especially those in the towns, to live lives based upon the gospels. Like Francis and his Little Brothers, those people wished to imitate the poverty of Jesus and His disciples. But many of those groups were very critical of abuses in the Church. They attacked Church leaders. Many would not accept Church authority, and became heretics. Francis was different. He never talked against the Church. In his great love for Christ, he just wanted the Franciscans to serve as an example for all in the Church.

The Rule of Francis Francis's rule made the gospel the way of life for his friars. In 1209 he went to Rome with eleven brothers to beg the approval of Pope Innocent III (1198–1216) for his rule. The pope agreed to allow the Franciscan way of life. Francis and his brothers were made members of the clergy and were allowed to preach. Their headquarters was a small chapel called the Portiuncula (pôrts'ē unk'ù lə), near Assisi.

The number of Franciscan friars grew very rapidly. By 1221 they numbered more than five thousand. Franciscans worked in France, Spain, and Germany as well as in Italy. Francis's simple little band had become an international organization grouped into large districts called provinces.

Some people are good at organizing and planning things; they are very practical. Others have a wider vision; they can inspire people with their ideas and their faith. Francis was the second type of person. He had the great ideal of absolute, Christlike poverty. But no organization can be utterly poor for very long. As an organization, even the Franciscans had to be concerned about houses to live in and money to live on. Although Francis's ideal of absolute poverty continued to inspire his friars, it became clear that his ideal had to be adapted to the needs of the times. In 1221, Francis's rule was changed. The Franciscans remained mendicant — an organized community of beggars who depended for their livelihood on acts of charity by others. They did not own income-producing lands as did the older monastic orders. But the friars were allowed to receive fixed, annual alms (ämz'), or donations.

In 1220, Francis appointed one of his brothers, Brother Elias, to act in his place as head of the community. Francis himself continued to be an example of great love and poverty. He lived and worked in the towns of central Italy. In August 1224, Francis built a little hut in a secluded place called Monte Alvernia (mônt'ē al vėr'nē ə), where he lived with Brother Leo, his secretary and confessor. While at prayer there in September 1224, Francis received the marks of Christ's wounds on his hands and feet. He tried, as much as possible, to hide those signs of our Lord's suffering by covering his hands with his habit and wearing stockings and sandals.

In 1230 the body of Saint Francis was secretly buried in the great church that Brother Elias was building at Assisi in his honor.

During the two years that remained of his life, Francis was almost constantly in pain. As his health failed, he also began to lose his sight. Obeying Brother Elias, Francis put himself in the care of the pope's own doctors. He was taken to many places for treatment, but nothing helped. Francis knew he was dying. He dictated a message to his brothers to love and observe the "Lady Poverty," and to love and honor the clergy of the Church. In 1226, while Francis was staying with the bishop of Assisi, doctors told him that he had only a few days to live. Ill and blind, Francis was carried to the Portiuncula to die. Urging his brothers to love God, poverty, and the gospel, and calling out "Welcome, Sister Death," Francis died on Saturday, October 3, 1226. He was buried in the church of St. George in Assisi.

In 1228, two years after his death, Francis was proclaimed a saint. We celebrate his feast on October 4. In the year 1230—out of fear that it might be stolen—Francis's body was secretly moved to the great church in Assisi that was being built in his honor by Brother Elias. It was only in 1818 that his relics, or remains, were found. They had been buried deep under the main altar of the crypt, or lower church.

Even during his lifetime, Francis was regarded as a saint. Gentle and simple, he was seen as a person very much like Christ. No other saint has won Saint Francis's popularity, not only among Catholics but also among non-Catholics and even non-believers. What Francis wrote and what he did still influence the lives of many people. Many still follow guidelines that Francis set down. Francis showed in his life what wonderful things could be done if you put Christ's message into practice.

The Lady Clare One of the people who lived like Saint Francis was a young woman of noble birth whose name was Clare. She

133

For forty-one years, from 1212 to her death in 1253, Saint Clare dedicated her life to Christ and to the service of the "Lady Poverty."

words, Clare slipped away from her home on Palm Sunday, 1212, and went to the Portiuncula, outside Assisi. There Saint Francis cut her hair and gave her a veil and also a habit like his own. Clare then dedicated her life to Christ and the "Lady Poverty."

Francis placed Clare with Benedictine nuns until a house could be built for her next to the church of St. Damian, outside Assisi. Soon many other young women joined Clare, including Clare's sister Agnes. Later, her sister Beatrice and her mother joined the new community of nuns. Saint Francis appointed Clare as superior.

Clare shared Saint Francis's desire to live a poor and simple life like Christ's. Her community grew. After a few years, monasteries of **Poor Clares**, as those Franciscan nuns came to be called, were founded in several places in Italy, France, and Germany.

Clare was a very brave woman. She did not want her nuns to possess any property that made money. In 1228, Pope Gregory IX tried to change that rule of strict poverty in order to make sure of the financial security of the Poor Clares. They were strictly cloistered (klois'tərd), and never left their monasteries. Clare told the pope, "I need to be absolved from my sins, but I do not wish to be absolved from the obligation of following Jesus Christ."

Clare herself never left the monastery of St. Damian. She remained superior for forty years, until her death in 1253. Two years later, in 1255, she was made a saint. Saint Clare had a wonderful devotion to Jesus in the Blessed Sacrament. When she spoke with her nuns and others about God and holy things, she held them spellbound. One account of the early life of Saint Clare described her in these words: "The Lady Clare, shining in name, more shining in

was born in Assisi about 1194. In the year 1212, when Clare was about eighteen, Francis came to her parish church to give a series of Lenten talks. Moved by his life, most shining in conversation . . . most pure of heart . . . wise and meek, and a marvellous lover of Christ." We keep her feast on August 11.

Recall and Reflect

1. Why did Saint Francis want to live like a poor man?

2. What name did Saint Francis give to his order?

3. Who were the Poor Clares?

4. Members of mendicant communities, such as the Franciscans, lived lives of poverty and worked to help poor people. What are some things that you could do in that same spirit of love to show your concern for the poor?

THE FRIARS PREACHERS

Dominic, Defender of the Faith The second great mendicant order of friars, the **Order of Preachers**, or the **Dominicans** (də min′-ə kənz), was founded in the early years of the thirteenth century. It was started by Dominic Guzman, a Spanish priest. Dominic lived at the time of Saint Francis of Assisi. He was born in the kingdom of Castile (ka stēl′), in northern Spain, some-time after 1170. He belonged to a noble family, and as a young man, he studied for the priesthood. Once a priest, Dominic became a canon of the cathedral in the town of Osma (äs′mə), Spain, around 1196.

As we saw in Chapter 6, canons are priests who are attached to a cathedral and who are in charge of the services there. The canons of the Osma cathedral lived a community life and followed a religious rule. Their rule was based on one made up by Saint Augustine, the great fourth-century Church teacher.

Around 1201, Dominic became prior, or superior, of his community when the former prior, Diego d'Azavedo (dē ā′gō daz ə vā′dō), became bishop of Osma. As a canon, Dominic had led a simple life of study and prayer. In the year 1203, how-ever, and again from 1205 to 1206, Domi-nic journeyed across Europe with Bishop Diego. The king of Castile sent the bishop on two trips to Denmark to arrange a mar-riage for his son. Bishop Diego took Domi-nic along for company. Although the king's marriage plans did not succeed, those trips across Europe were to change Domi-nic's life.

A Heresy in France On their way across Europe, Bishop Diego and Dominic passed through the south of France, also called the country of Languedoc (lang′gə däk′). They found that many people of Languedoc—especially in the towns and in the castles of the noble families—had left the Catholic Church and joined a heretical religious group known as the Catharists (kath′ər-ists), or the Albigensians (al′bə jen′sē ənz). The word *Catharist* comes from a Greek word that means "pure." *Albigensian* comes from Albi, a town in southern France that was a center of that heresy.

The **Albigensian heresy** began to spread in Europe during the second half of the twelfth century. It had been brought from the East by traders and by soldiers return-ing home from the crusades. Groups of Albigensians were to be found in many of the towns of northern Italy and in the Rhineland, in Germany. But the strongest centers of heresy were the towns of south-ern France, or Languedoc.

The Albigensians taught that all material things were evil. They believed that there were two gods—a good god who was purely spiritual and an evil god who made all material things. The good god created the angels and human souls. The evil god was responsible for human bodies. The Albigensians believed that human souls were "trapped" in bodies at the time of birth. The only way human souls could be freed from the evil, material world was, as far as possible, to give up all material things. That meant living a life of fasting and poverty.

Albigensians who tried to live in that heroic way were called "the perfect ones," or "the fulfilled ones." To become one of the perfect, a person had to give up marriage and live a hard, ascetic life. Perfect ones could never eat meat or eggs; they had to keep strict fasts and always travel on foot.

Most Albigensians, however, did not live like the perfect ones. Most were content just to honor their heroes. Albigensians of that type were called "believers." All that was asked of them was that they believe in the teachings of the perfect ones and promise to become like them before they died. Most believers tried to put off becoming perfect ones as long as possible.

Dominic and the Friars Preachers While Dominic was staying in the city of Toulouse (tù lüz′), the capital of Languedoc, he was able to bring an Albigensian heretic back to the Church. This experience convinced him that God wanted him to become a missionary. Bishop Diego shared Dominic's desire. Dominic and Bishop Diego went to Rome to offer their services to Pope Innocent III. They wanted to become missionaries to peoples of Eastern Europe who were still pagan. Pope Innocent, the same pope who had befriended Saint Francis of Assisi, asked Dominic and Bishop Diego to work instead for the conversion of the Albigensian heretics in southern France.

Like many popes before him, Innocent III worried about the spread of that heresy in southern France. He had already sent Cistercian monks into Languedoc as preachers against the Albigensians. But their work had had little effect. Returning from Rome, Dominic and Bishop Diego met with those Cistercian monks and watched them at their work.

Dominic and Bishop Diego soon became more and more certain that the chief reason the Cistercians were not able to reach the hearts of the heretics and draw them back to the Church was the Cistercians' way of life and method of preaching. When the Cistercians preached, they went about on horseback, with soldiers to guard them and with many servants. The Albigensian leaders, on the other hand, were poor and simple. Dominic was convinced that Catholic preachers would also have to be poor and live lives of prayer and penance. Bishop Diego returned to Osma, but Dominic remained in France and began to live and teach in that way.

Other men soon joined Dominic in working among the people of Languedoc. Dominic became the leader of a small group of preachers who went from town to town, preaching to the people and even debating with the Albigensian leaders. Dominic converted a number of women from the heresy. In 1206 he built a monastery in the town of Prouille (prü′ē′) for nine of those women. That little group became the first community of the mendicant order of Dominican nuns.

By 1215, Dominic had spent almost ten years preaching in Languedoc. All that time he had tried to follow the rule of Saint Augustine. But Dominic also wanted to organize his little band of followers into a new order, one of poor friars who would also be preachers. In 1214, the bishop of Toulouse approved Dominic's plan. In the next year, 1215, Dominic went to Rome to attend the **Fourth Lateran Council**, called by Pope Innocent III. Even though the council decided that no new religious orders were to be set up, Pope Innocent approved Dominic's new order of Friars Preachers. But the pope asked Dominic to choose an existing, approved rule as the basis for his own rule. Dominic chose the rule of Saint Augustine, who had also been a great preacher.

Dominic's rule called for a life of poverty and study to prepare his friars to be good preachers. When Dominic went to Rome again in October 1216, Pope Innocent III had died. The new pope, Honorius III, approved Dominic's rule for his new order.

The Friars Preachers became the second great mendicant order of friars in the Church. Dominican friars wore white habits. When they were journeying, however, they wore large black cloaks over their habits. For that reason, in the Middle Ages the Dominicans were often called "Black Friars."

Like the Franciscans, the Dominicans had only one superior general. As the order began to grow, Dominic spent his time traveling from place to place, setting up new communities. Wherever Dominic journeyed, he always preached to the people. By 1221 there were about sixty Dominican houses all over Europe; they were organized into eight provinces.

In the summer of 1221, Dominic became very ill, and knew that he was dying. He asked to be taken to the Dominican monastery in Bologna (bə lōn′yə), Italy. Dominic died there on August 6, 1221, at the age of fifty-two. He was made a saint in 1234. We celebrate Saint Dominic's feast day on August 8.

A Crusade in Languedoc Dominic's preaching did not stop the spread of the Albigensian heresy. In 1208, a papal legate in the south of France was murdered by an Albigensian. Innocent III called for a crusade against the Albigensians. Nobles from the north of France invaded the south. They fought against the nobles of Languedoc. Most of the nobles of Languedoc had allowed heretics to live at peace in their lands. Some of those nobles were also heretics or had family members who were. In those times a person was guilty of heresy if one merely gave a heretic something to eat or drink.

The **Albigensian Crusade** was a cruel war. The south of France was devastated. Many people died on both sides. By 1226, all of Languedoc was under the control of the king of France, and the Albigensian heretics were being persecuted in every town and village.

In all the years Saint Dominic preached against the heretics, he never separated his love for neighbor from love for the Church.

SIDELIGHTS ON CHURCH HISTORY

A Holy King of France

Louis IX was king of France from 1226 to 1270. He was known for his sense of justice and the holiness of his life. Long after his death the people of France looked back to the reign of "Good King Louis" as a time when the poor were defended and France was at peace. So great was King Louis IX's reputation for justice that other kings of Europe asked him to settle disputes.

King Louis would often hold public meetings with his people. At such times, any person who had a complaint against any officer of the king could speak to Louis freely. Once, one of the king's vassals, a nobleman, hanged three children who were caught hunting rabbits in his forest. King Louis IX would not allow the man to be tried by his fellow nobles, as was the custom. The king ordered him to be tried by the king's own judges. The nobleman was condemned to death. Louis later spared the man's life but imposed a huge fine and took away much of his land as a punishment.

During his reign, King Louis would not allow his feudal lords to wage personal wars among themselves. He ordered them to keep all treaties that they made. King Louis was concerned not only about peace but also about the welfare of his subjects. Every day he invited needy people to eat at his table. In Lent and Advent, King Louis himself often served the poor at table. He never spoke ill of anyone nor used bad language. His biographer wrote, "I was twenty-two years in the holy king's company, and never once did I hear him swear. . . ."

In 1239 the Latin emperor of Constantinople gave King Louis the relic of Christ's crown of thorns. Louis sent two Dominican friars to bring the crown to France. He and his whole court met the relic at the French city of Sens and carried it to Paris. To keep that holy relic, King Louis built a beautiful chapel, the Sainte Chapelle (sänt′ shə pel′), in his royal palace. That chapel still stands in Paris. The relic of the crown of thorns is now in Paris's Notre Dame (nō′trə däm′) Cathedral.

Although he loved peace, King Louis IX was also a brave soldier. Twice he went on crusade against the Moslems. In 1248, Louis led an army that attacked the Moslems in Egypt. King Louis took the city of Damietta (dam′ē et′ə) on the Nile, but he was later defeated and kept a prisoner in Cairo. He was ransomed together with his army and spent the next four years in the Holy Land. Unable to get more help from Europe, Louis returned to France. In 1267, King Louis began to prepare for a second crusade. This time he went to the Moslem country of Tunis in North Africa. The French crusaders landed in Africa in August 1270. Before fighting began, King Louis became very sick with a fever. He died in Tunis on August 25. His body was taken back to Paris and buried in the abbey church of St.-Denis. In 1297, King Louis IX was made a saint. During the French Revolution his tomb was broken open and his bones were lost.

The Papal Inquisition The thirteenth-century popes worried much about the spread of heresy among the people. The Albigensian heresy was popular. Its teachings appealed to many who had little or no schooling. It had always been the duty of a bishop to combat heresy in his diocese. The Albigensian heresy, however, spread so fast that the traditional system broke down. It was hard for local Church and civil leaders to know who was a heretic and who was not. Finally, investigation of heresy was taken over by the papacy.

In 1233, Pope Gregory IX set up special papal courts, known as **Courts of the Inquisition** (in′kwə zish′ən). The word *inquisition* comes from a Latin word that means "to find out." Dominican and Franciscan friars were put in charge of the courts. The friars were called inquisitors (in kwiz′ət ərz) and were responsible only to the pope. They went from place to place setting up the special courts, whose work was to track down heretics and bring them to trial. Since the inquisitors usually kept good records, we know much about the way they worked.

Courts of the Inquisition checked all charges of heresy made by people. Inquisitors could question anyone, even princes and bishops. After 1252, torture was allowed to be used in questioning accused people, just as it was used in secular courts of the time. The work of the Courts of the Inquisition was secret. Accused people were not told who had named them. Persons found guilty of heresy were punished. Sometimes they were ordered to make a pilgrimage to a famous shrine. Sometimes they were publicly beaten in the

In the papal Courts of the Inquisition, Dominican and Franciscan friars tried to find out who were heretics and who were not.

town square. Some convicted heretics were put in prison for life.

The inquisitors themselves never sentenced anyone to death. But people who were found guilty of heresy and who would not change their ideas were handed over to the local prince or ruler to be punished. Such people were then put to death, usually by being burned at the stake. A prince or ruler who refused to enforce a penalty could be excommunicated by the Church.

In the later Middle Ages, the Courts of the Inquisition were often used by kings and other lay rulers for purely political purposes. That was true in the case of Saint Joan of Arc, who was burned to death in 1431. It was also true in Spain, where the Inquisition, under royal control, was used to persecute Spanish Jews and take over their property. With their secrecy, use of torture, and terrible punishments, the Courts of the Inquisition were certainly not fair or just. Innocent people were often hurt, and even put to death. Although the Church has always guarded the truths of our faith, it has in its long history sometimes made mistakes in the methods it has used.

In its *Declaration on Religious Freedom,* the Second Vatican Council states that the "right to religious freedom has its foundation in the very dignity of the human person." The Council goes on to say that civil governments should not interfere with the religious practices of individuals or of groups. In fact a government should "assume the safeguard of the religious freedom of all its citizens, in an effective manner, by just laws and by other appropriate means."

In the thirteenth century, however, most people did not see things that way. And we have to remember that the men and women who made up the Church at that time in history were people whose points of view and ideas about government were shaped by the times in which they lived. They thought that heresy was the same as the crime of treason against the state or the king. Heresy, in fact, was thought to be treason against God. It was also a crime against the king or prince, who was God's representative on earth. Most of those people felt, therefore, that it was the duty of the Church and of civil governments to stamp out heresy.

A Great Pastoral Council The council that Pope Innocent III called in 1215 was one of the most important in the Middle Ages and indeed in the whole history of the Church. It was the fourth council to be held in the Lateran Palace in Rome and is known as the Fourth Lateran Council. It was attended by more than 1200 people from all parts of Christendom. As we have seen, Saint Dominic was a member.

Pope Innocent III (1198–1216) was one of the greatest popes of the Middle Ages. He studied at the universities of Bologna and Paris.

Those who attended the Fourth Lateran Council made important decisions that were to affect what was done by the Church for hundreds of years. At the Fourth Lateran Council, the Church was said to be one and universal. The sacraments were described as means of grace. It was decided that the Sacraments of Penance and Communion should be received together at Easter time. Today we call the reception of Penance and the Eucharist at Easter time "making our Easter duty."

The Fourth Lateran Council also made rules about how bishops were to be chosen, and the way of life of the clergy. Rules of monastic life were made more strict. And the Albigensian, or Catharist, heresy was also condemned. The Fourth Lateran Council was the last great work of Pope Innocent III—he died the next year—and stands as a monument to his talents as a leader and organizer.

Recall and Reflect

1. Who was the founder of the Order of Preachers?

2. What did the Albigensians teach about material things?

3. Name four decisions made by the Fourth Lateran Council.

4. Saint Dominic believed that to reach people who did not have the faith, it was important to live a life of prayer and penance. How can you give a good example to others in your own life?

THE FRIARS AND THE UNIVERSITIES

Dominican and Franciscan Scholars The thirteenth century has been called the most intellectual century in the history of the Church in the Middle Ages. It was a time when European thinkers discovered once again not only the writings of the Greek philosphers Plato and Aristotle but also the ideas of the Moslem philosophers. That huge mass of new ideas had to be made to agree with the teachings of the Church.

The work of putting together all those new ideas took place in the medieval universities. The leaders in that great task were Dominican and Franciscan scholars. It was in the universities that the new friars made their greatest and most lasting contribution to the Church. As a writer of history today has pointed out, "Without the towns, the friars would not have come into existence; without the universities, they would not have become great."

Dominicans had always made teaching a part of their work. As early as 1217, Saint Dominic had sent seven Dominicans to study at the University of Paris. Dominic wanted his friars to be learned men so they would be good preachers. But the Dominicans quickly found out that there was much good work to be done within the universities as well. Dominicans were soon teaching at the universities of Paris, Bologna, and Oxford, and in the newer universities that were being set up all over Europe.

Saint Francis did not reject learning, but he feared that too much love for books and higher education would make his friars proud and draw them away from the "way of holy simplicity, and most high poverty." Despite Francis's fears, the Franciscans also began opening houses of study at the universities, and Franciscan masters began to teach in them. Like the Dominicans, the Franciscans realized that a university education would make them better spiritual leaders, preachers, and confessors.

Thomas Aquinas Among the many friar-scholars, two stand out for their great learning and the holiness of their lives—

Saint Thomas Aquinas, a Dominican, and Saint Bonaventure, a Franciscan. Both made great contributions in bringing together the new learning and Catholic theology.

Thomas Aquinas, the youngest son of an Italian knight, was born about 1225 in the family castle of Roccasecca (rôk′ə sek′ə), near the town of Aquino (ä kwē′nō). His family was related to the German emperor Frederick II. When Thomas was about five, he was sent to study at the nearby abbey of Monte Cassino (mônt′ē kə sē′nō). His family hoped that Thomas would one day become a Benedictine and perhaps the abbot of Monte Cassino. In 1239 the abbot of Monte Cassino sent Thomas to the University of Naples to study. While in Naples, Thomas came to know the Dominicans. He was drawn by their life of poverty and study. In 1244 he became a Dominican against the wishes of his family. Thomas's mother set out for Naples to bring him to his senses, but Thomas had already left Naples for Bologna. He was overtaken on the way and forced to return to the castle of Roccasecca, where he was kept for over a year. When his family realized they could not make Thomas change his mind, he was allowed to rejoin the Dominicans in 1245.

Thomas was sent to Paris and then to Cologne, Germany, to study under a well-known Dominican teacher, Albert the Great. Albert was called "the Great" by his contemporaries, because of his wide knowledge. Albert's interest in natural science led him to study the works of the fourth-century-B.C. Greek philospher Aristotle. Like Abelard, Albert the Great used Aristotle's methods of inquiry.

Thomas was a large, stocky young man. His fellow students at Cologne did not think he was very bright, and they called him the "dumb ox." One of his fellow stu-

Saint Thomas Aquinas was a very successful teacher. He became known both for his great learning and for the holiness of his life.

dents set out to help Thomas and found that Thomas knew the subject matter better than anyone else. Albert the Great also saw how bright Thomas was. He remarked that soon all of Europe would hear the bellowing of "this ox." At Cologne, Thomas was ordained to the priesthood.

In 1252, Friar Thomas was sent to Paris to study. He became a doctor of theology and taught at Paris from 1256 to 1259. The years between 1259 and 1268 Thomas spent teaching in Italy. In 1269, Thomas was again teaching in Paris, but three years later the Dominicans sent him to teach their own friars at the University of Naples.

A very successful teacher, Thomas soon became well-known for his sytem of theology. Thomas, like his master, Albert the Great, used the writings of Aristotle as a basis for further reasoning. Thomas was able to show that the ideas of Aristotle and the writings of the Moslem philosophers did not go against Church teaching. In fact, using that philosophy, Thomas was able to build a whole system of theology—today called **Thomism** (tō′miz′əm)—that gave a Christian point of view on the universe.

Perhaps Thomas Aquinas's best-known work is his *Summa Theologiae* (sù′mə tā′ō lō jē′ə). The Latin word *summa* means "a whole or total summary." The *Summa Theologiae* was a summary of all the theological teaching of the time. It was begun in 1266, while Thomas was teaching in Italy. It was probably meant to be a classroom book for his Dominican-friar students. Large as it is, the work was never finished. On December 6, 1273, while Thomas was offering Mass, he received a special message from God. After Mass, Thomas did not write anymore. He told his secretary, "All that I have written appears to be as so much straw after the things that have been revealed to me."

In 1274, Pope Gregory X asked Thomas to attend the Second Council of Lyon (lyôn′) in France. Although ill, Thomas set out on his journey to the council. But on March 7, 1274, while he was still in Italy, Thomas died. Forty-nine years later, in 1323, he was made a saint. In 1567, Pope Pius V declared Saint Thomas a Doctor of the Church—that is, a special teacher of the Church. His feast is on January 28.

Saint Bonaventure Another great theologian of the thirteenth century was the Franciscan friar Bonaventure. He was born about 1217 into a wealthy family of northern Italy. Bonaventure studied at the University of Paris. While at Paris, Bonaventure became a Franciscan friar.

Like Saint Thomas Aquinas, Bonaventure also received his doctorate and taught at Paris. In 1257, however, Bonaventure became superior general of all the Franciscans. Despite his many duties and journeys, Bonaventure was able to write many important works in theology. Unlike Saint Thomas, Bonaventure mirrored an older tradition of Christian thought. Following Saint Augustine, whom we read about in Chapter 2, Bonaventure taught that divine revelation teaches us everything we need to know to serve God.

WORDS TO LIVE BY

Grant, Lord, that I may gladly share
what I have with the needy, humbly ask
for what I need from him who has,
sincerely admit the evil I have done,
calmly bear the evil I suffer,
not envy my neighbor for his blessings,
and thank you unceasingly
whenever you hear my prayer.
SAINT THOMAS AQUINAS

In 1273, Pope Gregory X made Bonaventure a cardinal and bishop. He was ordained a bishop at Lyon, France, in November 1273. The next year, while working at the Second Council of Lyon, Bonaventure died suddenly, on July 15, 1274, only a few months after his friend, Saint Thomas. Bonaventure was made a saint in 1482. He was named a Doctor of the Church in 1588.

The Franciscans and Dominicans gave many new ideas to people for their spiritual life. The rules of life of the friars let them move among the people more than could members of older religious orders, who lived in special monasteries. Because they were organized into worldwide orders, the friars could easily be sent from country to country. The friars did not need large estates to support their houses. They lived in and were part of the towns, and they lived on the free offerings, or alms, of the people.

Not only did the friars work in the universities but they were close to the people. Both Saint Francis and Saint Dominic wrote rules of life for people who wanted to live lives that followed more closely the teachings of the gospel without becoming monks or nuns. Today such groups are known in the Church as third order Dominicans and Franciscans.

The new mendicant friars, with their lives of poverty and service among the people, replaced the older monks as leaders in the Church. Many friars became bishops, and even popes. But most of all, the Franciscans and the Dominicans helped the Church to meet the needs of a new urbanized society.

Dominican and Franciscan friars made their greatest and most lasting contribution to the Church as teachers and scholars in the universities.

Recall and Reflect

1. Why did Saint Dominic encourage his followers to study?

2. What is Saint Thomas Aquinas's best-known work?

3. What did Saint Bonaventure teach about divine revelation?

4. Thomas Aquinas was a great thinker and teacher. Even today his writings help people to understand the faith. Is there some person in your life who has helped you to understand more about your faith? Tell something about him or her.

REVIEW AND CELEBRATE

Doctrinal Summary

As members of the Church, we are all called to holiness. Paul points out that we all share in "one Lord, one faith, one baptism" (Ephesians 4:5). Every way of life, every career, is worthy of honor, because whatever we do as Christians, we are building up Christ's Church. Today as in the thirteenth century, some men and women are invited to follow Christ as members of religious communities.

Religious Vocabulary

Franciscans	Poor Clares	Albigensian heresy	Courts of the
religious community	Order of Preachers	Fourth Lateran	Inquisition
mendicant orders	Dominicans	Council	Thomism
Friars Minor		Albigensian Crusade	*Summa Theologiae*

Review Questions

Answer the following questions on a separate sheet of paper.

1. What was it like for a person to be a member of the Friars Minor or the Poor Clares?

2. In what special ways did the Franciscans and Dominicans serve the needs of townspeople?

3. What special task did Pope Innocent III give to Saint Dominic?

4. What was the purpose of the Albigensian Crusade and the Courts of the Inquisition?

5. Why was the Fourth Lateran Council so important?

Prayer Celebration

Leader: Let us praise Christ the Lord with these words of Saint Francis:

All: "Most high, almighty, good Lord! All praise, glory, honor and exaltation are yours! . . .

Leader: "Praise to you, O Lord our God, for all your creatures: first, for our dear Brother Sun, who gives us the day. . . . "For our Sister Moon, and for the bright, shining stars:

All: We praise you, O Lord. . . .

Leader: "For our Mother Earth, who sustains us and feeds us: . . .

All: We praise you, O Lord.

Leader: "For those who forgive one another for love of you, and who patiently bear sickness and other trials. . . .

All: We praise you, O Lord.

Leader: "For our Sister Death, the inescapable fact of life. . . .

All: We praise you, O Lord.

Leader: "All creatures, praise and glorify my Lord and give him thanks and serve him in great humility.

All: We praise you, O Lord."

Built between 1334 and 1352, the Palace of the Popes at Avignon covers an area of 161,400 square feet (15,010 square m).

11

Popes in Avignon, and the Western Schism

On the evening of December 24, 1299, large numbers of people began visiting the Basilica Church of St. Peter in Rome. At that time in Rome, the new year began on Christmas Day. That new year, 1300, would mark the beginning of a new century. A tradition had grown up in the Church that the first year of each century was a time of special grace. Pope Boniface VIII, the pope at that time, seeing the crowds of pilgrims coming to Rome, decided to make the year 1300 a **Holy Year** for the whole Church.

Pope Boniface said that people coming to Rome during the year 1300 could gain special **indulgences** for their sins if they were truly sorry for them and visited the churches of St. Peter and St. Paul, both in Rome. An indulgence is the remission, in the sight of God, of the temporal punishment for sins that have already been forgiven in the Sacrament of Penance.

Large crowds of pilgrims visited Rome throughout the year 1300. In the church of St. John Lateran in Rome you can still see a fresco of Pope Boniface blessing some of those people. When Pope Boniface proclaimed 1300 a Holy Year, he said that the first year of each century would always be a Holy Year. Later popes proclaimed a Holy Year every fifty years. Today in the Church, we celebrate a Holy Year every twenty-five years. The last two such years were 1950 and 1975.

The pilgrims who flocked to Rome in 1300 from every country in Europe were signs of the Church's unity and universality. Unity, or oneness, and universality have always been seen as marks of Christ's Church. (We reaffirm these truths each Sunday at Mass, when we say in the Creed that "we believe in one holy catholic and apostolic Church.") We are joined together in our faith, and that oneness brings us to

A fresco in the church of St. John Lateran, Rome, shows Pope Boniface VIII blessing pilgrims during the Holy Year 1300.

God as a loving community of faithful. But the Church is also catholic—that is, universal—bringing together all nations and races.

Only through the Holy Spirit could so many different people be brought together in worship and faith. Now we shall see how the Church's unity and universality were greatly tested in the 1300s. For over a hundred years, the Church struggled with two serious crises. The first was the absence of the popes from their diocese, Rome, for seventy years. The second was a schism that tore apart the Church in the West.

That was not a pleasant period in Church history. But it is in difficult times such as those that we can see how the Church con-

tinues to be aided by the Holy Spirit and how God makes use of holy men and women to do His will.

THE AVIGNON PAPACY

A French King Attacks a Pope The first crisis that the Church faced in the fourteenth century was the fact that the popes lived outside of Rome for seventy years, from 1308 to 1378. The popes lived in the city of Avignon (av´ēn yōn´), on the Rhone River in what is now southern France. Locate Avignon on the map on page 193. That period in Church history is often called the **Avignon papacy**. The Avignon papacy was a result of a bitter fight between Philip IV, called "Philip the Fair," the king of France (1285–1314), and Pope Boniface VIII (1294–1303).

King Philip IV of France, the grandson of Saint Louis IX, was ruler of the largest and most powerful country in Europe. Philip believed that France should be a strong, centralized state in which everyone owed obedience to the king. He worked hard to gain complete authority over all the people in his kingdom. Like modern rulers, Philip thought of France as a "nation," or "national state," rather than as a "feudal state" in which the king was forced to share his authority with great nobles or Church leaders.

Also like the rulers of today's nations, Philip IV had a great need for money. He tried to solve his money problems in several ways. Philip imposed the first general taxes in French history. In 1302 he called the first States-General—a representative body of the French nobles, clergy, and townspeople—to help him. And in 1306 he drove all Jews out of his kingdom and seized their wealth.

One reason King Philip needed money was to finance a war he was waging against the king of England, Edward I. In 1296 Philip IV demanded that the French clergy give "voluntary gifts" to help him wage that war. Some French Church leaders complained to Pope Boniface VIII about what the king had done.

The Fourth Lateran Council, the great pastoral council that we learned about in Chapter 10, had ordered that the clergy was not to be taxed without the special consent of the pope. But later popes had sometimes agreed to special taxes for a crusade or for a war that was being waged for a just cause.

Pope Boniface VIII told the French clergy not to pay the tax for which King Philip had asked. The pope said that the war between the two Christian kings was not a "just" war. King Philip, in anger, refused to allow any French clergy to send money to Rome. That caused Pope Boniface much trouble, since he needed French money to run the Church. In 1297, therefore, Pope Boniface agreed that Philip IV could tax the French clergy in times of great need, such as at that time.

Today, as in the past, crowds of people, many of them pilgrims, visit St. Peter's in Rome and hope to catch sight of the pope.

Boniface VIII: Strong-willed Pope Boniface VIII was a strong-willed person who was determined to uphold the dignity of the papacy. He was born Benedict Gaetani (gä′ā tä′nē) and belonged to a wealthy Italian family. As a young man, Benedict studied canon law at the University of Bologna. He was made a cardinal in 1281 and quickly became a leader among his fellow cardinals. He was elected pope on December 24, 1294.

The trouble between Pope Boniface and King Philip had begun over money. In 1301 the quarrel began again. When a bishop from France was charged with a crime and condemned by Philip, the bishop went to the pope for help. Boniface said that Philip had no right to try the bishop. The French king in turn charged that the pope was meddling in French affairs and trying to become the ruler of France. Boniface then wrote a letter pointing out that "national" churches under the power of European kings put the unity of the Church in danger. In the summer of 1303 the pope excommunicated Philip IV.

In anger, King Philip attacked the pope directly. He charged Pope Boniface with many crimes and sent soldiers into Italy to arrest the pope. Pope Boniface, now sixty-eight, was staying at Anagni (ä nän′yē), a little town near Rome. Some of the French soldiers broke into the house where the pope was staying. They insulted him, and abused him, and demanded that he resign. Pope Boniface refused. The soldiers held him prisoner for several days, until the citizens of Anagni were able to rescue him. Pope Boniface was carried back to Rome. He died there on October 11, 1303.

Upon the death of Pope Boniface, the cardinals elected as pope a very holy and able man who took the name Benedict XI. But unfortunately for the Church, Pope Benedict died suddenly on July 7, 1304. The cardinals were once again called upon to choose a new pope.

The Popes in Avignon   The cardinals met in late January 1305 to elect a pope. They came together in the small town of Perugia, about a hundred miles (160.9 km) north of Rome. Fearful of what Philip IV of France might do, the cardinals decided it would be best to choose as pope someone who would be acceptable to the French king. In June 1305 they finally chose Bertrand de Got (ber′trän′də gō′). Although not a cardinal, he was the archbishop of Bordeaux (bôr-dō′), France, and a Frenchman. Bertrand took the name Clement V.

It would seem that Pope Clement V had every intention of residing in Rome, but he first wanted to make peace with the king of France. He decided not to go to Rome until the problems of the Church in France had been settled. In 1308, therefore, the pope settled in Avignon. This town on the Rhone River is now part of southern France. At that time, however, it was part of the Holy Roman Empire.

King Philip IV wanted Pope Clement to condemn the dead pope, Boniface VIII. Clement refused, although he tried as much as he could to please the French king. In 1307 Philip had moved against the military-religious order known as the **Knights Templars**. The Knights Templars were soldier-monks who had fought in the Holy Land until the crusaders were driven from Palestine in 1187. The Knights Templars then began dealing in banking and finance. By the fourteenth century the order was very rich. Philip IV attacked the Knights Templars because of their wealth. He falsely charged them with many crimes and with heresy. In 1307 he asked Pope Clement to begin a papal investigation.

A Knight Templar is shown in battle dress. The order of the Templars was one of the first military-religious orders.

men and good leaders. They remained at Avignon because it did not seem safe to return to Rome. Italy at that time was torn apart by wars. Armies of paid soldiers, known as mercenaries (mėr′sə ner′ ēz), fought each other and terrorized the people. Those troops were in the pay of cities such as Florence, Genoa, Milan, and Venice. Many Italian cities had become city-states and had their own governments. Some were republics, and some were ruled by princes or dictators.

Under the Avignon popes, the Church became more and more centralized. Most bishops were named by the pope himself instead of being chosen by representatives of the local clergy. Papal government was very efficient. Most legal cases were appealed to the papal courts, and that also multiplied papal income.

The Avignon papacy, however, created serious problems. Catholics in England, Germany, Spain, and other countries of Europe did not like the fact that the popes seemed to be under the control of the king of France. Most of the cardinals were also French. People resented the wealth and splendor of the papal court at Avignon. Clergy all over Europe were taxed to support that way of life, and they were unhappy.

Many people kept urging the Avignon popes to return to Rome. In 1367, Pope

Even though the king's charges were not proved, the pope suppressed the Knights Templars. Philip had already arrested all the Templars in France and had burned their major superiors at the stake as heretics.

The next six popes, all French, continued to live at Avignon. The great palace they built there still stands. The Avignon popes were for the most part hardworking

THE AVIGNON POPES	
Clement V	1305–1314
John XXII	1316–1334
Benedict XII	1334–1342
Clement VI	1342–1352
Innocent VI	1352–1362
Urban V	1362–1370
Gregory XI	1370–1378

Urban V did return with his cardinals. They remained in Rome for three years. But the continuing social and political unrest in Italy was so great that the papal court returned to Avignon. Pope Urban died a few months later.

It was the last Avignon pope, Gregory XI, who took the papacy back to Rome to stay. Gregory XI faced a great deal of opposition in that matter from his cardinals, most of whom were French. The papal return was also fought by the city-state of Florence, which feared papal political rule. On the other hand, many people wanted the pope to return to his diocese. One such person was a woman from Siena (sē en′ə), an Italian town to the north of Rome.

Catherine of Siena Catherine Benincasa (bā′nin kä′sä), the daughter of a well-to-do cloth dyer of Siena, was born about 1347. As a young woman, Catherine became a member of the Dominican third order. As we have seen, members of the third orders did not become friars and nuns. They remained laypeople, living lives of prayer and service to others.

Catherine continued to live in her parents' home—a house that still stands in Siena. She spent her time in prayer and in caring for the sick. In 1347 a terrible plague, or disease, spread throughout Italy and the rest of Europe. Called the bubonic plague (byü bon′ik plāg), it caused terrible epidemics. Over the next fifty years, it claimed the lives of about one third of the inhabitants of Europe. Since many of the victims of this sickness swelled up and turned black, it was also called the "black death." Catherine was untiring in her care and nursing of plague victims.

Catherine's reputation for holiness became so great in Siena and throughout Italy that many men and women were drawn to her. Her group of friends and disciples came to be called Catherine's fellowship, or family. The Dominicans appointed a holy and learned friar, Raymond of Capua, to be Catherine's confessor. Father Raymond would later become master general of the Dominicans and would write the life of Catherine.

Saint Catherine of Siena (1347–1380), shown with one of her disciples, carried her love of Christ to all those about her.

Catherine had written Pope Gregory XI several times, urging him to return the papacy to Rome for the good of the Church. In 1376 she visited Avignon in an unsuccessful effort to make peace between the pope and the city of Florence. When she saw Pope Gregory, Catherine pointed out that many of the Church's problems were due to the fact that for over seventy years the popes had been absent from Rome. Pope Gregory was moved to act. He left Avignon on September 13, 1376, finally entering Rome on January 17, 1377, to the great joy of the Roman people. Fourteen months later he would be dead.

Catherine returned from Avignon to Siena where she continued to work for peace in Italy. Her health had broken down, and she was in constant pain. On April 21, 1380, she suffered a stroke. She died eight days later, at the age of thirty-three. She was made a saint in 1461. We celebrate her feast on April 30.

Few young people have been given the opportunity to do what Catherine did in her lifetime. She was both a spiritual leader and a diplomat. She dictated over four hundred letters to popes and cardinals, to political leaders and military leaders all over Europe. A woman of deep faith and prayer, she also wrote letters of advice to friends, and spiritual writings that are still read. Above all, Catherine gave us an example of how much a dedicated person can do with God's help. She was able to work for peace and influence the leaders of her society. But Saint Catherine also knew great sadness and failure. Before she died, Catherine was aware that the Church was in the midst of one of its greatest crises—the Western Schism.

Recall and Reflect

1. According to the Creed that is recited at Mass, what are the marks of Christ's Church?

2. Where did the popes live from 1308 to 1378? What do we call that period in Church history?

3. What happened to Church government during the time of the Avignon popes?

4. Saint Catherine of Siena influenced many leaders and worked hard for peace during her lifetime. What woman today, do you think, could be described the same way? Explain.

THE WESTERN SCHISM

A Papal Election Picture to yourself a city with crowds of people roaming through the streets, shouting at the top of their lungs. Excitement is in the air, but there is also danger. A crowd can quickly become a mob—a thoughtless tool of destruction. That was the scene in Rome when Pope Gregory XI died on the evening of March 26, 1378. The Roman people were determined that the next pope should be a Roman or at least an Italian. They feared that if a French pope were chosen, he would take the papacy back to Avignon.

The sixteen cardinals who were meeting in Rome could hear the crowds. They knew the danger. They were divided and not able to choose a pope from within the College of Cardinals. Then, on the morning of April 8, the cardinals did elect an Italian pope.

They chose the archbishop of Bari, a town in southern Italy.

Since the archbishop of Bari was not in Rome, the cardinals had to send for him. He did not arrive until that evening. In the meantime, the cardinals dressed up one of the old Italian cardinals as the pope and presented him to the crowd. That prevented a serious riot. The people knew that an Italian had been elected. When the archbishop of Bari arrived, all the cardinals knelt before him and promised to obey him. The new pope took the name Urban VI. His reign began one of the most tragic periods of Church history.

High office does strange things to people. It sometimes brings out the best in a person. Or it may bring out the worst. One thing is certain: the office will always affect the man or woman called to fill it in ways one cannot foresee. That is what happened to the archbishop of Bari after he became Urban VI. The cardinals had known Urban as a trusted administrator. He had been an official at Avignon. And yet, less than two weeks after being chosen, Urban VI had angered most of the cardinals. He lashed out at the cardinals in public and insulted them. Urban VI did many other strange things and made many enemies. He had a violent temper and may have been mentally unbalanced.

Schism in the Western Church By the end of the summer of 1378, all the cardinals had left Rome. They put up a notice that read, "Urban resign: you are not pope." Then all the cardinals except one moved to the town of Fondi (fōn'dē), about 40 miles (64 km) south of Rome. There they elected one of their number as pope, Cardinal Robert of Geneva, who was the general of the papal army in Italy. Cardinal Robert took the name Clement VII, and returned to Avignon. A schism, known as the **Western Schism**, tore apart the Church in the West.

There were now two popes—one in Rome and one in Avignon. Since all but one of the cardinals who had elected him had returned to Avignon, Urban VI made twenty-nine new cardinals in Rome. There were now two papal courts and two papal governments. It was a split that would last thirty-nine years. For these thirty-nine years the Church would be torn apart, at first between two popes, and then for a short time between three of them.

Did the cardinals choose Urban VI in a valid election? *Valid* means "true," or "legal, according to law." The cardinals said later that when they elected Urban VI they did not act freely but in fear of the Roman people; therefore, the act they performed was invalid. The fact is that the cardinals were the only ones who knew if they were frightened to the point of not being free. Saint Catherine of Siena pointed out to the cardinals who had left Rome in order to elect another pope that many weeks passed during which they publicly accepted Urban VI as pope. Only after

POPES DURING THE WESTERN SCHISM

Rome

Urban VI	1378–1389
Boniface IX	1389–1404
Innocent VII	1404–1406
Gregory XII	1406–1415 (+1417)

Avignon

Clement VII	1378–1394
Benedict XIII	1394–1415 (+1423)

Pisa

Alexander V	1409–1410
John XXIII	1410–1415 (+1419)

In October 1978, cardinals met to elect a successor to Pope John Paul I. They chose a Polish cardinal, Karol Wojtyla, who became Pope John Paul II.

they saw what kind of person he was did the cardinals say his election was invalid. The same College of Cardinals elected two popes. To this day, there has never been an official Church pronouncement about the legality or illegality of either the Roman or the Avignon line of popes.

Religious Chaos in Europe The split affected nations, dioceses, religious orders, parishes, even families. Some nations accepted the Roman popes; others recognized those of Avignon for political reasons. France recognized Pope Clement VII of Avignon, so England, France's enemy, accepted Urban VI. Castile, Aragon, Scotland,

Naples, and Sicily accepted Clement. The Holy Roman Empire, Scandinavia, and most of Italy accepted Urban.

Each pope excommunicated the other. Each had his own College of Cardinals. In some dioceses there were two bishops— and in some parishes, two pastors—one named by each pope. There were holy and wise men and women on both sides. When Pope Urban VI died in 1389, the break continued. The Roman cardinals chose Pope Boniface IX (1389–1404) as pope.

Scholars at the University of Paris suggested three ways to end the schism. It could be ended (1) if both popes would step down, or (2) if both would agree to submit to the decision of an impartial court, or (3) if a general council of the whole Church were to decide the matter.

Since neither pope would resign, in 1409 the cardinals and other leaders of the Church from both sides decided to call a general council at Pisa (pē′zə) in Italy. It was there that both the pope at Rome—who was then Gregory XII—and the pope at Avignon—Benedict XIII—were said to be deposed. Then the cardinals of both "deposed" popes and the Council of Pisa chose another pope, who took the name Alexander V. Instead of ending the schism, however, the Council of Pisa did nothing except make another pope. Now there were three popes, each saying that he had full authority!

SIDELIGHTS ON CHURCH HISTORY

Saint Joan of Arc

Imagine a seventeen-year-old girl leading soldiers into battle. Imagine such a girl doing that not once but several times. It actually happened. The girl who showed that bravery was Joan of Arc. She became one of the Church's saints of the fifteenth century.

Joan of Arc was born in 1412 in the northeastern part of France, in what was then called the Duchy of Lorraine. When she was about thirteen, Joan began to hear "voices" that she believed to be those of saints. The "voices" told her to go to the as-yet-uncrowned king of France—Charles VII—and obtain from him an army to fight the English who had invaded France. (That was during the Hundred Years' War.)

In 1429, at the age of seventeen, Joan left home to meet Charles VII. The king concealed himself in a crowd of nobles. But Joan, who had never seen Charles, recognized him immediately. She was given the armor of a soldier, a horse, and the command of several thousand men. Although Joan carried a sword, she did not fight. Always at the head of her troops, even in battle, Joan won several great victories. In July 1429, because of her efforts, Charles VII was able to be crowned king of France.

On May 23, 1430, Joan was taken prisoner by French soldiers who were allies of the English. She was taken to the city of Rouen (rù än′) in northwestern France and put on trial as a heretic before a court of the Inquisition. During her trial, Joan answered her judges with simplicity and calmness. She showed herself to be a woman of deep faith. To the end, she proclaimed that she had truly heard the "voices" of her saints and that she had obeyed the will of God. Condemned as a witch and a heretic, Joan was finally sentenced to be burned at the stake. The sentence was carried out on May 30, 1431.

In 1449 the Church ordered Joan's case to be reopened. In 1456, after a seven-year investigation, Pope Callistus III overruled the decision of the Inquisition. Joan was declared to be a true servant of God. This simple farm woman is an example of bravery, Christian patriotism, and fidelity to God's will. More than 450 years after her death, then—on May 16, 1920—Pope Benedict XV declared Joan a saint. Her feast is May 30.

The End of the Schism It was the Holy Roman emperor Sigismund (sij´is mənd) who finally set in motion the events that would end the schism. First, Alexander V, the pope chosen at Pisa, died in 1410. Sigismund then made Alexander's successor, Pope John XXIII, call a general council to meet at Constance, a town in southern Germany.

Pope John XXIII opened the **Council of Constance** on All Saints' Day, 1414. Before the council ended in 1418, the schism would be over. Cardinals of all three popes attended the Council of Constance. Emperor Sigismund was there, as were political leaders from all over Europe.

The council persuaded Pope John XXIII to step down. The Roman pope, Gregory XII, also agreed to step down. But the Avignon pope, Benedict XIII, would not do so.

Benedict, a Spaniard, was one of the cardinals who chose Pope Urban VI in 1378. He was one of those who said that Urban's election was invalid. Benedict XIII firmly believed that he was the true pope. Nevertheless, in 1417 the Council of Constance deposed Pope Benedict XIII.

On November 11, 1417, twenty-two cardinals and thirty deputies from the countries of Europe elected a new pope. They chose an Italian, Oddo Colonna (ō´dō kō lō´nə), from a wealthy, old Roman family. He took the name Martin V, and the schism was over. On May 16, 1418, Martin V set out for Rome. He finally entered the city on September 28, 1420.

Gregory XII, the former Roman pope, died in October 1417. Benedict XIII fled to Spain. He lived there in a lonely castle until 1423, still saying that he was the true pope. The Pisan pope, John XXIII, was made the bishop of Frascati in Italy. He died in 1419.

When Pope Martin V (1417–1431) was elected at the Council of Constance, the Western Schism came to an end.

Once again there was unity within the Church, but problems remained. All the council members at Constance agreed that many things within the Church needed changing. In fact, the confusion within the Church mirrored that in secular society. In the fourteenth and fifteenth centuries, patterns of life that had been built up in the Middle Ages were giving way to new kinds of social, political, and economic organization. The world we call "modern" was coming into being. The Hundred Years' War (1338–1453), between the countries of France and England, was just one tragic example of the changes that were taking place.

All those changes affected the Church, the People of God. Still, the Church survived the crises. In Chapter 12 we shall see how the Church at the beginning of the sixteenth century would face even more serious trials than it had dealt with in the Avignon papacy and the Western Schism.

The Church's response to those trials would bring about reform and a renewed sense of mission to preach the gospel.

Recall and Reflect

1. How did Clement VII come to be pope?
2. What three solutions were offered by scholars of the University of Paris to settle the schism?
3. Who elected Pope Martin V?
4. Our Church is a living body that, just like a human body, is sometimes in need of healing. Can you think of a time when this was so? What do you think contributed to the healing of the Church?

REVIEW AND CELEBRATE

Doctrinal Summary

An ecumenical council is a gathering of all the bishops of the world, with the pope as the head. When a council teaches, it does so under the guidance of the Holy Spirit, both council and pope working together. The circumstances of the schism in the fifteenth century led some theologians to place the council over the pope. That cannot be. As the Second Vatican Council pointed out, harmony between the pope and the council is a sign of the Church's unity and its universality.

Religious Vocabulary

Holy Year	Avignon papacy	Western Schism
indulgences	Knights Templars	Council of Constance

Review Questions

Answer the following questions on a separate sheet of paper.

1. Why did popes live in Avignon rather than in Rome from 1308 to 1378?

2. Did good things come from the Avignon papacy? What problems did it bring to the Church?

3. What important advice did Saint Catherine of Siena give Pope Gregory XI? Did he take her advice?

4. Why is the papacy of Urban VI considered to be one of the most tragic periods of Church history?

5. What part did the Holy Roman emperor Sigismund play in ending the Western Schism?

Prayer Celebration

Leader: With the words of Psalm 46, let us pray.

All: "God is our refuge and our strength, an ever-present help in distress.

Therefore we fear not, though the earth be shaken
and mountains plunge into the depths of the sea;

Though its waters rage and foam
and the mountains quake at its surging.

The Lord of hosts is with us;
our stronghold is the God of Jacob."

Leader: God, our Father, we are Your Church on earth. Sometimes we are great. Sometimes we fall very short of the standards You set for us in Your gospel. We pray today for Pope John Paul, for our bishops, and for all who lead us in Your way. We pray, too, for ourselves. Lead us all to the fulfillment of Your kingdom through the power of Jesus Christ, Your Son and our Savior.

All: Amen.

UNIT THREE SUMMARY

We have looked at four hundred years of the Church's history, from 1100 to 1500, the period known as the Middle Ages. During that time the Holy Spirit, working through great men and women, helped the Church to realize its mission more fully. Older religious orders were reformed and new ones were created.

New life in the Church was not limited to new religious orders. During the 1100s, there was a great revival of learning in Europe. Schools formed around the cathedrals in Europe's towns, and scholars flocked to them. In 1110, Peter Abelard began teaching in the school of Paris. Abelard's new method of study by asking questions—the scholastic method—became the tool of learning in the Middle Ages.

The thirteenth century was a time of special greatness in the Church's long history. The revival of trade caused the renewal of city life. To meet the needs of townspeople, a new kind of religious community—the mendicant order—developed within the Church. In the early 1200s, two such communities were founded. Saint Francis of Assisi started his Friars Minor, or Franciscans. Saint Dominic Guzman founded the Friars Preachers, or Dominicans. The Franciscans and the Dominicans lived in the towns and ministered to townspeople, especially the poor.

The 1300s were a time of testing for the Church. Two serious crises—the Avignon papacy and the Western Schism—threatened the Church's unity and universality. For seventy years (1308–1378) the popes lived not in Rome but in Avignon.

In 1378 the same cardinals who elected Pope Urban VI soon declared his election invalid and elected another pope, Clement VII. Clement took up residence in Avignon. Thus began the Western Schism. For thirty-seven years (1378–1415) there were two popes in the Church—and for a short time there were three. The schism was finally ended with the election of Pope Martin V at a council held in Constance, Germany. But as we shall see in the next unit, the sixteenth century would bring even greater trials to the Church.

1098	Cistercians founded
1110	Peter Abelard begins to teach in Paris
1115	Saint Bernard becomes abbot of Clairvaux
1141	Gratian writes a collection of canon law
1153	Death of Saint Bernard of Clairvaux
1170	Thomas Becket, archbishop of Canterbury, martyred
1198	Innocent III becomes pope
1215	Fourth Lateran Council
1221	Death of Saint Dominic, founder of Friars Preachers, or Dominicans
1226	Death of Saint Francis of Assisi, founder of Friars Minor, or Franciscans
1233	Beginning of the Courts of the Inquisition: Suppression of the Albigensians
1253	Death of Saint Clare of Assisi
1266	Saint Thomas Aquinas begins to write his *Summa Theologiae*
1274	Deaths of Saint Thomas Aquinas and Saint Bonaventure
1294	Boniface VIII becomes pope
1308	Pope Clement V begins to live in Avignon
1378	Urban VI becomes pope: Beginning of the Western Schism
1415	Martin V becomes pope: End of the Western Schism

UNIT FOUR

The Church—Needing Reform

Martin Luther's desire to reform the Church led him to challenge papal authority. Those who follow his teachings are called Lutherans.

12

The Church and the Protestant Reformation

At noon on October 31, 1517, Halloween, a German friar nailed a notice to a church door in what is now the East German city of Wittenberg (vit′ən bərg). A church door at that time was like a public bulletin board, and posting a notice there was a common way of attracting attention. That particular church was a great pilgrimage center. It claimed to have the relics—that is, the bones or other remains—of over 17,000 saints. Since the next day was the Feast of All Saints, many people would be coming to the church to pray before the relics of the saints.

Those who read the notice learned that its author was a friar whose name was Martin Luther. Luther was a professor of theology at the University of Wittenberg. His notice listed ninety-five objections to Church practices about indulgences. As we saw in Chapter 11, an indulgence was the remission of temporal punishment for

About 6 B.C.	Birth of Jesus
About A.D. 29	Pentecost: Birth of the Church
A.D. 313	Edict of Milan: End of persecutions
325	Council of Nicaea
800	Pope Leo III crowns Charlemagne emperor
1049	Pope Leo IX elected: Church reform begins
1054	Schism between Rome and Constantinople
1095	Pope Urban II preaches First Crusade
1215	Fourth Lateran Council: Great pastoral council of Middle Ages
1453	Constantinople falls to the Turks
1521	Diet of Worms: Luther breaks with Church
1545	Council of Trent begins
1789	Crisis of the French Revolution
1870	First Vatican Council
1962	Second Vatican Council begins
1978	John Paul II becomes pope

sins that have already been forgiven. Martin Luther was offering to debate his ideas in public with anyone who did not agree with him. That, too, was a common practice at the time. But no one in Wittenberg in 1517—not even Martin Luther himself—had any idea that the act of posting a notice on a church door would later be looked upon as the beginning of a new religious movement. The movement would end the religious unity of Europe. Groups of people would break away completely from the Catholic Church. New churches would be formed, and Europe would be divided along religious lines.

In this chapter we will look at that new religious movement. We know it as the **Protestant Reformation**. In Chapter 13 we will look at the efforts of the Catholic Church to reform itself. We call that movement the **Counter Reformation**, or the **Catholic Reformation**. In Chapter 14 we will look at the Church's worldwide efforts to preach the gospel. This missionary work grew out of the Catholic Reformation.

The Protestant Reformation was not caused by one person alone. It came about because the time and place made such a religious break possible. We might say that the "climate" was right. By "climate" we mean the conditions of society in Europe in the 1500s.

In Chapter 11 we read about the Avignon papacy and the Western Schism. We also learned that many people wanted to reform the Church and correct the evils that existed. All those events had three major effects: (1) They weakened the Church's unity. (2) They lessened respect for the papacy, the center of that unity. (3) They caused many good people to believe it was impossible to correct abuses within the Church. In today's language, there was a "crisis of confidence" in the Church.

THE CHURCH IN A CHANGING WORLD

The Renaissance The break we call the Protestant Reformation was caused by more than the events outlined here. New ways of thinking and judging appeared in the late 1300s. That new spirit marked the end of the Middle Ages. In history that new view of the world has come to be called the Renaissance, which is a French word for rebirth.

The Renaissance brought about new interest in the ideas, the art, and the architecture of the Greeks and Romans. The peoples of Europe have always lived with the remains of that old civilization. In fact the Renaissance was not the first such rebirth. Several periods of Western history had seen revivals of Greek and Roman ideas and ways. Carolingian culture was that kind of rebirth. Another took place in twelfth-century Europe, at the time of Abelard. But the best-known and most far-reaching rebirth was the one that began at the end of the Middle Ages.

The Renaissance did not start all at once, nor was it the same in every place. It first appeared in the towns in Italy. There scholars and learned people—the bourgeoisie (bur'zhwä zē'), or new middle class—began studying the writings of the Greeks and Romans and imitating their art and architecture. Many Italian towns still had some old Roman buildings and statues, so the interest was not unusual. But the spirit of the Renaissance was new. People thought the works by the Greek and Roman writers and artists were better than works done in the Middle Ages.

Renaissance Thinkers Are Critical Greek and Roman culture was centered on men and women, on the human person and body.

Many Renaissance clergy, like the cardinal shown above in his study, began to study the writings of the ancient Greeks and Romans.

For that reason, the Greeks and Romans were often called humanists. Renaissance writers and artists also put great stress on people in their own writings and art. Renaissance thinkers were curious about every aspect of life. They began to question everything. In the Middle Ages there had been a great stress upon God as the center of all things. Questions had also been asked in the Middle Ages, but answers came from persons who believed in the Church.

At the close of the Middle Ages, some Renaissance humanists even began to have doubts about their faith. They became very critical of the Church, and especially of those religious ideas and practices that had

grown up in the Middle Ages. Renaissance scholars, for example, regarded the writings of pagan classical authors more highly than the writings of Saint Thomas Aquinas, Saint Bonaventure, and the other thinkers of the Middle Ages.

Instruments of Change Three things helped the new ideas and spirit of the Renaissance to spread across Europe. First, there was the invention of printing with movable type in the 1450s. Second, there was the growing power of kings and the birth of nation-states. Third, there was the continuing expansion of trade, the growth of towns and of the middle class.

The first large printed work was the Bible. It was printed in Latin. The work was done by Johann Gutenberg, a German goldsmith turned printer, in the city of Mainz, Germany. Although the exact date is unknown, Gutenberg's Bible was made shortly before 1455. A copy of that Bible can be seen at the Library of Congress in Washington, D.C. There are only several copies left.

The invention of printing with movable type was important because it meant that books could be made more quickly and accurately in larger numbers. In the Middle Ages, and before, people copied books by hand, one at a time. It was a slow process, and mistakes were sometimes made. Not all copies were the same. With the invention of printing, all copies of a book became identical. Many more copies could be made, and more people could read the same book. Thus ideas traveled farther and more quickly. In that way many people learned the new teachings of the Protestant Reformation.

In Chapter 11 we saw that European kings, like King Philip IV of France, were becoming more and more powerful. Feudal kingdoms were being changed into nation-states much like the countries we know today. Above all, that was true of France, England, Spain, and the Scandinavian countries. It was not true of Italy and Germany, which were parts of the Holy Roman Empire. In the Empire, princes and city-states were consolidating their power at the expense of the power of the emperor.

As the kings of Europe became stronger, they put the interests of their states before all else. They tried to control everyone and everything—including the Church—within their kingdoms. Confronted by that power, the popes became much weaker. Under the leadership of the papacy, the Church had always stressed its unity and universality. It was made up of all peoples and all nations. And, in fact, in the Middle Ages the Church had helped to build a common culture in Europe out of the beliefs of Christendom. Nationalism was an idea opposed to the idea of universality, both universality of culture and of belief.

The middle class had begun with the rise of the towns in the twelfth and thirteenth centuries. By the year 1500, many of Europe's towns and cities were free from control by local lords. But there were still conflicts between the towns and the bishops or abbots who had rights in them. The leaders of the towns were the new middle class, mostly merchants and bankers. Poorer townsfolk were craftworkers, such as weavers, metalworkers, and laborers in small industries and shops. All the people of the towns knew the value of work and the importance of making money. It was, however, the rich townspeople who were most influenced by Renaissance thinkers and artists and who gave much to support them.

Renaissance Popes Not only kings, princes, and rich people used their money to help thinkers and artists. The popes, too, became their patrons, and many popes were themselves humanist scholars. Pope Nicholas V (1447–1455) was the first of a long line of builder-popes. They tore down old buildings in Rome and built churches, parks, and palaces in the new Renaissance style, which was inspired by the buildings of Greece and Rome. Pope Nicholas's first interest, however, was books. He sent people everywhere to gather copies of the books of Greek and Roman writers, both pagan and Christian. Pope Nicholas founded today's Vatican Library, one of the great libraries of the world. Without the support of such Renaissance popes as Nicholas and his successors, the great works of art we admire in Rome today would not exist.

Unfortunately, those Renaissance popes, like many of the clergy of the time, adopted a life-style that was often more pagan than Christian. Like many of their clergy, they did not keep their promise of celibacy. Although those popes directed the affairs of the Church with skill and did not teach any doctrine that was false, they gave very bad examples.

Scholars from all over the world come to use the Vatican Library with its vast collection of books and Church documents.

A New Church of St. Peter in Rome The great church that the emperor Constantine had built over the tomb of the apostle Peter in Rome was in danger of falling down by the end of the Middle Ages. At the beginning of the sixteenth century, Pope Julius II (1503–1513) began building a great new church. Pope Julius II called many great artists to Rome to work on the new St. Peter's Church. It was Julius, for example, who hired Michelangelo to paint the interior of the Sistine Chapel in the Vatican, where popes are elected today. Michelangelo would later design the great dome that covers St. Peter's.

Much money was needed for such a huge building as the new St. Peter's. Pope Julius II had emptied the papal treasury to pay for wars he had fought to enlarge and defend the Papal States. Pope Julius decided to grant indulgences to those who would give offerings to rebuild St. Peter's.

Indulgences Today we rarely speak of indulgences. In the Middle Ages, however, indulgences were very popular. As we saw in Chapter 11, Pope Boniface VIII granted special indulgences to people who visited Rome during the first Holy Year.

In the early Church, people who had sinned seriously were forgiven in a public ceremony on Holy Thursday. They were forgiven only after they had done a penance. Even after the practice of private confession became common, people often had to do hard penances for their sins. If one had a good reason, the Church sometimes permitted a person to substitute an easier penance for a long, hard one. For example, one could be told to pray one hundred psalms each day for a year instead of to go on a pilgrimage. By the eleventh century, that practice was known as an indulgence. Sometimes the easier

The interior design of St. Peter's Basilica, the church begun by Pope Julius II in 1506, dates almost entirely from the 1600s.

penance might be offering money to the poor or giving money to a good cause—even giving money to build a church. Unfortunately, giving money could seem like "buying" an indulgence. The giving of money became the all-important thing.

By the 1500s, the granting of indulgences was often used as a wrong way of raising money. Popular preachers urged people to gain indulgences by giving money. Those speakers pointed out that one could get an indulgence not only for oneself but also for the souls in purgatory. Too often such preachers gave the impres-

sion that money given would automatically free a soul from purgatory. The people who understood their faith knew that such was not the case. But many people did not know better. Need for money turned the preaching of indulgences into a sale and made the church a market. It would also set the stage for the Protestant Reformation.

A New Archbishop In 1514 a young man of twenty-four was chosen archbishop of Mainz, now a city in Germany. He was Albert of Brandenburg, which was a territory in the Holy Roman Empire. Albert was already the archbishop of Magdeburg (mäg′də bərg) and the bishop of Halberstadt (häl′bər stät), two other German dioceses. Being bishop of three different dioceses at once was against Church law. Moreover, according to Church law, Albert was too young to become a bishop. Albert needed the pope's permission to keep his three dioceses.

Pope Leo X (1513–1521) allowed Albert to keep his three dioceses. But the archbishop was ordered to pay a large sum of money to the pope for that privilege. To raise the money, Albert had to borrow. He went to a bank in Augsburg, Germany, run by a great banking family called the Fuggers (fùg′ərz). The Fugger family often handled financial matters for European kings and princes as well as for the Church.

The Fuggers arranged for an indulgence to be preached in all of Albert's dioceses. The indulgence would be granted to all who gave money for the building of the new St. Peter's Church in Rome. Archbishop Albert would keep part of the money offered for the indulgences to pay off his debt to the Fugger family. The rest would be sent to Rome. Pope Leo X agreed to that financial arrangement in 1514. Neither Pope Leo X nor Archbishop Albert had any idea that their financial agreement would be the spark that ignited the Protestant Reformation.

Recall and Reflect

1. Name three things that helped Renaissance ideas to spread across Europe in the 1400s.

2. What was one important contribution of Pope Nicholas V?

3. How did the archbishop of Mainz's need for money help trigger the Protestant Reformation?

4. During the sixteenth century, some of the members and leaders of the Church lost sight of the most important goal of life. Can you think of a time in your life when you lost sight of an important goal? What did you do about it? Did anyone help you?

MARTIN LUTHER'S REFORMATION

A Storm Breaks A Dominican friar, Johann Tetzel, was given the task of preaching the new indulgence in Archbishop Albert's three dioceses. In January 1517, Tetzel preached in a small town near Wittenberg, where the friar Martin Luther was a professor of theology. People from Wittenberg who went to hear Tetzel told Martin Luther what had been said.

For some time, Martin Luther had been concerned about the abuses of indulgences in the Church. Luther became worried about Tetzel's preaching. Tetzel seemed to be making God's grace and forgiveness too easy to obtain. Tetzel did say that all who wished to receive the indulgence for them-

WORDS TO LIVE BY

In this one and only Church of God from its very beginnings there arose certain rifts. . . . But in subsequent centuries [more widespread disagreements] appeared and quite large Communities became separated from full communion with the Catholic Church—[developments] for which, [at times], men of both sides were to blame. . . . One cannot charge with the sin of separation those who at present are born into these Communities. . . . and the Catholic Church accepts them with respect and affection as brothers. . . . [People who are baptized are] brought into a certain, though imperfect, communion with the Catholic Church.

VATICAN COUNCIL II, DECREE ON ECUMENISM, 3

selves had to be in God's grace and to be sorry for their sins. But he also seemed to be saying that anyone could gain such an indulgence for the soul of a dead person simply by giving a donation to the new St. Peter's Church. To gain an indulgence for the dead, one did not have to be sorry for one's own sins or to be in God's grace. Tetzel is supposed to have said, "As soon as the coin in the coffer clinks, the soul into heaven springs." He probably did not say it in that way, but he certainly gave that idea to those who heard him.

Martin Luther Luther was thirty-four years old when he nailed his objections to the doctrine about indulgences to the church door in Wittenberg. He was born on November 10, 1482, in the small town of Eisleben (īs′lā′bən) (today in East Germany) and baptized the next day. Since November 11 is the Feast of Saint Martin of Tours, he was named Martin. His parents were of peasant stock. His father was a copper miner who later acquired some shares in a mine and had a comfortable income.

Luther's parents were very strict with their son. They sent him to grammar school in the nearby town of Mansfeld and later to the University of Erfurt (also in East Germany today). Luther had an active, quick mind. He graduated from Erfurt in 1502 and received a master's degree in philosophy in 1505.

In the summer of 1505, Luther began the study of law. His father wanted him to become a lawyer. That July, Luther had a very frightening experience. He was caught in the open during a terrible thunderstorm and was almost hit by a bolt of lightning. For some time Luther had been thinking about becoming a friar. He took that happening as a sign from God and decided to enter the religious life. He became a friar in

the Order of the Hermits of Saint Augustine—usually called the Augustinian Friars. It was a mendicant order that followed the rule of Saint Augustine.

Luther was a serious friar who studied and worked hard. On April 4, 1507, he was ordained a priest. At his first Mass he was so overcome with a sense of his own unworthiness and God's greatness that he hesitated a long time before saying the prayers of consecration. Luther had deep feelings about his own sins and God's perfection and power. For many years he was overwhelmed by those thoughts.

Professor of Scripture In the middle of his own difficulties, Luther was very busy. The Augustinians sent him to the University of Wittenberg, where he studied. Luther then taught Sacred Scripture at Wittenberg. While studying Paul's letter to the Romans, Luther found an answer to his feelings of doubt and unworthiness in God's sight. What he read in Romans 1:17 brought him peace of mind and a new understanding of Christian life. He read: "For in the gospel is revealed the justice of God which begins and ends with faith; as Scripture says, 'the just man shall live by faith.'"

The words "the just man shall live by faith" seemed to answer all Luther's doubts. It is faith—absolute trust in God—that makes Christians holy. Human beings must simply believe, and God will forgive them, no matter how sinful they are. Faith is total trust and confidence in God. Luther had arrived at his theory of justification by faith alone.

With his new insight, Martin Luther began to look at the Church and religion in a different way. It was faith alone that led the Christian to do good works. But good works, indulgences, relics, even the liturgical worship of the Church could never of themselves bring people to God. Although the Church had always looked upon the Bible as the Word of God, for Luther the Bible was all important. It was with that understanding of the Bible that Luther began to criticize many practices of the Church, including the practice of indulgences.

Printed copies of Luther's ideas about indulgences spread widely throughout Germany. Luther himself sent copies to people, including Albert, the young archbishop of Mainz. Soon everyone in Germany was talking about Luther. Many agreed with Luther's ideas in whole or in part. Some people saw Luther's writings as an attack upon Rome, and they were glad because for them the papacy was always looking for money.

Luther and Rome In 1518 a summary of Luther's ideas was sent to Rome. Pope Leo X asked the superior general of the Augustinians to silence Luther, but he was unable to do so.

Pope Leo X was a typical Renaissance pope. He was born Giovanni de Medici, and belonged to the powerful Medici family that governed the city-state of Florence at that time. Because of the Medici family's power, Giovanni's father, Lorenzo (called "the Magnificent"), was able to get Pope Innocent VIII (1484–1492) to make Giovanni a cardinal – even though the boy was only thirteen years old. At the age of thirty-seven, Giovanni, the young Medici cardinal, was elected pope.

Leo X was not a bad person. His tastes were those of a Renaissance prince. He liked the good things of life. He loved books, drama, and the sport of hunting. As pope, Leo X was of course head of the Church and ruler of the Papal States in Italy. But he was also head of the Medici

Pope Leo X lived like a Renaissance prince. He loved books, drama, and the sport of hunting, and was a generous patron of artists.

family, and he sought to promote their interests. Leo X was very generous to artists, writers, and poets. He had no idea, however, that the preaching of indulgences in the lands of the archbishop of Mainz would release a storm of protest against the Church. And he had no idea of the determination of the young Martin Luther, who was at the center of that storm.

In 1518, Rome sent Cardinal Cajetan (kaj′i tən), a great Dominican theologian, to Germany to question Luther. Luther appeared before Cajetan in October 1518. For the cardinal, the whole question was one of obeying the pope's authority. In the name of the pope, Cajetan ordered Luther to stop attacking indulgences. Luther was courteous, but he would not agree. In November 1518, Luther appealed from

Pope Leo to a general council of the Church. It was no longer a theological dispute about indulgences. Martin Luther seemed to be attacking the authority and place of the papacy itself in the Church.

Luther's Excommunication Luther went on writing and engaging in public debates. The most famous debate was with John Eck in July 1519 in Leipzig, a city now in East Germany. Eck, a famous theologian and a clever debater, pushed Luther into a corner. Eck tricked Luther into saying that an ecumenical council of the Church could make a mistake. It is Catholic belief that an ecumenical council of the whole Church headed by the pope is **infallible**— that is, it cannot make mistakes. By saying that, Luther set himself against the authority of the Church. Luther now said that Christ alone is head of the Church. He had come to believe that the papacy was built on human authority alone.

On June 15, 1520, Pope Leo X wrote a letter condemning some of Luther's teachings as heretical and threatening Luther with excommunication if he did not retract them. In December of 1520 Luther publicly burned a copy of the pope's letter in Wittenberg while college students danced around the fire. On January 3, 1521, Luther's excommunication was made complete. There were now two groups in Germany, those who supported the pope and those who followed Luther. Many German princes and nobles followed Luther for political reasons. Luther's desire to reform the Church became a revolt against it.

During the year 1520 Luther had stated once more his theory of justification by faith. He called upon the princes and nobles of Germany to reform the Church by destroying the pope's power in Germany. Even before his excommunication, Luther had attacked the idea of a sacramental clergy. He had written that the whole Church is a priestly body. All Christians could understand the Bible with the help of the Holy Spirit. Luther had also attacked the sacramental system and the Sacrifice of the Mass. He wrote that Baptism, Eucharist, and Penance were the only sacraments. Luther held those teachings because he believed them to be found in the Bible.

Luther at the Diet of Worms Charles V (1519–1556) had been elected ruler of the Holy Roman Empire only two years before Luther was excommunicated. Coming to Germany for the first time in 1520, Charles V called for the Diet—the representative body, or parliament, of the Empire—to meet at Worms, a city in southwest Germany. The Diet met in 1521 in the presence of the emperor, and Luther was ordered to appear before it. The emperor had promised him immunity from arrest.

Luther came before the Diet on April 16, 1521. He entered the great hall where the Diet was gathered before the emperor, who was seated on a throne. Luther was asked whether the books on the table before him were his. He replied Yes. He was then asked if he would take back what he had written in them. He asked for time to think, and was given twenty-four hours. On the next day, Luther returned to the great hall of the Diet. He told the emperor and the assembled princes and representatives of the Empire that he could take nothing back unless it was shown to him that what he had written was against the Bible. In a loud voice he said: "I cannot and I will not take back anything, for it is dangerous to act against one's conscience. May God come to my help. Amen."

When Luther left the meeting of the Diet of Worms, he also left the Church. By

Appearing before the emperor and assembled princes at the Diet of Worms in 1521, Luther declared that he could not act against his conscience.

so doing, the action that many had feared now took place—Christendom was divided. On May 8, 1521, Charles V placed Luther under banishment. Technically, that meant Luther was an outlaw in the Empire. Anyone could arrest him and hand him over to the soldiers of the emperor. Frederick the Wise, Luther's protector, had him "kidnapped" and carried to the safety of Wartburg (värt′bərg) Castle in Germany. The emperor's ban meant little or nothing, since not only Frederick the Wise but many other German princes and nobles backed Luther.

The Protestants Moved by Luther's teachings, the peasants in southern Germany took up arms against their lords. Luther was greatly alarmed and asked the German princes to put down the revolt through force. In 1529 those princes who accepted Luther's teachings had formed a political alliance. In that same year they also protested against the decision of the Catholic princes and the emperor to enforce Luther's condemnation. Those who made that protest came to be known as **Protestants**.

During the next twenty-five years, the religious division of Europe became a political one. The **Lutheran Church** came into being in Germany. Charles V tried many times to bring back the Lutherans to some kind of unity with the Catholics, at

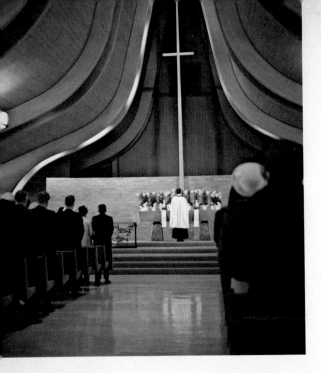

Although Lutherans do not stress the need for uniformity in worship, most Lutheran Churches follow rites that date from the time of the Reformation.

Death of Luther In 1546, Luther died at his hometown of Eisleben. He was sixty-two years old. In 1525 he had married a former nun, Katherine von Bora, and had several children by her. As Luther grew older, the movement he started was taken over by younger men. Luther did not start one big church. Rather, in each territory in the Holy Roman Empire over which a Protestant prince ruled, a state Lutheran Church was set up. Luther wrote a new Catechism, and new Church services in German. He also translated the Bible into German. Luther's translation of the Bible became a classic of the German language.

From the Catholic point of view, Luther did much harm to the Church. His actions divided Europe religiously and politically. For over a hundred years, wars of religion would tear Europe apart. Although Protestantism cannot be totally identified with Martin Luther and his writings, its spirit can certainly be found in Luther's own person. The struggle that occurred in Martin Luther's mind and soul led him to restate the message of the gospels and to show the German people that true religion meant living the gospel message.

least until a council could meet to discuss the differences between them. But he was unable to do so.

Pope Leo X died in 1521. In January of 1522, a Dutchman became pope. He took the name Adrian VI. Adrian was a hardworking, gifted man. He had been a professor at the University of Louvain in what is now Belgium. He had also been the teacher of Emperor Charles V. Unfortunately, Pope Adrian lived only a year. Had he lived longer, he might have had the honesty and the courage to reform the Catholic Church from within. (Adrian VI would also be the last non-Italian pope until the election of Pope John Paul II in 1978.) The next pope, Clement VII (1523–1534), was also a member of the Medici family. Pope Clement would not call a general council as Charles V wished. And he was also unable to solve the Lutheran problem.

Recall and Reflect

1. Why did Martin Luther find fault with Tetzel's preaching about indulgences?
2. How did Martin Luther's study of Saint Paul change his ideas about the Church?
3. How did the Church respond to Luther?
4. How did Martin Luther's followers come to be called Protestants?
5. The members of the Diet of Worms and Martin Luther could not agree. Luther left the Church and Christendom was divided. Have you ever been in a situation where you could not agree with a person or group? How did you settle it? What did you learn from the experience?

REFORM IN SWITZERLAND AND ENGLAND

Ulrich Zwingli The religious reform begun by Martin Luther spread quickly to other parts of Europe. Other people followed Luther's ideas about the sole authority of the Bible and the need to free the Church from the power of the papacy. One such reformer was a Swiss priest, Ulrich Zwingli (ul′rik tsving′lē) (1484–1531), who brought the Protestant Reformation to present-day Switzerland. Zwingli was a learned man who had been influenced by humanist ideas about the Church. He was ordained in 1506 and became a parish priest in the small town of Glarus, Switzerland. Luther's writings made a great impression on Zwingli. He was determined to reform the Church in Switzerland just as Luther had done in Germany.

Rich merchants and business people in many Swiss cities were attracted to Luther's ideas and tried to introduce Lutheran reforms. In 1518 such reform-minded citizens in Zurich offered Zwingli the post of "people's priest." Zwingli accepted, and set about reforming the Church in Zurich in the Lutheran way. In 1523 the city government, which was in the hands of the reformers, drew up a new religious code that set up the Protestant Church in Zurich. All those who did not accept Zwingli's ideas were made to leave the city. The Bible was accepted as the sole authority in religion. The Mass was done away with, and all relics and images were taken out of the city's churches.

Zwingli's ideas about the Eucharist led to a serious disagreement between Luther and himself. Luther believed that Christ's body was really present in the Eucharist. Zwingli, on the other hand, said that Christ was only symbolically present, not really present.

Luther and Zwingli talked the matter over in 1529 in the German city of Marburg, but neither man could make the other change his views.

The Reformation was very successful in Zurich. Under Zwingli's leadership most of the northern part of Switzerland became Protestant. But many Catholics fought the reformers, and that led to war in Switzerland. In 1531 the Catholics won a victory in the battle of Kappel, in which Zwingli was killed. The Protestants were then forced to agree that the government of each canton, or province, in Switzerland could decide the religion of its citizens. Zwingli's reformed Church continued in Zurich. And Protestant Churches were also set up in the Swiss cities of Basel, Bern, and Geneva.

John Calvin Even more important than Zwingli as a reformer was John Calvin (1509–1564). Calvin was one of those who helped set up the Protestant Reformation in Geneva. Calvin's thought and influence dominated the Protestant movement not only in Switzerland but also in France, the Netherlands, and Scotland. His ideas attracted many followers in England and parts of Germany and central Europe as well.

In fact, many Protestant Churches today look upon John Calvin as their spiritual father and theological guide. He came a generation after Luther and was able to consolidate much of Luther's work. Unlike Luther and many of the other reformers, Calvin had never been a priest; he was a layperson. If Luther began the religious movement that we call the Protestant Reformation, it was John Calvin who brought it to completion. In his writings, Calvin drew up an entire system of Protestant thought and belief. Luther had broken with many old Catholic traditions. Calvin forged a new Church law. Luther had stated Christian truths in a new way. Calvin gave that faith a clear, precise, and above all an orderly presentation.

John Calvin was born in the city of Noyon (nwä yōN′), France, in the year 1509 to a rich middle-class family. His father was a lawyer and financial agent for the diocese of Noyon. In fact, his father would later fight about money matters with the canons of Noyon's cathedral and would die excommunicated. Those difficulties would affect the young Calvin's views about the Church.

At the age of fourteen John Calvin was sent to Paris to study. He was preparing for a career as a humanist when he was ordered by his father to study law. Obeying his father, Calvin went to the University of Orleans to study law. In May 1531, Calvin's father died. Calvin returned to continue his humanistic studies in Paris. In the year 1533 or 1534, while still in his early twenties, Calvin decided to give his life to the reform of the Christian Church. Calvin had already drawn close to a small group of Lutherans who were working in France. In 1535 the French government under King Francis I began to attack those followers of the Lutheran Reform. Calvin fled with them to Protestant Switzerland.

Calvin's Reformed Church In March of 1536 Calvin published the first edition of what would be his greatest work, the ***Institutes of the Christian Religion.*** John Calvin would spend most of his life working on that book. The final edition appeared in 1559 and 1560. It treated Protestant theology in a clear, orderly way.

While on a journey in 1536, Calvin visited the Swiss city of Geneva. Geneva was the most important city in French-

When Calvin decided to give his life to Church reform, he used his great scholarship to write a clear, orderly treatment of Protestant theology.

speaking Switzerland. The city government had already set up a reformed Church before Calvin arrived. Those who remained Catholic had been driven out along with the bishop of Geneva. The Protestant leaders of Geneva persuaded Calvin to remain in the city. Except for a brief exile, 1538–1541, Calvin would live and work in Geneva until his death in 1564.

It was in Geneva that Calvin carried out his life's task of consolidating the Protestant Reformation. He was convinced that all that is required for salvation is found in the Scriptures and in them alone. That was the guiding principle for all his writings. Like Luther, Calvin taught the idea of justification by faith, but he parted from Luther over the Eucharist. In that matter, Calvin supported the views of Ulrich Zwingli.

Under Calvin's rule Geneva became a kind of religious city-state. In 1541, Calvin drew up a series of laws for what came to be known as the **Presbyterian**, or **Reformed, Church**. The offices, or ministries, of pastor, teacher, elder, and deacon were created. Every aspect of life was made to agree with the words and spirit of the Bible, both the Old and New Testaments. Geneva became the spiritual and intellectual center of the Protestant world. The French and the Dutch Protestant Churches followed Calvin's model. John Knox, a reformer from Scotland, studied under Calvin in Geneva and carried Calvinist teaching back to Scotland. From Scotland and England, Calvinist teaching would be carried to the New World by Puritans and Presbyterians.

Reform in England In England the Reformation was the work of the government. King Henry VIII (1509–1547) separated the English Church from Rome. Although there were Lutheran thinkers and writers in England, Henry VIII did not make the Church in England into a Lutheran Church. In fact, he rejected many of Luther's teachings. In 1521, Henry VIII wrote a book defending all the seven sacraments against Luther. The pope thereupon gave Henry the title "Defender of the Faith," a title that English rulers still use.

Although Henry VIII often attended three Masses a day and gave generously to the Church, he began to claim more and more power over the English Church. For Henry, as a Renaissance ruler, regarded himself as having absolute power in both Church and state. Handsome, vain, and strong-willed, he was used to having his way.

One of Henry's chief concerns was to have a son so that his family's hold on the throne would be more secure. He had married Catherine of Aragon, the daughter of Ferdinand and Isabella, the rulers of Spain. Catherine had been married to Henry's brother, who died very young. Henry had married her with a **dispensation** from the pope. A dispensation is a permission to set aside a Church law for a good reason. In this case, Church law did not allow marriage between brother-in-law and sister-in-law.

Henry and Catherine had six children, but only one daughter lived. That daughter would one day be queen of England as Mary Tudor. Still, Henry wanted a son. He believed, or made himself believe, that God was punishing him because he had married his dead brother's wife. He decided to set the marriage aside. In 1527, Henry asked the pope, who was Clement VII, to declare that his marriage to Catherine had not been a true marriage and

Although preaching is central to Presbyterian worship, the hymns and prayers of Sunday services stress the importance of Christian fellowship.

that the dispensation was therefore unlawful. Catherine of Aragon insisted with all her strength that she was the king's lawful wife. Moreover, Catherine was the aunt of Emperor Charles V.

Henry had another reason for wanting his marriage to be declared unlawful. He was in love with Anne Boleyn, who was a lady-in-waiting, or an attendant, to Queen Catherine. For that reason, Henry wanted his marriage with Catherine to be set aside very quickly. Pope Clement VII hesitated a long time before making his decision. He did not want to offend Henry, and he did not want to offend the emperor. In 1529 he called Henry's case to Rome to be judged.

The Break Henry VIII became more and more angry at the pope's delay. Finally, in 1529, Henry set about bringing the English Church under his own control and cutting it off from Rome. He forced the English bishops to recognize him as head of the Church "as far as the law of Christ allows." Parliament passed laws forbidding any appeals to Rome and transferring all papal rights and duties to the king. The archbishop of Canterbury, Thomas Cranmer, who was secretly a Lutheran sympathizer, declared the marriage between Henry and Catherine unlawful. In 1533, Henry married Anne Boleyn. Unfortunately for Henry, Anne too had only one child who lived. That child, a daughter named Elizabeth, would also one day rule England as queen.

In 1536, Henry VIII had Anne Boleyn beheaded for adultery. The king then married Jane Seymour, who bore him a son, Edward. But Jane died twelve days after childbirth. In 1539, Henry married a European princess, Anne of Cleves. That young lady did not like England; the marriage was

Anglican worship, based on Archbishop Thomas Cranmer's Book of Common Prayer, *is very similar to the liturgy of the Roman Catholic Church.*

dissolved, and Anne was sent home. In 1542, Henry married Catherine Howard; shortly after, he charged her with adultery and had her beheaded. In 1543, Henry married the sixth and last of his wives, Catherine Parr, who survived him.

Henry's Reform The break between the English Church and Rome came slowly. In 1534, Parliament, which represented the nobility and the burghers, declared that the king was "the only supreme head on earth of the Church of England." This was made into an oath—a statement that all citizens had to swear to. It became known as the Oath of Supremacy. Anyone who denied that statement was declared guilty of treason, a crime punishable by death. *Treason* means "action against one's country." Thus English Catholics who refused to take the oath because they did not agree with what Henry had done could be put to death.

Very few English Catholics objected to what Henry VIII had done. Most people, including almost all the bishops, accepted him as head of the Church in England. Many people thought that the separation

---

SIDELIGHTS ON CHURCH HISTORY
Two Brave Men

Among the English Catholics who refused to take King Henry's Oath of Supremacy were two well-known scholars. One, John Fisher, was a bishop. The other, Sir Thomas More, was a layperson.

John Fisher, the chancellor, or head, of the University of Cambridge, was also the bishop of Rochester in England. He had upheld the validity of King Henry's marriage to Catherine of Aragon. In April of 1534, he was brought to the king's palace to take the Oath of Supremacy. He would not do so. Reminded that all the other English bishops had taken the oath, Bishop Fisher said that he did not "condemn any other men's conscience. Their conscience may save them, and mine must save me."

Bishop Fisher was imprisoned in the Tower of London, a castle that served as a prison for political prisoners. While he was in prison, Pope Paul III made John Fisher a cardinal. Henry VIII, on hearing that news, exclaimed: "Let the pope send him a [cardinal's] hat. I will so provide that whensoever it cometh he shall wear it on his shoulders, for head he shall have none to set it on." On June 22, 1535, Bishop John Fisher was beheaded.

Two weeks later Sir Thomas More, a Catholic layperson, met death in the same way for the same reason. Like John Fisher, Sir Thomas More was well-known as a learned humanist and scholar. He was also a brilliant lawyer. Henry VIII had

made Thomas More lord chancellor of England in 1529.

Unable to approve of the king's divorce nor his actions against the Church, More resigned as chancellor in 1532. Sir Thomas More would not speak publicly against the king, but like Bishop John Fisher, More refused to take the Oath of Supremacy.

Sir Thomas More was imprisoned in the Tower of London. He would live for little more than a year in a damp cell. His health deteriorated. His wife and his favorite daughter, Margaret, often visited him. Thomas More's family and many of his friends could not understand why he took the position that he did regarding the king as head of the Church. Later, after a special court had found him guilty, Thomas More spoke out: ". . . this Realm, being but one member and small part of the Church, might not make a particular law disagreeable with the general law of Christ's Universal Catholic Church. . . ." Thomas More understood that the Catholic Church was universal.

On July 6, 1535, Thomas More was beheaded. Well-known for his sense of humor, Sir Thomas More joked with the man who helped him up the steps of the platform—where he was to be executed: "See me up safely, but let me shift for myself when I come down." In May 1935 both John Fisher and Thomas More were declared saints of the Church.

would only be temporary. Henry VIII died in 1547. His nine-year-old son, Edward VI, became king. He would die in 1553 at the age of fifteen. Many Protestant reforms were introduced into the English Church while Edward ruled.

Mary Tudor was queen from 1553 to 1558. She tried to reestablish the Catholic religion. It was only during the long reign of Queen Elizabeth, 1558–1603, that the **Church of England**, or the **Anglican Church**, became firmly established as a Protestant Church. In liturgy it remained very similar to the Roman Catholic Church. Its theology, however, reflected the influence of Protestantism.

Results of Reformation Luther, Calvin, and the other religious reformers were sincere people who were searching for religious truth. Unfortunately, their desire to reform the Church and to restate and rethink Christ's message ended in revolt against the Church. As separate Churches came into being, the religious unity of Europe was destroyed. Instead of the united Western Christendom of the Middle Ages, Europe was now divided along religious lines. As the map on page 193 shows, by the year 1600 the Roman Catholic Church remained strong in the south of Europe and in Poland, Hungary, and parts of the Holy Roman Empire. Lutheran Churches were set up in what is now Germany, in the Baltic lands, and in Scandinavia. Calvinist, or Reformed, Churches were set up in Switzerland, the Netherlands, and Scotland. The Church of England, or Anglican Church, became the official Church in England.

Minority religious groups were to be found in all those geographic regions. Calvinist Churches were to be found in France and in parts of Germany and Hungary.

Some Catholics lived in England and Scotland. In most cases those religious minorities were attacked by the government. In France, for example, the Reformed Churches were only tolerated after the **Edict of Nantes**, in 1598. And that toleration was taken away in 1685 by King Louis XIV of France.

All efforts at reconciliation among the Churches failed in the years after the Protestant Reformation. From the very beginning, political and economic matters played a large role in keeping Europe divided along religious lines. Kings tried to control religion and the Church within their lands. Often that led them to break with Rome. As religious disputes and splits continued, the doctrines and beliefs of the individual Churches became more and more rigid and fixed. Those religious disputes became mixed with European political struggles. For over one hundred years, wars of religion brought suffering and death to many European peoples.

The Protestant Reformation attacked the authority, teachings, and traditions of the Roman Catholic Church. In the next chapter we shall see how the Catholic Church began to counter those attacks.

Recall and Reflect

1. Name two leaders of the Protestant Reformation in Switzerland.

2. Why did Geneva, Switzerland, become a religious center for a great part of the Protestant world?

3. Who carried Calvinist teachings to Scotland? To the New World?

4. Who caused the break between England and the Roman Catholic Church?

5. What particular things might you do in your parish to bring about better understanding of and sharing with the Protestant young men and women of your community?

REVIEW AND CELEBRATE

Doctrinal Summary

As Pope John XXIII pointed out, Protestants are "our separated brethren." We are brothers and sisters because we have many things in common: the love of Christ, Baptism, the Holy Bible. Through discussion and dialogue, Catholics and Protestants will better understand each other's views and the things that unite us as well as those that divide.

Religious Vocabulary

Protestant Reformation
Counter Reformation
Catholic Reformation
infallible
Protestants

Lutheran Church
Institutes of the Christian Religion
Presbyterian Church
Reformed Church

dispensation
Church of England
Anglican Church
Edict of Nantes

Review Questions

Answer the following questions on a separate sheet of paper.

1. How did Renaissance ideas affect the papacy?
2. How did the need for money lead to abuses of the idea of indulgences in the Church?
3. What effects did Martin Luther's reforms have on the Church in Europe?
4. Why is John Calvin considered a spiritual father by many of the Protestant Churches today?
5. How was the map of Europe divided religiously in the year 1600?

Prayer Celebration

Leader: Lord God, we pray for a spirit of unity in the words of Psalm 133.

All: "Behold, how good it is, and how pleasant,
    where brethren dwell
        at one!"
It is as when the precious ointment
    upon the head
    runs down over the beard, the beard
        of Aaron,
    till it runs down upon the collar of
        his robe.
It is a dew like that of Hermon,
    which comes down upon the
        mountains of Zion;

For there the Lord has pronounced
    his blessing,
    life forever."

Leader: We know, Lord, that You have called us to live together in love, and instead we build walls to separate ourselves from one another. We want to welcome Your Spirit into our hearts so that we may learn to build bridges instead of walls. We ask to be able to do this through the power of Jesus Christ, Your Son and our Savior.
All: Amen.

Saint Ignatius Loyola founded the Society of Jesus. His followers became leaders in Church reform and in the fight against Protestantism.

13

The Church Reformed

In 1521, the year in which Martin Luther broke with the Catholic Church, a thirty-year-old soldier lay ill in a Spanish castle not far from the French border. His name was Ignatius Loyola. Though often wild and reckless, Ignatius was a very brave soldier and loyal to his king.

On May 20, 1521, while helping to defend the Castle of Pamplona against a French attack, Ignatius was struck in both legs by a cannon ball. His left leg was wounded, and his right leg badly broken. The doctor did not set the right leg correctly and it was not healing. It had to be rebroken twice before it began to mend.

Ignatius bravely stood the pain, but he almost died from infection. During the long, dull months of healing, he wanted books to read. None were to be had except a life of Christ and some lives of the saints. Ignatius began to read those. When his right leg was finally healed, his heart had

also been touched. The tough, brave soldier who had sought glory in war and honor from an earthly king was transformed into a soldier for Christ. Ignatius decided to serve God for the rest of his life. He became one of the Church's great leaders and the founder of a new religious order, the **Society of Jesus**, or **Jesuits**. In this chapter we will learn how Ignatius and his new order helped to further the great spiritual revival and movement for reform within the Catholic Church that we call the Counter Reformation, or the Catholic Reformation.

THE COUNTER REFORMATION BEGINS

A Great Spiritual Awakening The term *Counter Reformation* was coined in the 1800s by Protestant historians to describe a great spiritual awakening in the Church. The Counter Reformation, however, was not just a reaction to the Protestants. It had begun in the Church even before Martin Luther. It was that spiritual awakening in the Church which would lead to a Catholic, or Counter, Reformation.

The Protestant Reformation had left many Church leaders confused. The Church was not prepared for attacks on its authority, teachings, and traditions. It lost many members, both laypeople and clergy. But by the end of the sixteenth century, the Church had met and checked Protestant challenges. It had also reformed itself.

The Counter Reformation took place on many levels. Politically, the Church had the help of Catholic rulers and princes who checked the Protestants on the battlefield. Spiritually, there was a great renewal in the Church. Under the Holy Spirit, many Catholics led very holy lives. Their good example helped the Church to change. New religious orders were founded. An ecumenical council carefully restated the Church's beliefs and reformed its discipline. Finally, as the Church changed from within, its new vitality gave birth to new forms of art, architecture, and culture.

Religious Wars From the very beginning, the tensions caused by the Reformation had broken out into wars between Protestants and Catholics. As we saw in Chapter 12, those wars always had political and social sides as well as religious ones. That was true of the wars of Switzerland and the Netherlands, the civil-religious wars of France, the Catholic uprisings in England, and the wars within the Holy Roman Empire.

Within the Empire, the disputes between Lutheran and Catholic princes and leaders led to a compromise settlement in 1555. At a Diet in Augsburg, Germany, it was decided that the religion of the prince or ruler would also be the religion of his subjects. Those who did not believe as their prince believed had to leave and find a place where their religion was officially accepted. In a few places within the Empire, religious minorities could practice their religion openly. But it would be a long time before most European rulers would accept the right of all people to have religious freedom.

During the 1600s and 1700s, political-religious wars continued to bring death and suffering to many people in Europe. The most bitter and cruel of those wars was the Thirty Years' War (1618–1648). It was fought on German territory. When it was finally settled by the Peace of Westphalia in 1648, the religious divisions that can be seen on the map on page 193 had become fixed. They would remain for almost three hundred years.

Politically, the Counter Reformation would not have been possible without the help of the Catholic rulers of Europe—the kings of France and Spain and the Catholic princes of Germany and the Holy Roman Empire. In Chapter 12 we saw that the Reformed Church in France had legal rights after 1598. But the Catholic Church had reformed itself. And in France that reform was supported by the government. Only a minority of the French people became Calvinist.

The Society of Jesus Many times in history, new religious orders have helped the Church to reform itself or to meet some new need. In Chapter 10 we saw how the Franciscans and Dominicans helped the Church meet the needs of people who lived in towns. New religious orders now

The Thirty Years' War, the cruelest and bitterest of all the religious wars, caused terrible suffering and destruction in Germany.

helped to bring about a spiritual renewal within the Church in the sixteenth century. The most important of those new orders was the Society of Jesus, or the Jesuits, founded by Ignatius Loyola.

Ignatius Loyola was born in 1491 into a noble family of northern Spain. He was the youngest of eleven children. Like most sons of such families, Ignatius was trained to be a soldier. As we have seen, he followed that career until he was gravely wounded in 1521.

Ignatius Loyola was thirty years old when his wounds healed. He decided to become a soldier for Christ. Ignatius first went as a pilgrim to the famous Benedictine abbey of Montserrat (mänt′sə′rat′), high in the mountains of northeastern Spain. The abbey of Montserrat was, and still is, a

famous shrine dedicated to the Blessed Virgin. It has an old statue of Mary that is blackened by candle smoke and known as the Black Virgin of Montserrat. Ignatius left his sword as a gift before the Virgin's statue. He made a confession of his life and spent the whole night in prayer, going to Mass and receiving Communion the next morning. Ignatius began his new way of life at Montserrat. He went to the nearby town of Manresa (män rā′sə) and lived there for ten months. He begged for his food and spent long hours in prayer. That long retreat helped prepare him for his future work.

Like Saint Francis of Assisi, Ignatius wanted to live and work in the Holy Land. In 1523, Ignatius left Manresa and sailed from Spain to Italy. In Italy he went to

185

Venice and set sail for Jerusalem. Ignatius longed to stay in Jerusalem, but the Franciscan friars who were in charge of the Holy Places were afraid Ignatius would do something rash. They refused to let him stay, so he returned to Spain.

Ignatius now began to plan for his future work for Christ. He realized that he needed to study theology. To do so he first had to learn to read Latin. Thus, in 1524, at the age of thirty-three, Ignatius began his studies in a Latin school for boys in Barcelona. Ignatius then tried to study at two universities in Spain, but his ascetical way of life brought him to the attention of the Spanish Inquisition. He was questioned, and even put in prison for a while. In 1528, Ignatius went to Paris to study.

The Society Begins Its Work It was at Paris that the Society of Jesus was born. A natural leader of men, Ignatius had a way of attracting followers. Those men shared his enthusiasm for a life of poverty and service for Christ. On August 15, 1534, Ignatius and six of his friends made vows of poverty and chastity. They also vowed to go to the Holy Land. If they could not do that, they promised to offer themselves to the pope to serve Christ and His Church wherever the pope wished to send them.

Ignatius now began the study of theology. Because of sickness, he had to go back to Spain for some months. In 1537,

Ignatius again joined his companions—now ten in number—in Venice, Italy. They went to Rome, where Pope Paul III gave permission for all those not yet priests to be ordained. After his ordination, Ignatius prepared himself for a whole year before offering his first Mass.

By 1538, it had become clear that it would not be possible for Ignatius and his companions to go to Jerusalem. They decided to form themselves into a new religious order. To their vows of poverty and chastity they added the vow of obedience to a superior and the vow to go wherever the pope wished to send them. On September 27, 1540, Pope Paul III approved the new order. It was called the Society of Jesus. Ignatius was elected the first superior general.

The Jesuits were not founded to fight the Protestants. But from their beginnings they were active in the defense of the Church against Protestant attacks as well as in reform efforts within the Church. Ignatius wanted his order to be ready to do any work for the Church and the greater glory of God. Ignatius wrote the constitution, or rule, for his society. Jesuits did not have to pray the Divine Office as a group like the older communities. They did not wear a special habit or uniform. The rule was balanced and moderate. Ignatius wanted both the minds and the bodies of his members trained for hard work in the field.

The Society of Jesus grew rapidly. By the time Ignatius died in 1556, they numbered almost one thousand. The Jesuits quickly spread throughout Europe. Ignatius sent some of them on mission to the New World, Africa, and Asia. The Jesuits preached against heresy. They became theologians, philosophers, and scientists. They became preachers and spiri-

WORDS TO LIVE BY

Soul of Christ, be my sanctification;
Body of Christ, be my salvation;
Blood of Christ, fill all my veins;
Water of Christ's side, wash out my stains. . . .
ATTRIBUTED TO SAINT IGNATIUS LOYOLA

Pope Paul III has been called the first reform pope by Church historians. In 1540 he approved the new order of the Society of Jesus, or Jesuits.

Ignatius spent the rest of his life running his order. Although he never left Rome, he kept in close touch with members of his order by letter. Over six thousand of his letters have been printed. They show that Ignatius was wise and prudent, and above all kind and loving. Charity was the crown of all his virtues. He took for his own motto and that of his order the words "to the greater glory of God." In the fifteen years that he was superior, Ignatius had often been ill, but he died suddenly and unexpectedly on July 31, 1556. Ignatius was made a saint in 1622. We keep his feast on July 31.

The Society of Jesus was only one of many new orders that were founded in the sixteenth century. Like the Jesuits, most of those new orders served the new needs of the Church. They ran schools, hospitals, orphanages, and houses for the poor, disabled, and aged. The older religious orders also began to change and to direct their work to the needs of the time. The work of those orders, with their active social missions, helped quicken and revive Catholic religious life in Europe. The orders would also carry throughout the Church the reforms of an ecumenical council.

tual directors and advisers to popes, kings, cardinals, students, and others.

Jesuit Schools The most famous work of the Society of Jesus was and still is in the field of teaching. Everywhere the Jesuits went they started schools. They began teaching in Roman slums and soon were teaching the sons of kings and nobles. Jesuit teaching methods worked so well that the Jesuits became known as the "schoolmasters" of Europe.

Recall and Reflect

1. What was the Counter Reformation?
2. How did the Diet of Augsburg in 1555 try to settle the religious problems in the Empire?
3. How did Ignatius Loyola want his followers to live for the Church?
4. What was and still is the Jesuits' most famous work?
5. During the time that he was very sick, Saint Ignatius Loyola made an important decision about his future. Do you ever take special time to pray and think about your life? How often do you do this? Is it a helpful experience?

THE COUNCIL OF TRENT

A Difficult Start From the beginning of the Reformation, Protestants and Catholics had called for a Church council to deal with the crisis. Luther, Calvin, Henry VIII, Charles V—all asked for a council to reform the Church. The popes and other Church leaders truly desired to correct abuses and to meet the Protestant challenge. But only the pope could call a general council. Many things kept the post-Reformation popes from calling one. On the one hand, there was the rivalry between Catholic countries, especially between France and the Holy Roman Empire. On the other hand, many Church leaders feared losing their own power if changes were made in the Church.

Demand for a council remained strong, however. Finally, Pope Paul III (1534–1549) had the courage to call one. In 1545, Pope Paul called for a general council to meet in Trent, a town in northern Italy. The choice of Trent was itself a compromise. The emperor Charles V had said that any council should be held in Germany, or at least in his Empire. The pope wanted it to meet in Rome. The pope and the cardinals were agreed that any council should be under the presidency of the pope or his legates. (As we learned in Chapter 7, a papal legate is a person who speaks for the pope and acts in his name and with his authority.) Trent at that time was German speaking and was a part of the Holy Roman Empire. But it was also on the south side of the Alps, in Italy. Communication with Rome was not too hard.

The Council Under Way On December 13, 1545, the **Council of Trent** opened with only twenty-eight bishops present. It was to last for eighteen years, 1545–1563. It was interrupted twice, and can be divided into three periods: the first, 1545–1547; the second, 1551–1552; the third and last, 1562–1563. The pope did not attend the Council of Trent in person. He was represented by legates to whom he sent letters.

From the beginning it was decided that the attending bishops—who were aided by learned theologians—would treat both the Church doctrine and Church discipline at the same time. Important points were discussed by the scholars and theologians. The bishops listened and questioned. It was the bishops, however, who voted on the conclusions of the scholars and passed the laws, or decrees, of the council.

The decrees of the Council of Trent were worded with great care. Though they stated the main Catholic beliefs and traditions, the decrees were not meant to attack Protestants but to bring them back to the Church. In many ways, the first period of Trent was the most important. The council fathers made it clear that justification was a matter not only of faith but also of hope and love. They said that the Church rested not only on the Bible but also on those traditions "which have always been maintained by the Catholic Church." The council restated the Church's belief in seven sacraments. It said that the Mass was not just a memorial, or a Communion service, but a real sacrifice.

The first period of Trent ended in April 1547. The following month a plague struck Trent. Pope Paul III wanted to move the council to Bologna. The emperor refused to let the German bishops attend there. In September 1549, Paul III was forced to suspend the council. Two months later the pope died.

The Second Period The new pope, Julius III (1550–1555), called the Council of

The Council of Trent restated traditional Catholic beliefs and began a vital and lasting program of Church reform.

Trent back for its second period. Work began again in May 1551 and lasted until April 1552. During that period certain Lutherans were present at Trent. Though the council had been called to heal the differences between the Protestant Churches and the Catholic Church, that was the only time that Protestants attended. As it happened, neither the Lutherans nor the Catholics were able to talk about the ideas that separated them. Mutual trust and respect have to be present for a true dialogue. It has only been in our own time, at the Second Vatican Council which opened in 1962, that dialogues have taken place between the Protestant and Catholic Churches. In April 1552 the Council of Trent had to stop again, now because of war. The council would not meet again for ten years.

Pope Julius III died on March 22, 1555. He was followed by Pope Marcellus II who ruled only 22 days (April 9 to May 1, 1555). Marcellus II was a firm believer in the Council of Trent and probably would have reopened it soon if he had lived. His successor, Pope Paul IV (1555–1559), an old man of seventy–nine, felt that he did not need the Council of Trent to reform the Church.

Paul IV was a very severe and harsh pope. He relied upon the Courts of the Inquisition to track down heresy in every part of the Church. He also used the Inquisition to look into the private moral life of individuals. Paul IV drew up a list of books that Catholics were not allowed to read. Known as the *Index of Forbidden Books*, it was published in 1559. It was so long that almost everything ever printed seemed to be on it. A less sweeping list was printed in 1564 after the pope's death. Pope Paul IV's rule was so harsh that the Roman people rioted at his death. They pulled down his statue and stormed the buildings of the Inquisition. They burned many of its records and set free the prisoners.

The Council Ends The next pope, Pius IV (1559–1565), reopened the Council of Trent. Its third and last period began in January 1562. It would close on December 4, 1563. In that last meeting, Trent dealt chiefly with disciplinary matters in the Church. It directly attacked the abuses that had brought about the Protestant Reformation. The office of indulgence preacher was abolished. Bishops were told to live in their dioceses. Clergy were not allowed to hold more than one office at one time. The rule of celibacy was to be followed in the Church. Those decrees of Trent became the rules for reform of the Catholic Church.

One important act of Trent was the setting up of **seminaries**, or schools to train young men for the priesthood. As you learned in Chapter 9, during the Middle Ages there were no such seminaries to train young men who wanted to become priests. Such students were taught by the parish clergy, the cathedral canons, or at the universities. The Council of Trent ordered every bishop in a diocese where there was no university to set up a seminary to train boys and young men for the priesthood.

The Council of Trent touched upon every aspect of Catholic life. It called upon people to receive Holy Communion and to confess more often. Indeed the work of the Council of Trent was so careful that it

Seminaries are found in most Church dioceses. These young men are studying for the priesthood at St. Michael's Seminary in Gambia, a country in West Africa.

A Woman of the Counter Reformation

Many devoted men and women were involved in the great Catholic, or Counter, Reformation of the sixteenth century. Among them was Angela Merici, who founded the first teaching order of women in the Church. Angela was born about 1474 in northern Italy. Her parents were poor, and both died before Angela was ten. She was raised by a wealthy uncle. Angela wanted to give her life more completely to God. She became a member of the third order of Saint Francis. Like Francis she wanted to possess nothing of her own and to live only for God.

After her uncle's death, Angela, then about twenty-two, found her life's work. She began to teach religion and reading skills to young girls of poor families. Most of her work was done in the northern Italian city of Brescia, not far from Milan. Soon Angela had gathered around her other young women who shared her desire to teach poor girls. At that time such education for the poor was almost unheard of in Europe.

Angela had no intention of beginning an order of nuns. It was her desire to gather together a group of women who would pray together and live a life of service to others. The young women would live with their own families but keep the vows of poverty and chastity. They would meet together for classes and worship. Each member was to seek out poor girls and teach them.

Angela Merici founded her group in 1535. She chose Saint Ursula as its protector. Saint Ursula was a legendary early Christian martyr. From the Middle Ages she had been honored as the protector of universities and as a leader of women. The members of Angela's new group were soon called Ursulines. Angela Merici became their superior.

The idea of young, unmarried women living outside a monastery was not accepted in the sixteenth century. After Angela Merici's death in 1540, her little band of women was changed into a religious order of nuns who wore habits and lived in convents. But Angela Merici's daughters, the Ursulines, have continued her work of teaching young girls. Ursuline nuns today are found all over the world, teaching and serving the poor. Angela Merici was declared a saint of the Church in 1807. Her feast is on January 27.

set the tone for Catholic thought, attitudes, and ideals for the next four hundred years. Because the Protestants attacked the tradition of honoring the saints, the council fostered many new ways of praying to them and to Christ in the Eucharist. The kind of.Benediction of the Blessed Sacrament we know today comes from Trent.

The Council of Trent ordered that the language of the Mass continue to be Latin.

That had an important effect on Catholic practice. In the 1500s, Latin remained the language of higher studies, but it had little meaning in daily life. The use of Latin made the Mass remote to many people who did not understand the language. People did not "participate" in Mass; they "assisted" at it. People went to Mass and said private prayers rather than the prayers of the Mass.

Counter-Reform Bishops The Council of Trent passed reforms for the whole Church. Still, laws mean nothing unless Church leaders are willing to carry them out. That was especially true of the decrees of the Council of Trent. The new measures called for bishops who were willing to work for change. The Holy Spirit guided many good men to become bishops and Church leaders at that time. Many today are saints of the Church. One is Saint Francis de Sales (1567–1622), bishop of Geneva. Another is Saint Philip Neri (1515–1595), the founder of the **Oratorians**—priests who lived together in community but without vows. The Oratorians helped many people to lead holy lives. Oratorians became confessors, preachers, and scholars. Saint Philip Neri himself worked among the clergy of Rome, teaching the ideals set forth in Trent.

One bishop who changed his diocese was Charles Borromeo, archbishop of Milan, Italy (1560–1584). Charles Borromeo was born in 1538 to a northern Italian noble family. His mother was a sister of Pope Pius IV. From childhood, his family wanted Charles to have a career in the Church. At the age of twelve he was made a member of the clergy. That allowed him to receive Church offices with their income but without any of their duties. All of that was part of the abuses in the Church at the time. Charles became an archbishop at twenty-one and a cardinal at twenty-two. When his uncle was chosen pope as Pius IV, Charles was called to Rome to become the cardinal secretary of state. That too was an abuse. Popes often gave high offices to their nephews and other family members. Often those persons were unworthy or were not able to do the work they were given.

Charles Borromeo, however, used his high office to further the work of the Council of Trent at Rome and within the papal court. He became his uncle's most valued helper during the third period and the close of the council. In 1563, Charles's older brother died suddenly. That greatly affected Charles. He began to reform his own life-style. On July 17, 1563, he was ordained to the priesthood and began to preach sermons. It was so unusual at that time for a cardinal to preach that the Roman people flocked to hear him. Charles worked hard to bring about reform in Rome and in the whole Church. He helped to write a catechism and to revise the **breviary** (brē′vē er′ē), as ordered by the Council of Trent. The breviary is a book that has the prayers of the Divine Office. Diocesan and religious priests pray the breviary every day.

After the death of Pope Pius IV in 1565, Charles gave up all his Church offices except that of archbishop of Milan. He had been made archbishop of Milan when he was made a cardinal. Charles Borromeo went to live in Milan. He was the first archbishop in many years to actually live there. For eighteen years Charles worked hard putting into practice the reforms of Trent. As the council had ordered, he called diocesan synods, or meetings, and visited every part of his huge archdiocese. He began a society of diocesan priests to help him. He set up not one but three seminaries in his archdiocese.

Charles Borromeo also taught by example. He often cared for the sick and dying, especially during the outbreak of plague in 1576–1577. Charles set up regular catechism classes for children. He lived a simple life and was known for his kindness. Charles Borromeo died on November 3, 1584. He was only forty-six. He was made a saint on November 1, 1610. We keep his feast day on November 4.

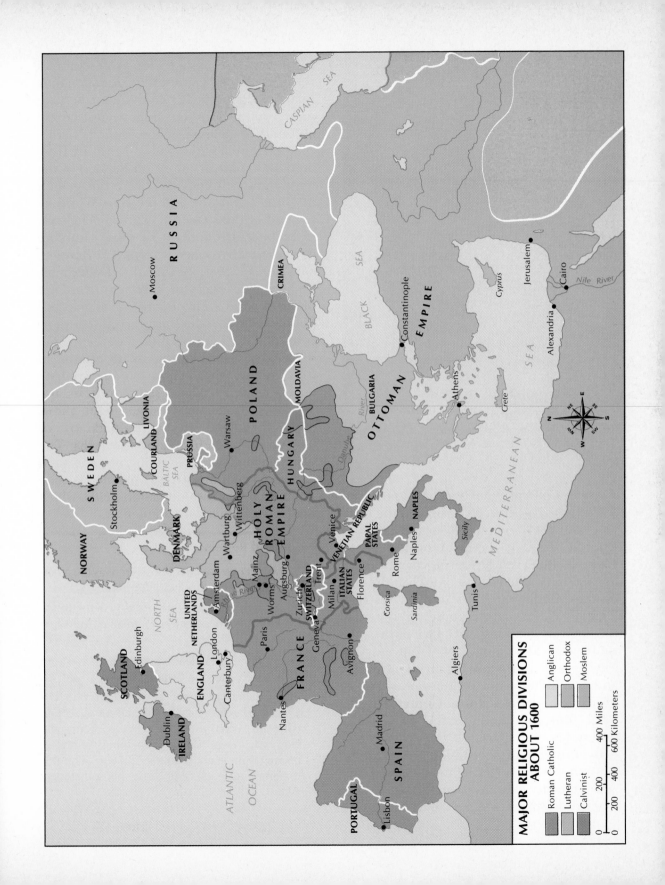

MAJOR RELIGIOUS DIVISIONS ABOUT 1600

Roman Catholic		Anglican
Lutheran		Orthodox
Calvinist		Moslem

0   200   400 Miles
0   200   400   600 Kilometers

ATLANTIC OCEAN

NORTH SEA

BALTIC SEA

MEDITERRANEAN SEA

CASPIAN SEA

BLACK SEA

RUSSIA
Moscow

SWEDEN
Stockholm

NORWAY

DENMARK

POLAND
Warsaw

PRUSSIA

COURLAND

LIVONIA

CRIMEA

MOLDAVIA

HUNGARY

BULGARIA

OTTOMAN EMPIRE
Constantinople

Athens
Crete
Cyprus
Jerusalem
Cairo
Alexandria
Nile River

HOLY ROMAN EMPIRE
Wartburg
Wittenberg
Mainz
Worms
Augsburg
Zurich

SWITZERLAND
Geneva

UNITED NETHERLANDS
Amsterdam
Rhine River

ENGLAND
London
Canterbury

SCOTLAND
Edinburgh

IRELAND
Dublin

FRANCE
Paris
Nantes
Avignon

SPAIN
Madrid

PORTUGAL
Lisbon

ITALIAN STATES
Milan
Florence
Trent
Rome

PAPAL STATES

VENETIAN REPUBLIC
Venice

NAPLES
Naples

Corsica
Sardinia
Sicily
Tunis
Algiers

Danube River
Dnieper River

N E S W NE SE SW NW

Saint Charles Borromeo put the reforms of Trent into practice in his archdiocese. He also taught by example, caring for the sick and dying of Milan.

A New Cultural Vitality The Council of Trent was the Church's answer to the challenges of the Protestant Reformation. The Church through Trent reformed all of Catholic life. Trent's reforms corrected the abuses that existed in the Church at the end of the Middle Ages. Its decrees restated Catholic beliefs in response to the new theological teaching of the Protestant reformers. The Council of Trent marked the beginning of a new era for the Church and for Catholicism. In many ways, it set the course of the Catholic Church for the next four hundred years, up to our own times.

By the end of the 1500s, the Catholic Church was no longer fighting for survival. Although the map on page 193 shows that much of Europe was lost to the Church,

some areas that earlier were Protestant had returned. As the Counter Reformation took hold, new generations of Catholics became more confident in their fight against heresy and in their defense of the Catholic faith.

The Church's new-found sense of freedom and spirit of joy could be seen in the many new churches that were being built in Catholic Europe and the New World by the end of the sixteenth century. The style of architecture and art of those churches is called baroque (bə rōk'). Baroque churches have beautiful decorations. Ceilings and walls in such churches are often covered with pictures of angels and saints in glory. Statues are carved that show Jesus and the saints as if they were moving, their clothing billowing as if caught in some mighty wind. Those churches radiate energy. The baroque style, with its use of color, contrast, curves, and light, shows the self-confidence, peace, and joy of the Counter Reformation Church. The Church's new understanding of its mission and sense of purpose was also to be seen in the new worldwide mission fields, which will be the subject of Chapter 14.

Recall and Reflect

1. Why did Pope Paul III choose Trent as the meeting place for the Council of Trent?

2. What two main topics did the bishops at the Council of Trent decide to treat at the same time?

3. Name three great leaders who helped reform the Church after the Council of Trent.

4. The Council of Trent was an effort of the Church to reform itself. Tell about a time in your life when you took steps to change the way you were doing something—studying, playing on a team, working. Do you think it is important for each of us to do that sometimes? Why?

REVIEW AND CELEBRATE

Doctrinal Summary

The Second Vatican Council declares that the human person
has a right to religious freedom. No one should be forced to
act in a manner contrary to his or her beliefs. Nor does any
country have the right to interfere with such religious
freedom. In the sixteenth century neither Catholics nor
Protestants believed in that principle of religious freedom.
Although the Church itself has not always practiced the
principle. Every person's response to God must be a free
response, and God respects that freedom.

Religious Vocabulary

Society of Jesus	Council of Trent	seminaries	breviary
Jesuits	*Index of Forbidden Books*	Oratorians	

Review Questions

Answer the following questions on a separate sheet of paper.

1. What were some of the things that helped renew the Church spiritually during the
   Counter Reformation?
2. How did the Society of Jesus help meet the special needs of the Church during the 1500s?
3. What was the purpose of the decrees of the council? Why weren't Catholics and
   Protestants able to talk to each other at the Council of Trent?
4. Why do we say that the Council of Trent "set the course of the Church for the next four
   hundred years"?
5. Why is Saint Charles Borromeo considered to be a good example of a Church leader
   after the Council of Trent?

Prayer Celebration

Leader: God our father, we pray to you in
the words of Saint Ignatius Loyola.

All: "Lord, I freely yield all my freedom to
you. Take my memory, my intellect, and my
entire will. You have given me everything I
am or have; I will give it all back to you to
stand under your will alone. Your love and
your grace are enough for me; I shall ask for
nothing more."

Leader: Let us also praise God for His constant love in the words of Psalm 103.

All: "Bless the Lord, O my soul;
 and all my being, bless his holy
 name.
Bless the Lord, O my soul,
 and forget not all his benefits;
He pardons all your iniquities,
 he heals all your ills. . . .
He fills your lifetime with good;
 your youth is renewed like the
 eagle's. . . .
Bless the Lord, O my soul!" Amen.

The Church continues to grow among African peoples. In 1975 over 6,000 people attended this ordination Mass in Ouagadougou, capital of Upper Volta.

14

The Missionary Church

On Saturday, December 3, 1552, a Spanish priest lay dying of fever on a lonely island close to the southern coast of China. The island was about a hundred miles (160 km) southwest of today's city of Hong Kong. The priest's name was Francis Xavier (zā′vē ər). Love for God and for His people had taken Francis Xavier halfway around the world to preach the gospel and to teach the Catholic faith. Only forty-six years old when he died, Francis Xavier had more excitement and adventure than most people who live much longer.

Francis Xavier's life and missionary work were part of the great wave of exploration and expansion in the 1400s and 1500s. During those years Europeans crossed the oceans and sailed around the world. He was part of the age that Columbus opened up when he sailed west under the flag of Spain in search of China and Japan.

While the Church in Europe was reforming itself and defending itself against Prot-estants, Portuguese and Spanish missionaries, like Francis Xavier, were carrying the Christian faith to the peoples of Africa, East Asia, and the Americas. Thus the 1500s was not only a time of European exploration and discovery but also an age of great missionary work by the Catholic Church. In this chapter we will learn about that period. We will read about the greatest expansion of Christianity since Saint Boniface converted the peoples of Germany in the early Middle Ages.

THE CHURCH IN AFRICA AND ASIA

Portuguese Control Their Missions In the 1400s the kingdom of Portugal had become strong and united. It had set up trading centers in Africa, India, and Southeast Asia where goods could be traded with the people who lived there. Portugal hoped to become rich by controlling trading rights.

The Portuguese did not interfere in local affairs except to protect their trade.

Wherever the Portuguese went they took missionaries with them. As Christians, they wanted to gain souls for Christ just as they wanted to gain wealth. Priests were also needed for the care of the merchants, sailors, and government people who lived in the trading posts. The Portuguese took the faith with them wherever they went. They also took charge of all the work of the Church in the lands they ruled. In all Portuguese overseas possessions, the Church was under the authority of the Portuguese king and his government.

A Christian King of the Congo As the Portuguese worked their way down the west coast of Africa, missionaries began to work among the black peoples who lived along the coast. In 1484 a Portuguese ship captain discovered the mouth of the Congo River—between what today are the countries of Angola and Zaire (zä ir′). Going upstream the Portuguese came into the ancient kingdom of the Congo. In 1491, King Nzinga (nə zing′gə) and some members of his family were baptized by Portuguese missionaries.

When King Nzinga died in 1506, his oldest son, Afonso, who was also a Catholic, fought his pagan brother for the throne. With the help of some Portuguese soldiers, Afonso won. He ruled as Afonso I from 1506 to 1543. With Afonso's help, Christianity spread through much of his kingdom. Letters between King Afonso and the kings of Portugal—Manuel I (1495–1521) and John III (1521–1557)—tell of Afonso's desire for priests, teachers, doctors, carpenters, stonemasons, and other skilled workers. A Portuguese priest wrote to the king of Portugal that Afonso I "studies the Holy Gospels [and] when the priest has finished saying Mass, [Afonso] asks for his blessing then he begins to preach to his people with great generosity and charity."

African Slaves The Portuguese wanted Afonso I to allow them to carry on the slave trade in his kingdom. Slavery had never completely died out in Europe after the end of the Roman Empire. Most slaves in Europe were found in the Mediterranean countries of Portugal, Spain, Italy, and Sicily. They were mainly household servants living within the family. Throughout most of the Middle Ages, those slaves had come generally from Eastern Europe. Later they came from North Africa and the Arab countries. The Arabs and the Portuguese took black slaves into Europe during the 1400s.

A priest in Kinshasa, Zaire, offers Mass. There have been many vocations to the priesthood among the peoples of Africa in our times.

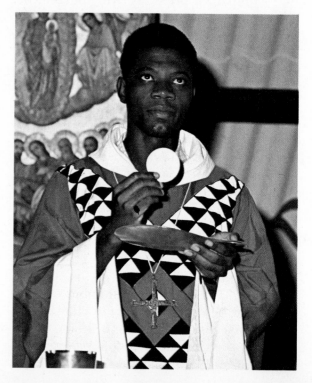

King Afonso sent slaves to the king of Portugal. No doubt Afonso thought of slavery in Europe in terms of the family slaves that were also found in Africa. It soon became clear, however, that the Portuguese wanted more and more slaves. The last years of Afonso's reign were years of sadness. He bitterly complained to the king of Portugal about merchants who made slaves of his people. The Portuguese, he said, attacked villages, kidnapped his subjects, and sent them to Portugal as slaves. Afonso pointed out to the Portuguese king that not only merchants and soldiers acted in that way but even some of the priests who had been sent as missionaries to the Congo.

One of Afonso's sons, Prince Henry, was sent to study in Portugal. Henry became a priest, and Pope Leo X made him a bishop. He returned to the Congo in 1518 and worked there until his death in 1535. Afonso I had hoped to use Bishop Henry as a means of building a Church in the Congo that would be African, and directly subject to Rome instead of to the king of Portugal. Bishop Henry's death ended that hope.

Afonso I died in 1543. Despite his bitter disappointments, he remained a faithful Catholic to the end. The faith survived in the Congo, but the Church did not do well. The memory of Afonso I, however, has lived to this day among the African people. Sadly, the Church remained a foreign influence because of its ties with Portugal. The work of Afonso I was defeated by the Portuguese slave-trading. Afonso was not able to plant the Catholic Church in African soil as an African institution with African roots. Such an "Africanization" of the Church would only begin in our own times.

Francis Xavier, Apostle of Asia In 1539, King John III of Portugal asked his ambassador to the papal court to get priests for his new

overseas lands in India and Southeast Asia. King John had heard of the new Society of Jesus. He hoped some Jesuits could go overseas for Portugal. Saint Ignatius Loyola promised the ambassador two priests and asked Francis Xavier to be one of them.

Francis Xavier was born in the small castle of Xavier in the northern part of Spain on April 7, 1506. His family belonged to the minor nobility of the area. In 1525, Francis Xavier went to Paris. He became a friend of Saint Ignatius when they were both students in the University of Paris. In 1534 Francis Xavier was one of the small group that, with Ignatius, began the Society of Jesus. Together with Saint Ignatius, Francis Xavier was made a priest in 1537. Francis acted as secretary for Saint Ignatius until, to his great joy, he was chosen to be a missionary.

Francis Xavier left Lisbon for India on April 7, 1541. It was his thirty-fifth birthday. He would never return to Europe. Two young Jesuit seminarians sailed with the two priests. The trip took over a year. They reached Goa in May 1542. Goa, Portugal's trading center in India, was already a diocese. During the ten short years of life that remained to him, Francis Xavier set out from Goa on missionary journeys that took him to the far reaches of Asia.

India, Sri Lanka, Japan After five months in Goa, Francis went to the south of India. With great difficulty he learned the language of the people who lived there. Francis Xavier always lived very simply among the people to whom he preached Jesus. He had great success and made many converts. Some days he baptized so many people that he could scarcely move his arm.

From southern India, Francis Xavier went to the island of Sri Lanka (srē läng′kə), then called Ceylon (sə län′). From there he went to Malaysia and to what is now the country of Indonesia. He ministered to Portuguese sailors and merchants, and preached the gospel to the peoples in all those lands.

Saint Francis Xavier always tried to learn the language of the people among whom he worked. He preached with great success and baptized thousands.

In 1549, Francis Xavier became the first Christian missionary to enter the country of Japan. He was accompanied by three Japanese converts. The group arrived in Kagoshima (käg′ə shē′mə), on the southernmost tip of the southern Japanese island of Kyushu (kē ü′shü). Francis set about learning Japanese. By the time he left Japan in 1551, there were almost 2,000 Japanese Christians. While he was in Japan, Francis Xavier heard much about the great Chinese Empire. He decided that he must try to work there. In 1551 he returned to Goa to prepare for a journey to China.

In April of 1552, Francis began his last missionary voyage. He left Goa with great enthusiasm because he expected, at long last, to make his way into China. He was not to get his wish. Xavier's ship anchored at the small island of Sancian, or Shang-chwan (shäng′chwän′), off the southeast coast of China. There he waited patiently for a boat to take him the last hundred miles to the great city of Canton. He was disappointed. China was closed to all foreigners. No one dared take him into the country. Then, on November 21, 1552, a fever seized Francis. Despite all medical help, Francis died on Sancian on December 3, 1552.

Francis's body was buried on the island. Two months later it was dug up to be sent back to Goa. When the coffin was opened, his body was found to be preserved. It is now in the Church of the Good Jesus in Goa. Francis Xavier was declared a saint in 1622. We keep his feast on December 3.

Saint Francis Xavier did not have time to set up well-organized local churches. He was a herald of the gospel, an "advance man" for later missionaries. He opened the way more by his strong and generous personality than by his good planning. Above all, Saint Francis Xavier knew how to draw

Mission work takes many forms. Catholic-school girls in Bangladesh are trained to teach poor people how to make salable articles out of jute.

people to Christ despite the barriers of language, custom, culture, and race. In 1927, Pope Pius XI declared Saint Francis Xavier one of the patrons of the Church's missions.

Recall and Reflect

1. How did King Afonso want to use his son, Prince Henry, in building up the Church in the Congo?

2. Name three places in Asia where Saint Francis Xavier did missionary work.

3. Why has Saint Francis Xavier been called a "herald of the gospel"?

4. Saint Francis Xavier attracted many people to Christ because of his strong and generous personality. What special qualities and gifts has God given you? How can you use them to attract people to Christ?

THE CHURCH IN THE AMERICAS

Spanish Missions The Portuguese carried out the work of the Church in Africa and Asia. Both the Spaniards and the Portuguese spread the faith among the Amerindians, or American Indians. Those peoples lived in the newly conquered lands of the West Indies and the Americas. But the problems facing the Church in the New World were much different from those it faced in Asia. The Portuguese in Asia had met civilizations and religions that were very old and strong. In the Americas, the Spanish and Portuguese missionaries met peoples whose cultures and religions were much different from European ways. In the Americas, to convert the Indians was also to teach them the ways of European culture.

Perhaps the greatest problem for missionaries in the New World came from the Spaniards. They came to the Americas to settle and to find wealth. Soon they needed many workers to raise crops on their large farms, or plantations, and to work newly found gold and silver mines. The Indians, a ready source of cheap labor, were divided among the Spanish landowners as slaves. In return, the landowners were to teach the Indians the Catholic faith and protect them. The Indians were not used to working in that way. Many did not live long under such treatment. Some Spanish slave owners treated the Indians with great cruelty. There were many fights about the Indians between the settlers and the missionaries.

Spanish missionaries established the Church very quickly in the West Indies and in Mexico and South America. On his second trip, in 1493, Columbus had brought twelve Franciscans to work among the settlers and to convert the Indians. As early as

1512 there were dioceses in San Domingo (now Santo Domingo, the capital of the Dominican Republic) and in San Juan, Puerto Rico. By 1582 there were fifteen bishoprics in the Americas. Convents and schools were built in all the Spanish colonies. In 1544 the first university in America was set up in Mexico City, Mexico. By the year 1600 there were also universities in Lima, Peru, in Bogota, Colombia, and in San Domingo.

Defender of the Indians As the Church worked among the Indians, many missionaries continued to speak out against the cruel treatment of the Indians. One who protested was a Dominican friar named Bartolomé de las Casas (bär′tō lō mā′ də läs kä′säs).

Bartolomé was born in Seville, Spain, in 1474. His father and his three uncles had sailed with Columbus on his second voyage. In 1502, Bartolomé de las Casas also sailed to the New World. Bartolomé was already a member of the clergy when he left Spain. But he was not yet a priest. In 1512 he became the first priest to be ordained in the Americas.

Bartolomé became a landowner in what is now the country of Cuba. Like other settlers, Las Casas farmed his land in Cuba using Indian slaves. He treated them kindly, but at first he thought very little about their plight.

Dominican friars who were missionaries in the Spanish settlements began to preach against making slaves of the Indians. By 1514, Las Casas also had become convinced that enslaving Indians was morally wrong. Bartolomé de las Casas made up his mind to work on behalf of the Indians for the rest of his life. He gave up his possessions in the Americas, joined the Dominican order, and returned to Spain.

Bartolomé de las Casas crossed the ocean fourteen times to help the Indians. In 1517 the Spanish king gave him the title "Defender of the Indians."

For the next thirty-six years Las Casas went back and forth between the royal government in Spain and the colonies in the New World. He planned, he pleaded, he wrote, and he preached on behalf of the Indians and against the injustice and cruelties done to them. Bartolomé was hated by many colonists, but he did make an impression on the Spanish government. In 1542, new laws were passed that made the Indians and the Spanish settlers equal before the law. Yet many of the rights Las Casas won for the Indians were ignored by some Spanish governors and colonists in the New World. Far from central government control, they continued to rob, kill, and make slaves of Indians.

In 1543, Bartolomé de las Casas was made the bishop of Chiapas, in what is now the country of Mexico. As bishop, Las

Casas ordered all confessors to refuse absolution to those colonists who would not free their Indian slaves. There was a great outcry, and Las Casas had to resign his diocese. He returned to Spain in 1551.

Las Casas spent the rest of his life writing books that defended the Indians. In Spain he publicly debated those theologians who agreed with the practice of making slaves of the Indians. Bartolomé de las Casas died in 1566 at the age of ninety-two.

The missionary expansion of the Church was part of the overseas expansion of Europe in the 1500s. The life of Bartolomé de las Casas is one example of how the Church taught the faith and tried to work for social justice and human rights. Bartolomé de las Casas was not alone in that fight for human dignity. Many other missionary bishops and priests raised their voices on behalf of the defenseless.

Black Slaves in America Bartolomé de las Casas has often been criticized as one of those who urged that African slaves be used in the Spanish colonies in place of Indian slaves. The blacks were more likely to survive because they had already been exposed to diseases carried by the Europeans. Many of the Indian tribes in the West Indies and Central America died out chiefly because they had no immunity to European diseases. Bartolomé de las Casas said openly that he had given such advice in 1516 and in 1518. But in later years he bitterly regretted what he had done. He had learned about Portuguese cruelty and injustice in capturing African slaves. He had also seen the cruel results of slavery as a system in the colonies.

Spanish colonists, in fact, had begun buying African slaves from the Portuguese as early as 1501. By the middle of the 1500s, blacks were being brought to both Spanish

SIDELIGHTS ON CHURCH HISTORY
A Black Saint

Martin de Porres (də pôr′ez) was born in 1579 in the city of Lima, today the capital of Peru. He was the son of Anna Velasquez (vā läs′kāth), a free black woman who had once been a slave, and John de Porres, a Spanish noble who served for a time in the colonial government.

As a boy, Martin was trained in nursing and pharmacy. When he grew older, Martin wished to give his life to God. At that time, the laws of the Spanish government would not permit anyone who was black or Indian or even a mixture of white and black or Indian to enter the religious life or to become a priest. Martin therefore asked to become a lay helper in the Dominican monastery of Lima. He worked there for nine years in this way before he was finally permitted to take vows as a Dominican lay brother.

Martin was a Dominican brother for forty years. He served his fellow monks as infirmarian, or nurse. But Martin also became an apostle of charity to all the poor and the suffering in sixteenth-century Lima. In that colonial society that placed so much importance on color, culture, and class, Martin de Porres organized charitable aid for the poor and the outcast. He gave food and shelter to black slaves, poor Indians, and Spaniards. He established an orphanage and set up a hospital for abandoned babies, the first of its kind in the New World. Martin's nights were spent in doing penance, and in long periods of prayer. Martin de Porres lived that kind of life until his death in 1639. He was declared a saint in 1962. His feast day is November 3.

A sixteenth-century Spanish friar baptizes a Mexican Indian. Missionaries became champions of the Indians' human rights.

and Portuguese colonies in the Americas in ever growing numbers. They were made to work on the great plantations and in the mines. Soon most of the slaves in Latin America would be black.

Missionary Activities As we have seen, missionaries who carried the Church to the Indian peoples in the Americas often found it necessary to defend the native peoples from cruel exploitation by European settlers and colonial governments. The missionaries were not always successful. And it is understandable that many who lived in those lands did not accept a Christianity that seemed so far from Christ. Still, in the 1600s and later on, there were Spanish and Portuguese missionaries who did wonderful work on behalf of African slaves and Indian tribes.

During the sixteenth century, the Church had not been able to work directly in the overseas mission fields. The mission Churches were under the complete control of Portugal and Spain. By the seventeenth century, however, that control had weakened. In 1622 the Church took over the direction of its missionary activity all over the world. In Rome a special department was set up. It was known as the **Congregation for the Propagation of the Faith**. (The verb *to propagate* means "to spread.") All mission work was put under papal control. It could now be separated from national interests.

Even so, the Church was not able to free the work of the missions from all interference by the European nation-states—especially in Portuguese and Spanish colonies. It was also hard to keep some missionaries from thinking too much about their own countries. They did not understand how harmful that could be to those they hoped to serve. That European outlook on the part of some missionaries would be damaging for the Church later on, when colonialism came to an end.

Recall and Reflect

1. Why were the Spaniards the greatest problem for the missionaries in America?

2. How did Bartolomé de las Casas try to help the Indians?

3. Why were black slaves brought to the Americas?

4. What was the purpose of the Congregation for the Propagation of the Faith?

5. Many missionaries have worked and continue to work among people who are treated unfairly and with great cruelty by others. Do you know of people in your school or in your local community who are being treated unfairly? How could you help to bring about fair treatment?

REVIEW AND CELEBRATE

Doctrinal Summary

By its very nature, the Church must be missionary. As the Second Vatican Council states, the "work of evangelization is the basic duty of the People of God." All members of the Church participate in some way in this missionary activity of the Church. Often this is simply the witness of one's own life, a life faithful to Jesus.

Religious Vocabulary

Congregation for the Propagation of the Faith

Review Questions

Answer the following questions on a separate sheet of paper.

1. How did the Portuguese and the Spanish peoples contribute to the spread of Christianity in the fifteenth and sixteenth centuries?

2. What was the most important accomplishment of Saint Francis Xavier to the missionary work of the Church in Asia?

3. How did the problems of the missionary Church in the New World differ from those it faced in Africa and Asia?

4. How did Las Casas and the other missionaries help to advance social justice and human rights?

5. What caused the most suffering and hardship for the inhabitants of mission lands in the 1500s? What did the Church in Rome do about it in 1622?

Prayer Celebration

Leader: Lord God, Father of all peoples, You have created Your Church with care and charged it with a purpose—a mission. You have given us Your word that we might speak it to all people. Let us listen to a reading from Saint Luke's gospel, Chapter 9, verses 1 to 9.

Reader: "Jesus now called the Twelve together and gave them power and authority to overcome all demons and to cure diseases. He sent them forth to proclaim the reign of God and heal the afflicted. Jesus advised them: 'Take nothing for the journey, neither walking staff nor traveling bag; no bread, no money. No one is to have two coats. Stay at whatever house you enter and proceed from there. When people will not receive you, leave that town and shake its dust from your feet as a testimony against them.' So they set out and went from village to village, spreading the good news everywhere and curing diseases."

Leader: Father, You sent Your Son to sow the seed of the word.

All: Enable us also to spread Your word. Amen.

UNIT FOUR SUMMARY

In this unit we have seen how the Church through its renewal met the challenges of the Renaissance and Reformation. We have also learned how the Church in the 1500s had its greatest growth since the early Middle Ages. The faith was carried to Asia, Africa, and the Americas.

In 1517, Martin Luther, a German monk, attacked the Church's teaching about indulgences. The granting of indulgences was often used by the Church as a means of raising money. Luther attacked not only that grave abuse but the Church's teaching as well.

The Reformation was carried to England by Henry VIII and the English government. By the time Queen Elizabeth I died in 1603, the Anglican Church was firmly established in England. As the map on page 193 shows, in the 1600s Western Christendom was no longer of one faith.

A great Counter, or Catholic, Reformation began in the 1500s. The Church was filled with new life and vigor. In 1540, Pope Paul III approved the Society of Jesus, founded by Saint Ignatius Loyola. Pope Paul also called the Council of Trent (1545–1563). Trent clearly stated Catholic beliefs and traditions. It also reformed Church discipline and practice. So well did Trent do its work that it shaped the history of the Church for the next four hundred years.

Revitalized by Trent and by the work of the Jesuits and other new religious orders, the Church created a new culture in Europe—the Baroque. It also began a great expansion. Portugal and Spain carried the faith to all parts of the world.

But those new missions also gave the Church many problems. The Europeans made slaves of blacks and Indians and treated them cruelly. Missionaries like Bartolomé de las Casas had to work hard to defend their converts. In 1622, Rome set up the Congregation for the Propagation of the Faith. Gradually that group was able to get control of all the Church's missions. In Unit Five we shall learn how the Church faced up to the challenges of revolutionary change.

1400s	Renaissance scholars criticize the Church: Portuguese and Spaniards spread the faith in Africa, Asia, and the Americas
1453	Constantinople falls to the Turks
1455	Gutenberg's printed Bible
1491	Nzinga, king of Congo, converted
1517	Luther attacks doctrine of Indulgences
1521	Diet of Worms: Luther breaks with Church
1536	John Calvin begins Reformed Church in Geneva
1540	Pope Paul III approves the Society of Jesus
1545	Council of Trent begins
1549	Saint Francis Xavier in Japan
1556	Deaths of Saint Ignatius Loyola and Bartolomé de las Casas
1559–1560	Final edition of John Calvin's *Institutes of the Christian Religion*
1584	Death of Saint Charles Borromeo
1603	Death of Queen Elizabeth I: Anglican Church firmly established in England
1622	Congregation for the Propagation of the Faith set up in Rome
1648	Treaty of Westphalia ends Thirty Years' War: Last of religious wars in Europe

UNIT FIVE

The Church—Meeting New Challenges

By 1792 leaders of the French Revolution began to view the Church as an enemy. Mobs assaulted Paris's Notre Dame, a symbol of the Church.

15

The Church and Revolution

The term *revolution* can mean the movement or the revolving of one thing around another. We say that a wheel makes a revolution around its axis, or that in one year our earth makes one revolution around the sun. In history the term *revolution* can have many other meanings. It can mean the overturning of a government. And it can mean a social or economic movement that turns around the whole life-style of a people. Very often the changes that take place in a revolution are done violently.

Such violent changes affect society much as an earthquake affects the earth. After the main shock there are many spreading aftershocks. In an earthquake, many houses and buildings fall to the ground. Many of the houses are brought down because they are old or in need of repair. Something like that happens in a revolution when many political and social institutions within a society are also destroyed by it.

The French Revolution (1789–1799) was like an earthquake in world history. Not only did it overturn the kings of France, but it changed the whole of French society. It also brought down many institutions, including some within the Church, that dated back to the early Middle Ages. In fact, the French Revolution of 1789 changed all of European society. The Revolution affected ideas, human values, even the worlds of art and science.

Following the shock of the Revolution of 1789 came the aftershocks of other revolutions in other countries throughout the nineteenth century and up to our own day. Since the French Revolution, the Church has had to adapt to a world that is new and strange. That world is the one we live in today. It was born out of blood and suffering, and it began in France in 1789.

In this unit we will see how the Church has met its new challenges and adapted to our present-day world. In this chapter we will learn how the French Revolution affected the Church and how, with difficulty, the Church began to come to terms with our contemporary age. In one way, the French Revolution of 1789–1799 was not settled finally until the Second Vatican Council began to meet in 1962.

BACKGROUND OF THE FRENCH REVOLUTION

The Church and the Old Regime The system of government that was destroyed by the French Revolution is often called the old regime (ri zhēm′). The word *regime* comes from a Latin word that means "rule" or "government." In the 1700s the term meant much more than the government of France. The old regime meant the kind of society that existed until 1789—not only in France but in all the countries of Europe. The old regime was a culture and society dominated by privileged classes. People of those classes had special rights before the law.

In the 1700s the social classes in France were called estates. Society was divided into three estates. The clergy of the Church made up the first estate. Nobles were the second. The largest class of all, the third estate, was made up of all the people in France who were neither clergy nor nobility. Peasant farmers were members of the third estate. So were the middle classes, the townspeople or bourgeoisie, whose beginings we learned about in Chapter 10. If we were to draw a diagram of French society before 1789, it would look like a triangle. At the top was the king, who believed he ruled by the will of God. Below the king were the privileged classes of clergy and nobility. Below them were the common people, or the third estate.

The Catholic Church had a special place in the old regime. In the 1700s most of the bishops in France were members of the nobility. They were all named by the king. There was a large gap between ordinary priests and their bishops. In France many bishops did not live in their dioceses. Many lived at the royal court of Versailles (vər sī′), just outside of Paris. Such bishops could not know the problems of their people or their priests. Many monastic communities of men and women in France were open only to members of the nobility. In many ways the Church of the old regime was divided like society itself, along the lines of social classes. Such a state of affairs could only bring disaster if the old regime was destroyed. That disaster happened in the French Revolution of 1789.

The Enlightenment Ideas are like smoke. It is almost impossible to keep smoke fumes from getting into even a locked room. Nor can ideas be kept from reaching all groups of a society. The eighteenth century has been called the Age of Enlightenment. It was a time when people in Europe were strongly influenced by new ideas in scientific thought. In 1687 a scientist in England, Sir Isaac Newton, was able to explain all movements—both in the heavens and on earth—through his three laws of motion, or gravity. Other scientists made new discoveries in the heavens with the aid of new telescopes, and there were many new advances in mathematics. As people began to learn the secrets of the universe, they began to question all accepted ideas.

Those scientific discoveries had two main results. One was that many things once thought to be mysterious works of God were found to have reasonable explanations. The other result was that people saw the value of learning by the careful sifting of facts discovered through observation. All of this gave many people great confidence in human reasoning and in natural science. It also made people want to observe and test things around them by critical observation. They did not want to accept things on faith or on someone else's word.

Some people began to look at all religious truths in the same way. Can there be some explanation, other than the will of God, for things happening as they do? If there is, can it not be changed or controlled? If that is so, can it be simply God's will? Ought we not to question everything? Can we not demand proof? Such ideas caused doubts among educated people. The new ideas seemed to call religion into question.

Many people felt that reason could, with time, explain all mysteries. They believed it could solve all problems and lead to greater progress. That is why the 1700s have become known as the Age of Enlightenment.

Scientists, like those below using a quadrant and a telescope to observe the heavens, greatly influenced thought in the Age of the Enlightenment.

Many men and women of the Enlightenment in Catholic countries saw the Church as standing only for faith instead of faith and reason. For such people the Church stood for backwardness instead of progress. Educated people often made fun of the practices of the Church. They felt, however, that religion was necessary to keep poor, uneducated people happy.

Educated members of the clergy often shared the ideas of the Enlightenment. They often lacked strong religious beliefs. That lack of leadership seriously affected the Church throughout the 1700s.

Enlightened Rulers As we learned in Chapter 11, by the end of the Middle Ages, kings in many European countries had become very powerful. As kings became stronger, their kingdoms became more like the nation-states of today. After the Renaissance, the kings tended to become even more powerful. The European nation-states began to play a more important role in the lives of individual citizens.

It was felt that kings, as heads of governments and as enlightened rulers, often had to act for reasons of state. That meant they worked for what they thought was the good of the whole country. Catholic kings and princes felt that reasons of state could sometimes allow them to act against the wishes of the pope. They felt that their own bishops and clergy should always work for the good of the country. Catholic kings sometimes refused to allow papal laws or letters to be published in their countries.

Suppression of the Jesuits Catholic kings and princes and their governments tried to control not only the relationship between Rome and the local churches but also the activities of the religious orders in their kingdoms. In 1773, for example, great pressure from the kings of Spain, France, and other Catholic countries led Pope Clement XIV (1769–1774) to suppress the Jesuits. To *suppress* means "to end or do away with."

By the beginning of the 1700s, the Society of Jesus had become very unpopular in many Catholic countries. The Jesuits supported the popes and fought against royal power in the Church. False stories were spread about Jesuit wealth and power. Many diocesan clergy did not like Jesuit influence in all parts of society. Some Jesuits made mistakes in handling their business affairs. That caused them to be investigated in France. For good and bad reasons, the Jesuits were feared and often hated. Theological controversies in the 1600s and 1700s also led important groups of Catholics to oppose the Jesuits.

Many Catholic countries drove the Jesuits out. In 1759, Portugal expelled all Jesuits from its territories everywhere. Over a thousand Portuguese Jesuits were put aboard boats and taken to the Papal States as refugees. In 1764, France declared the Jesuits to be illegal both in France and in its colonies. In 1767, Spain expelled all Jesuits from Spain and all its colonies. More than five thousand Spanish Jesuits were taken to the Papal States.

When Pope Clement XIV suppressed the Jesuits, he said he was doing so for the peace of the Church. The pressure under which the pope acted was a clear sign that the Church was at the mercy of the Catholic governments in the 1700s.

Suppression of other Orders Some of the monks and nuns in the time of the Enlightenment were not very holy. In many monasteries, the huge buildings housed only a few monks. Most monasteries were rich and had much land. For many thinkers in the 1700s, religious orders seemed useless.

The above engraving shows Pope Clement XIV announcing the suppression of the Society of Jesus to the Spanish ambassador in Rome in 1773.

In 1766 the government in France set up a commission, or group, to regulate religious life there. Many orders besides the Jesuits were suppressed by that group. In many cases the decisions were perhaps right. But it was the state that was making the decisions and setting the rules, not the Church.

The same thing happened in other parts of Europe. Emperor Joseph II of Austria suppressed all monasteries of men and women that did not teach or did not care for the sick or aged. He also closed diocesan seminaries and made all students for the priesthood study in special seminaries set up by the state. Joseph II considered himself a good Catholic. But he felt that he knew what was best for the Church in the Austrian Empire. Because he was even concerned with little details, such as the number of candles that should be on the altar,

Joseph II was called the "sacristan-emperor." A sacristan is a person who is in charge of the altar. A sacristy is a room or place where Church vestments, chalices, and other ornaments are kept.

Recall and Reflect

1. How was French society divided before the French Revolution?

2. What was the place of the Church in the old regime?

3. What effect did the new ideas in scientific thought have on the way people viewed religious truths?

4. Why were the Jesuits so unpopular in Europe in the 1700s?

5. Sometimes when people discover the wonderful things that they are able to do, they decide that they do not need God anymore. What do you think about that attitude? What part, do you think, does God play in our accomplishments?

THE FRENCH REVOLUTION AND ITS AFTERMATH

The Financial Crisis, 1788–1789 During the course of the 1700s, the government of France under the old regime became more and more unworkable. Taxation was unfair. Neither the nobles nor the clergy paid their fair share. Taxes fell heaviest on the middle class and peasants. Although French society was prosperous, by 1788 a number of money crises had brought the royal government of France to the point of bankruptcy. As a last resort, the government called for a meeting of the Estates-General, a kind of parliament, or legislative body. The Estates-General had not met since 1614.

When the Estates-General was called together in 1789 to deal with the money situation, the French people, particularly the middle class, took affairs into their own hands. The Estates-General was made up of three groups or bodies: the clergy, the nobility, and the representatives of the third estate.

Historically, all three groups had always met and voted separately. In 1789, however, power was seized by the third estate because many priests in the first estate voted with the third estate to have all three groups meet together. In a very real sense, the lower clergy and the third estate made the French Revolution possible. It was that combined group which became the National Constituent Assembly in the month of June 1789. In time that body would become the new revolutionary government of France.

When the Estates-General met in 1789, members of the clergy were present. There was little evidence of a desire to destroy Catholicism.

French Church Reorganized On August 4, 1789, the nobles and clergy, now a part of the new National Assembly, voted to give up all their special rights and privileges. All citizens were now to be equal before the law. In November 1789, in order to take care of the government's money problems, all the property of the Church was declared to belong to the nation. The state took over the support of the clergy.

In 1790, religious orders in France were suppressed by the Revolution. Only orders of nurses or teachers were allowed to continue. In July 1790, the number of dioceses in France was cut from 134 to 83. Diocesan boundaries were now the same as those of the 83 departments, or states, into which France was now divided. All bishops were to be publicly elected, just like the representatives to the National Assembly. Parish priests were also to be elected by the people. All the clergy had to take an oath. They had to promise to support the new **Civil Constitution of the Clergy** that had been passed by the Assembly. The oath that was required of the clergy was simply to make sure that bishops and priests would be loyal to the Revolution.

King Louis XVI was at the head of the government in 1790. However, he now shared power with the National Constituent Assembly. Though Louis XVI was not very bright, he was a sincere person. He was pious and he loved the Church. Louis XVI asked the pope what should be done about the new Civil Constitution of the Clergy. The pope was Pius VI (1775–1799), who had one of the longest reigns in the eighteenth century. Of noble birth, Pius really did not understand the deep changes that were taking place in France. What is more, Pius was not a strong leader. He could not decide what to do. He finally condemned the Civil Constitution of the Clergy, but he took five months to make up his mind. By that time, Louis XVI had signed the Constitution into law.

There was great confusion in France. The clergy had to decide for themselves about taking the oath. Many of the bishops joined many of the nobles in leaving the country. Four bishops and almost thirty thousand priests took the oath. About twice that number, as well as the rest of the bishops, refused to take the oath. Some priests who took the oath rejected it after Pius VI finally condemned the Civil Constitution. The revolutionary government now began to persecute all French clergy who refused to take the oath.

The Civil Constitution of the Clergy marked the beginning of the split between the Revolution and the Church. The Church in France was soon divided between those who upheld the Civil Constitution and those who followed the pope. New bishops were ordained for the Constitutional Church. All parish churches and cathedrals were placed in their hands. But most of the people in the countryside supported only those clergy who refused to take the oath.

Persecution in France In 1792 the government in France, now called the National Convention, became much more radical. Louis XVI and his family were put in prison. France was declared a republic. In January 1793, Louis XVI would be put to death.

War broke out between France and the other countries of Europe. The war created fear in France. That fear caused a hatred of all who were thought to be traitors to France and thus supporters of the enemy. The clergy who would not take the oath to uphold the Civil Constitution were called traitors.

Carmelite Martyrs of Compiègne

On July 17, 1794, sixteen Carmelite nuns were taken to a public square in Paris. The oldest nun was seventy-eight; the youngest, in her late twenties. One by one they climbed a platform in the center of the square. They were beheaded by the falling blade of the guillotine (gil′ə tēn′).

The sixteen nuns belonged to the Carmelite Order, a religious order in which nuns devote their lives entirely to prayer and penance. Their convent was in the town of Compiègne, about sixty miles (96 km) north of Paris. In 1790 the French Revolution suppressed all religious orders that did not engage in teaching or nursing. The Carmelite convent of Compiègne was closed. The nuns continued their religious way of life in hiding. After two years the revolutionary authorities discovered them. They were taken to Paris and put in prison with other priests, nuns, and laypeople who had already been condemned to death.

The sixteen Carmelite nuns were also sentenced to death. There was no evidence to prove that the nuns were "enemies of the French people," but the judge accused them of being "fanatics." One of the nuns asked him what he meant by the word. "I mean by it," he replied, "your attachment to childish beliefs and your silly religious practices." The nun turned to her sisters and said, "You see! We are condemned for clinging to our holy religion. We have the happiness to die for God."

The nuns were beatified by Pope Pius X on May 13, 1906. Their beatification was the first official declaration by the Church that there had been true martyrs for Christ among the many victims of the French Revolution. The feast day of the Martyrs of Compiègne is July 17.

At first such clergy were sent into exile. Several thousand went to England. But the situation became worse. Political leaders who hated all religion began making speeches that stirred up the people. In September 1792, a raging mob broke into the prisons of Paris where many priests and some bishops were being held. They were all asked to take the oath to support the Civil Constitution. When they refused, they were killed. The Church looks upon all those clergy as true martyrs for their faith. In 1929, those September Martyrs, as they are called, were declared **blessed** (bles′id) by the Church. **Beatification** (bē at′ə fə cā′shən) is the act by which the Church declares a person to be blessed—that is, to have been truly holy or to have suffered true martyrdom for the faith. There were 191 martyrs in that group. At the same time, other members of the clergy were killed in other parts of France.

The September massacres marked the beginning of government violence in France. The next two years (1793–1795) have been called the Reign of Terror. Many people were put to death for their faith. The French Revolution became more and more anti-Christian. Even the Constitutional Church was persecuted. In 1793, non-Christian forms of worship were introduced by the government. A new calendar was adopted in which weeks had ten days. Sundays were no longer kept as holidays. The year 1792 became the year one of the Revolution.

The Revolution Spreads Even though they suffered, most people in France remained Catholics. Many priests secretly continued to say Mass and give people the sacraments. In 1795 still another revolutionary government, known as the Directory, came to power. The bloody persecution of the

Reign of Terror was stopped. By 1795, France had also defeated the armies of Austria, Prussia, and other European countries. Now the French were able to take the offensive. The Revolution spread to Holland, Belgium, the Rhineland in Germany, Switzerland, and Italy. In many of those places the Church began to be attacked. Religious orders were suppressed, and Church property was taken away.

One of the leading French generals was a military genius named Napoleon Bonaparte. By 1797, Napoleon had conquered northern Italy for France. An agreement was worked out with Pope Pius VI. Napoleon's brother was made France's ambassador to the Papal States. But a riot broke out in Rome and a French general was killed. The French army then seized the city. On February 15, 1798, Pope Pius was deposed and the Papal States became the Roman Republic.

Pope Pius VI was now eighty years old and in very bad health. He was made a prisoner by the French. The pope was moved from place to place—finally to the small city of Valence (va läns´) in southeastern France. Pius VI died there on August 29, 1799.

Recovery of the Church Many Europeans thought that Pius VI would be the last pope. Everything seemed to indicate that the last days of the papacy had come. Napoleon, who had fought a series of battles against the British in Egypt, stopped in Valence on his way back to Paris. He learned how Pius VI had been mistreated, and he promised to let the pope's followers leave France. Back in Paris, Napoleon seized control of the French government. He called himself first consul. And in 1804 he would declare himself to be the emperor of the French people. Napoleon

announced that the French Revolution was over.

Pope Pius VII, the pope who followed Pius VI, was chosen in the city of Venice in northern Italy. Thirty-five of the forty-six cardinals met in Venice on December 8, 1799. They finally elected Cardinal Barnaba Chiaramonti (kyä´rä môn´tē) on March 14, 1800. He took the name Pius VII to show his respect for the exiled pope he followed.

A quiet, gentle man, Pius VII was pope from 1800 to 1823. Until the defeat of Napoleon by the other European countries in 1814, Pius VII had a difficult time. In 1800, Napoleon had let it be known that he wanted to settle all religious problems in France. Pope Pius sent his secretary of

Pope Pius VII has been called the "pope of the new age." He tried to find ways the Church could work with the new society born of the French Revolution.

217

state, Cardinal Consalvi, to Paris. In 1801, Cardinal Consalvi was able to work out an agreement that let the Church work in France. Such a public treaty, or agreement, between the Church and a national government is called a **concordat** (kon kôr′dat).

The **Concordat of 1801** governed relations between the Church and France until the year 1905. In it the Catholic Church was said to be the religion of the majority of the French people. The Church in France was to have freedom of action and worship. The number of dioceses was to be reduced to sixty. Napoleon was to have the right to name all bishops. But the pope was to approve and appoint them. All clergy were to take oaths to obey the government. The Concordat of 1801 was an example of Pope Pius VII's sincere efforts to help the Church come to terms with the new society born of the French Revolution.

Napoleon soon violated some of the terms of the Concordat. Pope Pius VII protested, and relations between the papacy and the French government became difficult. In 1809, French troops occupied Rome. For the next five years the pope was kept a prisoner in France. After Napoleon's defeat in 1814, Pius VII was able to return to Rome. Napoleon was exiled to the island of St. Helena in the South Atlantic. He died there in 1821. Pius VII showed much kindness to the former emperor and gave help to members of his family who found safety in the Papal States.

Pius VII also restored the Jesuits in 1814. He tried to improve government in the Papal States and to establish better relations with the governments of European countries. New religious orders were founded, and the older religious orders were revived. New centers of Catholic learning were set up. A new spirit of devotion and piety appeared in the Church.

The program of re-Christianization begun by Pius VII was continued by the popes who followed him. But some of the popes were much more cautious. They were less willing than Pius VII to adapt to the new conditions brought about by the Revolution of 1789.

Pope Pius IX Revolutions continued in Europe during the 1800s. In 1848 a revolution broke out in the Papal States. Pope Pius IX (1846–1878) had been pope for two years. He had to flee Rome and could only return in 1850 with the help of French soldiers. That experience turned the pope into a very conservative ruler.

Pope Pius IX was pope for thirty-one years. His papacy was the longest in history. During his long **pontificate,** or reign, Pius IX had to face many problems. As

The papacy lost political power while Pius IX was pope. But people looked to Pius IX and the popes who came after him as world spiritual leaders.

pope, Pius was also the ruler of the Papal States. In all the parts of Italy, including the Papal States, there was a desire on the part of the Italian people to unite into one country. By 1860 almost all of Italy had actually been united under King Victor Emmanuel II, of Piedmont in northern Italy. Even part of the Papal States had become part of the new Italian nation.

The only obstacles to completely uniting the country were the remaining Papal States and Pope Pius IX as a temporal ruler. In 1870 war broke out between Prussia and France. The French soldiers who had been kept in Rome to protect the pope were called back to France. Soldiers of Victor Emmanuel II then entered Rome, which became the capital of the united Italy.

Pius IX protested the loss of the Papal States. He refused all offers from the government of Italy for a financial settlement. He declared himself a "prisoner of the Vatican." From 1870 until 1929 all the popes would think of themselves as "prisoners." It was only in 1929 that a concordat was signed between Pope Pius XI (1922–1939) and the government of Italy. By that agreement the pope was recognized as the independent ruler of Vatican City in Rome.

Under Pope Pius IX the papacy lost nearly all of its political power. On the other hand, people began to look to Pius IX and the popes who came after him as spiritual leaders. The popes were able to speak to the whole world with great moral authority.

First Vatican Council Pius IX carried out two major accomplishments. Both have affected Catholic theology and practice in modern times. He proclaimed the **dogma** of the **Immaculate Conception,** and he called the **First Vatican Council.**

In 1854, Pius IX solemnly declared the Immaculate Conception to be a dogma of

WORDS TO LIVE BY

Young persons exert very important influence in modern society. . . . As the awareness of their own personality matures . . . they assume their own responsibility, and wish to play their part in social and cultural life. If this zeal is [filled] with the spirit of Christ, . . . it can be expected to be very fruitful.

VATICAN COUNCIL II, *DECREE ON THE APOSTOLATE OF THE LAITY,* 12

the Church—that is, something to be firmly believed by all Catholics. The doctrine states that the Mother of God was free from original sin from the moment of her conception. That was true because of the merits of her Son, who was to save everyone by His death and resurrection.

In 1869, Pius IX opened the twentieth ecumenical council in the Church's history and the first one since the Council of Trent. The council is known as the First Vatican Council. It lasted less than a year, closing before all of its work was finished. In 1870 the withdrawal of the French troops from Rome and the arrival of the Italian troops forced the council to suspend its meetings. Before it stopped, however, the council defined the dogma, or teaching, of **papal infallibility.** Papal infallibility means that when the pope speaks in Christ's name he is kept from all error in matters of faith and morality. The pope is infallible whenever he speaks, intending to use the full authority of his office. The teaching of infallibility reminded the modern world that the pope as head of the Church has a power greater than any earthly power. His authority is to teach and to reconcile as Christ's representative on earth.

Forty-eight archbishops and bishops and one abbot from the United States were among the 700 delegates at the opening of the First Vatican Council.

Pope Pius IX died in 1878 at the age of eighty-six. In many ways the Church was far stronger and more spiritual than it had been at the end of the eighteenth century. The French Revolution and the many trials of the nineteenth century purified the Church in a remarkable way. The loss of the Papal States actually made Pius IX freer and more independent than popes had been before the Revolution. Pius IX took a tough stand against many modern ways of thought. Today we would call him a very conservative thinker. In Chapter 16 we shall learn how the popes who came after Pope Pius IX used modern thought to face new problems. Popes in the twentieth century have never hesitated to employ science to teach the truths of faith.

Recall and Reflect

1. What did the Civil Constitution of the Clergy demand of the French clergy?

2. Why did the French Revolution begin to persecute the Church?

3. Why was the Concordat of 1801 important in the history of the French Church?

4. Name two major accomplishments of Pope Pius IX.

5. The years of the French Revolution were difficult and painful for the Church. Even so, the Church survived and was even stronger spiritually in Europe after the Revolution than it had been before. Can you think of a time in your life that was particularly difficult for you? Tell something about it. What do we learn from such an experience?

REVIEW AND CELEBRATE

Doctrinal Summary

The Catholic Church proclaims the truth that all people
have rights. Pope John XXIII reminds us in his encyclical
Peace on Earth (1963): ". . . Every human being is a person,
. . . with intelligence and free will. . . . [Every human being]
has rights and duties. . . ." One of those duties is to respect
such rights in others.

Religious Vocabulary

Civil Constitution of the Clergy	Concordat of 1801	First Vatican Council
Blessed	pontificate	papal infallibility
Beatification	dogma	
concordat	Immaculate Conception	

Review Questions

Answer the following questions on a separate sheet of paper.

1. Why are the 1700s called the Age of Enlightenment? According to men and women of
   the Enlightenment, what were the purposes of religion?

2. Why did Catholic kings put pressure on the pope to suppress the Jesuits?

3. Briefly describe the split in the French Church caused by the Civil Constitution of the Clergy.

4. List three things Pope Pius VII did to help the Church recover from the French Revolution.

5. What was accomplished at the First Vatican Council?

Prayer Celebration

Leader: Mary, you are our Mother and the
Mother of the Church. We pray with you in
the words of your Magnificat (Luke 1:46–55).
All: "My being proclaims the greatness of
    the Lord,
    my spirit finds joy in God my savior,
  For he has looked upon his servant in
    her lowliness;
    all ages to come shall call me
    blessed.
  God who is mighty has done great
    things for me,
    holy is his name;
  His mercy is from age to age
    on those who fear him.

He has shown might with his arm;
  he has confused the proud in their
    inmost thoughts.
He has deposed the mighty from their
    thrones
  and raised the lowly to high places.
The hungry he has given every good
    thing,
  while the rich he has sent empty
    away.
He has upheld Israel his servant,
  ever mindful of his mercy;
Even as he promised our fathers,
  promised Abraham and his
    descendants forever." Amen.

Vatican Council II has helped the Church respond to the problems of our times. Over 2,540 people were at the opening session, October 11, 1962.

16

The Church in Recent Times

The past one hundred years have been breathtaking in the history of the world and in the history of the Church. It has been a century of rapid changes. It has been a time of giant advances in science and technology. These years have seen great social and political upheavals. The changes have led people to look at traditional values in new and fresh ways.

The Church, the People of God, has also changed. The Catholic Church is a teacher. It must change and adapt so that it can teach the timeless truths of our faith in a way that all peoples can understand. That has always been the challenge for the Church. In the past hundred years the challenge has been especially difficult. All the areas of human life have presented and continue to present new questions for the Church to answer and new problems to which the Church must respond.

In this chapter we shall look at some of the major challenges the Church has had to face in the past one hundred years. And we shall see how the Church has responded and continues to respond to the crises of our modern world.

THE CHURCH IN THE INDUSTRIAL SOCIETY

The Church and the Factory Workers When Pope Pius IX died in 1878, Cardinal Gioacchino Pecci (jō′ä kē′nō pet′chē), a man of sixty-eight, was chosen pope. He took the name Leo XIII (1878–1903). In many ways Leo XIII was different from Pius IX. He was more willing to listen to people with new ideas and more ready to adapt the Church to the changes that were taking place in the world. Leo XIII would be pope for twenty-five years. During his long pontificate, or reign, Leo XIII wrote many important **encyclicals** (en sik′lə kəlz), or papal letters. In those letters he explained the Church's teaching on many questions. An encyclical is a pastoral letter written by the pope for the whole Church. It is called a pastoral letter because in it the pope, as pastor of the whole Church, deals with Catholic beliefs and practices.

Perhaps the most important of Leo XIII's encyclicals was *Rerum novarum* (rā′rüm nō vär′üm) (1891). A papal letter is usually written in Latin. It is called by its first words. *Rerum novarum,* or *On the Condition of the Working Man,* dealt with the rights of the factory worker in an industrial society.

By the 1830s a new social and economic order had appeared in Western Europe. It was based upon making goods cheaply in large factories. That change in European society is sometimes called the industrial revolution. It created serious social problems. The new inventions that made the factories possible also created a new kind of worker who had only his or her labor to sell. Factories were built in cities, and workers lived nearby in the cheap city slums.

Life was hard for the factory workers and their families. In the industrialized countries, men and women and even children worked fourteen or fifteen hours a day, six days a week, for very low pay. There was little concern for the workers' health and safety. The effect of all that on family life, on education, and on morals was very bad.

In *Rerum novarum,* Pope Leo XIII set down a guide that the Church still follows in working for the rights of factory workers. Leo XIII pointed out three important ideas. First he wrote of the rights of workers to a just wage. Then he said that the duty of the state is to see that factory workers are treated justly by factory owners. Finally he noted the value of labor unions, or organizations that would help workers defend their rights. The social and economic ideas of Leo XIII have been developed by later popes. Pius XI (1922–1939) and John XXIII (1958–1963) both stressed the dignity of the factory workers and the need for mutual trust between owners and workers. In his letter *Mater et magistra* (mä′tär et mä jis′trə), *Mother and Teacher* (1961), Pope John said, "If the organization and structure of economic life be such that the human dignity of workers is compromised, or their sense of responsibility is weakened, or their freedom of action is removed, then we judge such an economic order to be unjust. . . ."

Kolping and von Ketteler One of the greatest challenges the Church would have in Europe in the 1800s and 1900s would be to win back the factory workers. Many working-class people felt cut off from the Church. They stopped going to Mass and the receiving sacraments.

In the 1800s two Catholic leaders in Germany were among those who took the side of the poor and the workers. One was a priest, Adolph Kolping (kōl′ping) (1813–1865). The other was the archbishop of Mainz, Germany, Wilhelm von Ketteler (ket′ə lər) (1811–1877).

Adolph Kolping was born close to Cologne, in what is now West Germany. The son of a poor shepherd, he was a shoemaker by trade. Only later in life was he able to begin studying for the priesthood. He was thirty-two when he was ordained. Father Kolping devoted his whole priestly life to the service of the young laborers and factory workers in Germany. For those young workers, he set up an organization called the Young Catholic Workmen's

Society. Branches were set up all over Germany. Popularly called Kolping Houses, the branches had places for workers to live. They were also centers of education, recreation, and culture. Father Kolping's society still works for the social and religious betterment of young workers. Today there are over two thousand Kolping Houses in the United States alone.

Archbishop Wilhelm von Ketteler was born in northwestern Germany to a wealthy, noble family. When he was in his late twenties, von Ketteler decided to study for the priesthood. He was ordained in 1844. Father von Ketteler also became a defender of the poor. He attacked those rich factory owners who exploited their workers. He taught, wrote, and worked to make people aware of the need for **social justice**. He pointed out that followers of Jesus have the duty to see that their neighbors are treated justly. Everyone must work for the good of the whole community.

In 1850, von Ketteler became the archbishop of Mainz. His writings and ideas about social justice began to spread outside Germany. Archbishop von Ketteler called for the creation of labor unions. Workers should be guaranteed a just wage. Child labor should be stopped. And governments must see that there are good working conditions in factories. Archbishop von Ketteler became one of the first to speak for a Catholic or Christian program of social justice. He insisted that the Church must work to preserve the family and the human dignity of each person. It was Archbishop von Ketteler, more than any other person, who influenced Pope Leo XIII's teaching about the rights of the factory worker.

Pope Leo XIII and Learning Pope Leo XIII also brought a new interest in scholarship to the Church. The pope encouraged Cath-

Father Neil Connolly isn't out to change the world. Just the South Bronx.

Father Connolly's parishoners are poor. Many of their problems are social and economic—race prejudice, lack of jobs, poor housing, and health care.

olics to study their religion. This would help them to understand the problems they faced.

A useful tool in such study, said Pope Leo, were the writings of Saint Thomas Aquinas. In 1879, a year after his election, Pope Leo XIII wrote a letter in which he asked seminarians, priests, and other Catholic scholars to study Saint Thomas and use his methods when treating the problems of society. In 1882, Pope Leo XIII helped set up a special graduate school of Thomistic (tō mis′tik) philosophy at the University of Louvain (lü van′) in Belgium. This is one of the most important and oldest of the Catholic universities in Europe.

Pope Leo XIII encouraged the study of Church history. In 1880 he opened the

Vatican Archives to students of history. Archives are places where official records and historical documents are kept. The Vatican Archives contain the documents and records of the popes from the early Middle Ages to modern times. They are a rich source of historical material. Before Leo XIII it had been very hard for historians to use them. Leo XIII stated that the Church had nothing to fear from the truth. In a letter of 1883, Pope Leo said, "The first law of history is to dare not to lie; the second is not to fear to speak the truth—and to leave no room for prejudice." In a way, Leo XIII was insisting that a good Catholic should never hide the unpleasant sides of Church history and should not be afraid to print those facts along with the good. In doing both, the Church will be seen as truly a human institution responding in every age to God's call.

Finally, Pope Leo XIII gave encouragement to the scientific study of Scripture. In an encyclical published in 1893, students of the Bible were told to study languages such as Hebrew and Greek. This would help them understand better the meaning of Holy Scripture. The Bible was to be studied in the seminary. And modern methods of scholarship were to be adopted.

Pius X: Pope and Saint Giuseppe Sarto (jü zep′ā sär′tō) followed Leo XIII as pope in 1903. Sarto, from a small town in northern Italy, had been ordained in 1858 and had worked in a parish for many years. In 1884, Father Sarto was made the bishop of Mantua in northern Italy. Leo XIII made him a cardinal in 1893 and appointed him archbishop of Venice.

Cardinal Sarto took the name Pius X when he became pope. Pope Pius X was a very holy person. He did not, however, act in the same ways Leo XIII had acted. In

his first encyclical letter, Pope Pius X said that his goal was to "renew all things in Christ, so that Christ may be all, and in all [things]."

Pope Pius X has been called the "pope of the Eucharist." He encouraged frequent and even daily Communion. Today it is understood that at every Mass all people may, and are urged to, receive Communion. At the beginning of this century, just the opposite would have been the case. Pope Pius X also lowered the age at which children could first receive Holy Communion. The pope believed that a child who was able to know the importance of the event was to be allowed to receive the Sacrament of the Eucharist.

Pope Pius X taught that children could be invited to Communion when they knew the difference between the Bread of the Eucharist and ordinary bread.

Another achievement of Pope Pius X was the reworking of the Church's Code of Canon Law. As we saw in Chapter 9, a scholar by the name of Gratian made a great collection of Church laws in the twelfth century. Gratian's work was carried on all through the Middle Ages and into modern times. In 1904, Pius X asked a group of scholars to study all those documents and write a new Code of Canon Law. That code was published in 1917, three years after Pius X's death. Today, Church law is being updated once again.

Pope Pius X strongly believed that the pope was to be the shepherd of the whole Church. Simple and modest, he was loved by all. In August 1914, Pius became ill with a lung infection. He died on August 21 at the age of seventy-nine.

Very soon after the death of Pius X there was a strong movement in the Church to make him a saint. His life and work were looked into for that purpose. In 1954, Pope Pius XII canonized Pius X a saint in St. Peter's Square before many thousands of people. His feast is kept on August 21.

Recall and Reflect

1. What led Pope Leo XIII to write the encyclical *Rerum novarum*?

2. What people are served by the Kolping Houses?

3. Name three ways in which Pope Leo XIII influenced the field of learning.

4. Why has Pope Pius X been called the "pope of the Eucharist"?

5. We have seen that the Church has often had to change its way of teaching the faith because of changes in society. Sometimes change is difficult. Have you ever had to change the way you have always done something—studied your lessons, solved a problem, pitched a ball—because you learned something new? Was it easy to change? Why, or why not?

THE CHURCH BETWEEN TWO WORLD WARS

Pope Benedict XV Pope Pius X died just at the beginning of the First World War. His successor, Benedict XV (1914–1922), followed a policy of strict neutrality; that is, he took neither side in the dispute. But both sides accused the pope of showing favoritism. The French called Pope Benedict the "German pope." The Germans called him the "French pope."

World War I lasted four years, 1914–1918. It involved most of the countries of Europe. In 1917, the United States entered the war. World War I took more than nine million lives and caused terrible suffering and destruction.

During the war, Pope Benedict did what he could to work for peace. But his peace plan of 1917 was not accepted by either side. Benedict also did much to help prisoners of war, refugees, and many other victims of the war. He set up a missing-persons bureau in the neutral country of Switzerland. He gave generously to war-relief efforts.

When peace finally came in 1918, Pope Benedict XV was not able to send representatives to the peace settlement at Paris. That was because of the opposition of the Italian government. The papacy was not allowed representation in the League of Nations, the international organization that was set up after the war to keep world peace. Benedict XV died a disappointed man in 1922.

Pope Pius XI The man who became pope after Benedict XV took the name Pius XI. His seventeen-year papacy (1922–1939) would last until the beginning of an even more terrible war. We know it as World War II. Under Pope Pius XI a concordat,

World War I caused the destruction of many churches. This cathedral in St.-Quentin, a town in northern France, was almost reduced to rubble.

government is one in which a single political party claims all power. In it all citizens exist only for the state.

The Church and Totalitarian States The kingdom of Italy became a totalitarian state in 1922, when Benito Mussolini became the prime minister. Even though Italy had been on the winning side in the war, its economy was crippled and there was much suffering among its people. Mussolini promised to solve the problems. At first some Italian bishops took a sympathetic view of Mussolini. But he became a dictator. Mussolini's government began to interfere with the education of the youth. Pius XI reacted strongly. The pope died just as he was preparing to make an appeal against Mussolini to the Italian bishops.

Adolf Hitler and the Nazis came to power in 1933 in Germany. That country had been defeated in the First World War. Hitler promised to make Germany strong again. Hitler's doctrine was based upon the false idea that the German people were superior to other peoples and therefore had the right to rule the world. All other peoples were to be kept in a lower place.

Hitler attacked the Jewish citizens of Germany. They were not allowed to take part in German public life. Every year more of their freedoms were taken away. Eventually, Jews were rounded up and placed by the millions in concentration camps. During the Second World War those camps became death camps. Hitler's government killed more than six million Jews from all over Europe. And Jews were not the only people killed in the Nazi concentration camps. The feeble-minded, those with incurable illnesses, and all those who opposed the Nazi rule were also put to death. Many Catholic priests and Protestant ministers were among Hitler's victims.

or treaty, was signed in 1929 between the papacy and the Italian government. In that agreement, known as the **Lateran Treaty,** the Church officially accepted the country of Italy with Rome as its capital. The Italian government recognized Vatican City as a completely independent state with the pope as its ruler, or head of government.

Under Pope Pius XI the Church faced many problems. World War I had toppled many governments and changed boundaries of Europe's countries. Many new nations had come into being. A revolution made Russia a Communist state. Both Italy and Germany came under the control of totalitarian governments. A totalitarian

Brave Germans, both Protestant and Catholic, opposed those terrible acts. Two German bishops, Cardinal Faulhaber (foul′hä′bər) of Munich and Cardinal von Galen (gä′lən) of Münster (min′stər), condemned the policies of Hitler. Pope Pius XI also condemned the Nazis in an encyclical letter addressed to the German people.

A Period of Growth The years between the two world wars was a time of growth for the Church. Both Benedict XV and Pius XI were concerned with the missionary Church. In an important letter written in 1919 on the missions, Pope Benedict XV asked missionaries not to join forces with European colonial governments in Asia and Africa. The pope called for vocations to the priesthood and religious life from among the people who lived in mission countries. Pope Benedict called for native rather than European Church leaders. He expected the priests to be well schooled. He called on missionary parishes in those lands to help one another. He asked, too, that missionaries give themselves completely to their work.

Benedict XV set down a guide for the Church in its world missions. He ordered that the work of teaching the faith must never make people of different races feel in any way inferior.

Pope Pius XI carried on that interest in the missions. In 1926 he ordained six Chinese bishops at St. Peter's in Rome. It was one way of saying that the Church was universal—made up of all races, peoples, and countries. The Church, had to be planted and must grow among every people throughout the world.

A Modern Missionary Pioneer One modern missionary had great influence on the Church's approach to mission work. He was a Belgian priest, Vincent Lebbe (leb′ā). Born in 1877, Vincent Lebbe went to China in 1901 to work as a missionary. He was ordained a priest in Peking.

China was a huge empire ruled by a weak central government. Some countries of Europe, as well as the United States, enjoyed special economic benefits in the country. France also had the right "to protect" the Catholic missionaries in China. Most of the Catholic bishops in China were from France. None were Chinese. Chinese priests were kept away from European priests. Vincent Lebbe would not accept that. It put Chinese Catholics in a lower place in their own country. Father Lebbe learned Chinese. He lived and dressed in the Chinese way. He became, in fact, thoroughly Chinese.

In 1912, Father Lebbe began the first Chinese-language Catholic newspaper. It was a weekly. And in 1916 he founded a daily newspaper that quickly became very popular among the Chinese people. Father Lebbe criticized European actions in China. He tried to see things from a Chinese point of view. Church leaders did not like Father Lebbe's involvement in the political life of China. He was sent to work in the far south of China.

Father Lebbe was a man who never gave up. He knew how to talk to the ordinary people of China. Church leaders saw him as a political danger to the Church in China. In 1920 Father Lebbe was sent back to Europe. There he became a chaplain for Chinese students studying in European universities.

Father Lebbe spent six years in Europe. He visited Rome. There he gave his views about the Church in China to Pope Benedict XV and to the officials of the Congregation for the Propagation of the Faith. As we saw in Chapter 14, the Congregation for

Maryknoll, an American community founded in 1911, began work in China in 1918. Brother Michael Hogan, M.M., posed with his Chinese pupils in 1925.

the Propagation of the Faith is in charge of all the Church's missions. Many at the Congregation agreed with Father Lebbe that the Catholic Church in China had to become truly Chinese.

Father Lebbe was able to return to China in 1926. He went back with the six Chinese bishops who had been ordained by Pope Pius XI. All the bishops had been taught by Father Lebbe in China.

Father Lebbe became a Chinese citizen. He also began a religious order for Chinese monks and nuns. In 1940, Father Lebbe was captured by Chinese Communists, who were trying to seize control of the country. He was imprisoned for about six weeks and badly treated. When released, he was gravely ill. He died in China on June 24, 1940. Thanks to Father Lebbe and other missionaries like him, the Church was better prepared to meet the challenges after World War II, when many countries in Africa and Asia became independent.

The Liturgical Movement As we saw earlier in Chapter 4, liturgy is the public worship that the Church offers to God. Between the two world wars a **liturgical movement** began in the Church. It tried to help the people better understand the Mass and the other liturgical ceremonies.

We may forget, today, that up until the 1960s the official prayers of the Church were almost all said in Latin. The Mass was in Latin, and all the sacraments were given in Latin. Many Catholic people were not able to understand the Latin prayers. Mass was said at an altar by a priest facing away from the people. Very often the ceremonies of the Mass were not fully understood.

People sometimes used other, private prayers at Mass. All that began to change through the work of several priests and Benedictine monks.

Benedictine monks for hundreds of years had celebrated the liturgy in a solemn and beautiful way. It was not surprising, then, that some monks should seek to share with others their own love for the prayers, the music, the ceremonies, and even the art that were part of the liturgy. Many Benedictine monks felt that parish priests and their people should not be deprived of the beauty and richness of the Church's public prayer. All that was needed to reach that goal was to teach and train the priests and the people to know and love the liturgy.

Lambert Beauduin (bō dwaɴ′) (1873 – 1960) was a young monk at the Benedictine Abbey of Mont César in Belgium. He believed that all members of the clergy should learn more about the liturgy. They should preach about it and teach it to the people in their parishes. In 1910 the monks at Mont César started a liturgical magazine under Beauduin's direction. They also began to publish leaflet missals in French. Thus the people could follow the Latin Mass in their own language. At the same time, special courses on the liturgy were organized at Mont César for parish priests.

An Austrian Augustinian priest, Father Pius Parsch (1884 – 1954), developed a more pastoral approach to the liturgy. Everything, said Father Parsch, should be written in a way that all people in a parish church might understand. Father Parsch also helped people to a better understanding of the Bible. As the liturgical movement spread, Catholics began to read and study the Bible more.

The liturgical movement has continued in the Church. In 1963, the Second Vatican Council reminded us that the liturgy "is the outstanding means whereby the faithful may express in their lives, and manifest to others, the mystery of Christ and the real nature of the true Church." The Church wants us to assist at Mass. It does not want us to be silent spectators. We are called to be participants and to have a good

Benedictine monks concelebrate the Eucharist. Since Vatican II, such celebrations by many priests have become a common liturgical practice.

understanding of the ceremonies and prayers. One result of the council is that Masses today are offered in our own language.

An Ecumenical Movement We first met the word *ecumenical* in Chapter 2. As we have seen, it comes from a Greek word. It means worldwide, or universal. For Catholics, *ecumenical* is most often used with *council* to mean a general council of the whole Church. In modern times, however, the term **ecumenical movement** has been used to describe efforts among Christian Churches to work for Church unity.

As we have already seen, from the beginning of the Church's history there have been heresies and schisms. The Roman Catholic Church has always worked to bring back all those who are no longer one with it. The twentieth century has seen the beginnings of the new ecumenical movement. It began among several Protestant Churches.

The Catholic Church did not take part in the beginnings of the modern ecumenical movement. Its leaders were found in the Episcopal Church in the United States and in the Anglican Church of England. Before the First World War, those two Churches formed several interfaith groups for common work and discussion. They continued the work on a larger scale after the war. There were two international conferences. One was held at Lausanne, Switzerland, in 1927. The other was held at Edinburgh, Scotland, in 1937. In 1948, movements toward unity led to the organization of the **World Council of Churches** in Amsterdam, the Netherlands.

A Protestant clergyman preaches at an ecumenical service held during the 1977 Catholic Eucharistic Congress in Philadelphia, Pennsylvania.

Individual Catholics sometimes joined together with Protestants to talk about the things that divided them. They also talked about the things they both had in common. Such talks first took place between representatives of the Roman Catholic Church and the Anglican Church. The Anglican Church had kept many Catholic traditions and teachings. A group in the Anglican Church also wanted closer ties with Roman Catholicism.

Between the years 1921 and 1926, interfaith talks were held between Catholics and Anglicans at Malines (ma lēn′) or Mechelen (mek′ə lən), a city in northern Belgium. Inspired by Lord Halifax (1839–1934), a devout member of the Church of England, several Anglican and Catholic scholars met at Malines. They met four times under the leadership of Cardinal Désiré Joseph Mercier (mer′syā′) (1851–1926), the archbishop of Malines. As news about them leaked out, the conferences became highly controversial. Neither English Catholic nor Anglican bishops would support them. Similar talks between Anglicans and Roman Catholics would not start again until after Vatican Council II (1962–1965).

Lambert Beauduin, one of the leaders of the liturgical movement, is also known for his ecumenical work with the Eastern and Orthodox Catholic Churches. In 1925, Father Beauduin set up a monastery in Belgium where the Byzantine liturgy was offered in both Slavonic and Greek. He also arranged meetings between Orthodox and Roman Catholic scholars. He encouraged Westerners to study the theology, history, and traditions of the Eastern Churches. The monastery Father Beauduin set up still exists in Belgium. Lambert Beauduin, often misunderstood and criticized by some Catholics, had very great influence on the ecumenical movement.

Recall and Reflect

1. What were some of the things Pope Benedict XV did during the First World War to promote the cause of peace?

2. What important points were agreed to in the Lateran Treaty between Italy and the Church?

3. What principles did Pope Benedict XV establish for mission work?

4. What contributions have been made by the Benedictines to the liturgical movement?

5. One result of the liturgical movement is that Catholics have been encouraged to read and study the Bible. Do you take time to read the Bible regularly? How often? What is your favorite scripture passage? Why is it your favorite?

THE CHURCH SINCE WORLD WAR II

A Pope of Peace Pope Pius XI died on February 10, 1939. Cardinal Eugenio Pacelli (pä chel′lē), who had been papal secretary of state, was elected pope on March 2, 1939. He took the name Pius XII. Between March and September, Pope Pius XII worked hard to keep war from again breaking out in Europe. In an address to the world in August, Pope Pius declared, "Nothing is lost by peace: everything is lost by war." He was unsuccessful. On September 1, 1939, the German army invaded Poland. World War II had begun.

World War II (1939–1945) involved a struggle between two very different sets of ideas about the nature of the state. On one side were the totalitarian countries of Germany and Italy. On the other side were the democratic countries of Great Britain, France, and the United States.

World War II killed more people and caused more suffering and destruction than any other war in history. During the war,

During World War II, Pope Pius XII worked hard for peace. He was not afraid to change many customs to help the Church adapt to new ways of living.

Pope Pius XII worked constantly for peace. He helped war refugees, especially the Jews. He worked against the war aims of both Hitler and Mussolini. Pope Pius remained in Rome throughout the war. His presence, more than anything else, kept Rome from being destroyed.

The Communist Threat During the war, Russia, a totalitarian Communist state since 1917, also fought against Hitler. In many countries that were taken over by the Nazis, Communists were often leaders in the fight against them. With the end of the war, many of the countries of Eastern Europe fell under the control of the Soviet Union. Between 1945 and 1947, Communist governments took over Poland, Romania, Bulgaria, Yugoslavia, Hungary, Czechoslovakia, and the eastern half of

Germany. Conflict between the Church and the Communist governments followed. For the Communists, all religion was simply a means to control the working people in order to keep them in poverty.

In all countries under the Communists, the Church suffered a loss of freedom. Church leaders were arrested and often put in prison. Cardinal Stepinac, the archbishop of Zagreb in Yugoslavia, was in prison until 1951. He was then kept under house arrest until his death in 1960. Cardinal Mindszenty in Hungary, Cardinal Beran in Czechoslovakia, and Cardinal Wyszynski in Poland were also persecuted by Communist governments. Many other bishops, priests, and laypeople suffered for their faith.

It was the same story for the Church in China, North Korea, and Vietnam. Communist governments attacked the Church as European and foreign, even though all of those countries now had their own native bishops and clergy. Pope Pius XII spoke out against the Communist attacks. In 1949 he excommunicated all those who supported Communist parties or who joined them.

Changes in Church Practices The Second World War had brought many changes in the way people lived and worked. During the war, people worked both day and night. Members of the same family often worked on different shifts. Pius XII was not afraid to change many Church customs to adapt to the new ways of living. In 1953 he gave permission for evening Masses. The Eucharistic fast before Communion, which had once prohibited the taking of all food or drink after midnight, was also changed. Today we have to keep from food and drink—except water—for only one hour before receiving Holy Communion.

SIDELIGHTS ON CHURCH HISTORY

Two Modern Martyrs for Christ

During the Second World War the Nazis set up many concentration camps in Germany and in other countries of Europe. One of the most notorious was located at Oswiecim (ôsh vyeɴ′tsēm) in southern Poland. The German name for the camp was Auschwitz (aůsh′vits′). Auschwitz was a Nazi death camp. Hundreds of thousands of Jews and Poles were sent there to die of starvation or in gas chambers. Two of the victims were Edith Stein, also known as Sister Teresa Benedicta of the Cross, a Carmelite nun, and Maximilian Kolbe, a Polish Franciscan priest.

Edith Stein was born in Breslau, Germany (now Wroclaw [vrôt′släf′], Poland), in 1891 to a devout Jewish family. She lost her faith while still a young girl. Highly intelligent, Edith studied philosophy in the German university of Göttingen (gət′ing ən). While a student, she came into contact with Catholicism. After a time of struggle, she became a convert through reading the autobiography of Saint Teresa of Avila, a Carmelite nun.

Edith Stein became well-known in Germany as a philosopher, teacher, and writer. Nazi persecution of the Jews ended her public career in 1933. Edith became a Carmelite nun at Cologne, Germany. Now known as Sister Teresa Benedicta of the Cross, she continued to write scholarly books. In 1938 the Nazis began to persecute Jews who had become Catholics. Sister Teresa was sent to a Carmelite convent in the Netherlands. After the Dutch bishops publicly denounced the Nazi persecution of the Jews, the Germans, now in control of the Netherlands, arrested a number of priests and religious who were of Jewish origin. Edith Stein, Sister Teresa, was among those arrested. She was sent to the camp at Auschwitz. On August 9, 1942, she died in a gas chamber.

Father Maximilian Kolbe, a Polish Franciscan, was born in 1894 at Lodz (lüj), a town in central Poland. He began and edited a devotional magazine written to spread devotion to Mary. After the German invasion of Poland in 1939, Father Kolbe was arrested twice. The second time he, too, was sent to the death camp at Auschwitz.

A prisoner in Father Kolbe's cellblock escaped. The German guards then took ten other prisoners, chosen at random, to be executed. One of the ten, a young Polish soldier, was also the father of a family. Father Maximilian Kolbe offered to take his place among the ten, and the offer was accepted.

The ten victims were placed in a bunker, or concrete blockhouse, and left to die of starvation. On August 14, 1941, Father Maximilian Kolbe was the last of the ten to die. He was beatified by Pope Paul VI in 1971. Both Edith Stein and Maximilian Kolbe are modern martyrs for Christ. They gave their lives for their faith.

Under Pius XII the English language began to be used in giving some sacraments. Later it would be used in parts of the Mass. The services of Holy Week were no longer held in the morning. They were restored to evening hours, as in the ancient Church. Many more liturgical changes would come later, but changes began while Pius XII was pope.

Worker-Priests As we have seen, the working classes in France, Belgium, and other industrialized countries of Europe had fallen away from the Church. They were hostile to the Church, which seemed to meet only the needs of the middle class. When France was defeated during the war, many French workers were sent to work in German factories. The French bishops asked young priests to go along as workers and to secretly minister to the others. Young men from French working-class families were brought into contact with priests for the first time in their lives. And young French priests became aware that the Church was not meeting the needs of the working classes. Some bishops in France and Belgium saw the need for a new kind of priestly work that would bring the priests closer to the workers.

From 1944 to 1954 a small group of worker-priests began to work in factories, to live in urban slums with the other workers, and to share their lives. The worker-priests also began to take part in the activities of labor unions. In France a large number of workers were Communists. They were in charge of most of the unions. Many of the worker-priests came to feel close to the Communist workers because the priests shared their problems. There was fear on the part of some of the pope's advisers that the worker-priests would soon stop being priests. For that reason Pope Pius XII in 1954 ordered the worker-priests of France to stop their activity. The French bishops were aware of the great good the worker-priests had done. They also knew the risks the worker-priests had taken. The bishops asked Rome to reconsider its decision. As a result, the pope allowed the worker-priests to continue their mission among the factory workers and in the city slums. But the methods and the way of life of those priests were modified.

Pope John XXIII Pope Pius XII was an extraordinary leader in very difficult times. He led the Church with great wisdom. When he died on October 9, 1958, at the age of eighty-two, there was worldwide respect for the papacy. On October 28, another remarkable man, Angelo Guiseppe Roncalli (rōng käl′lē), was elected pope. He took the name John XXIII. Pope John was seventy-seven when he was chosen pope. People said that he would not live long and that he would not make many changes. They were partly right. Pope John was pope for only five years. But in those five years he made more changes in the Church than any other pope in modern times.

Pope John XXIII quietly began to change the style of the papacy. A man of humble origins, he believed in simplicity. He warmly greeted all who came to him. To Jews who came to see him, Pope John said, "I am Joseph, your brother." He spoke of Protestants as "our separated brethren in Christ." One of his first acts as pope was to visit a Roman prison and speak to the prisoners because, as he said, "they could not come to me."

Clearly, John XXIII knew how to inspire love and affection from all kinds of people. He was also an experienced diplomat. He had served as papal delegate in Bulgaria, Turkey, Greece, and France during the most trying times. Pope John was a shrewd judge of character. He had a broad understanding of humanity. From his vast experience outside of Italy, he had come to understand that the world was changing in profound ways. He knew that the Church itself had the ability to respond to the changing world.

A Pastoral Council John XXIII had been pope for only three months when, to the surprise of the whole world, he announced that he was calling an ecumenical council. It would be the twenty-first such council in the Church's history. It would be known as the Second Vatican Council (1962–1965). That council has had a tremendous effect on all Catholic life, on the other Christian Churches, and on the world at large.

Pope John was deeply interested in the ecumenical movement. He was the first pope to give it his total support. He called for a "reunion" of the Churches, not for their "submission" to Rome. For that reason, he invited all the Churches to send observers to the council. Pope John also invited laypeople as observers. Here, too, he was responsible for the new roles that the laity would take in the Church.

The Second Vatican Council opened on October 11, 1962, in St. Peter's Basilica in Rome. Pope John gave an opening address that was full of hope. "We feel we must disagree with those prophets of gloom, who are always forecasting disaster, as though the end of the world were at hand," he said. He also said that the Church "must look to the present, to the new conditions and new forms of life introduced into the modern world which have opened new avenues to the Catholic apostolate." Finally, Pope John said that the council's work was not so much to discuss the doctrines of our faith but to present those doctrines in a

On December 26, 1958, Pope John XXIII visited one of Rome's prisons. He was reviving a custom of Pope Pius IX, who visited prisoners every Christmas.

way that men and women might understand and appreciate them. The council was to be, above all, a "pastoral council." It was to be concerned with the needs of people. It was to be pastoral in the same way that John himself was pastoral.

Pope John XXIII did not live to see the end of his council. He died on June 3, 1963. Just before his death he published his last encyclical, called *Pacem in terris* (pä'chem in ter'is), or *Peace on Earth*. In that letter Pope John wrote on the rights and duties of all peoples. He reminded all peoples of the dignity of working people and the new place of women in public life.

He noted the disappearance of European colonies and the new nations that were replacing them. No people, said the pope, could ever be thought inferior to others. He called for the end of racial discrimination. Pope John wrote that all people have the huge task of "restoring the relations of the human family in truth, in justice, in love and in freedom. . . . Every believer in this world of ours must be a spark of light, a center of love, a vivifying leaven to others." When Pope John XXIII died, a newspaper headline proclaimed, "The father of us all has died." Catholics, Protestants, Jews, non-Christians, Communists, and those with no religion—all mourned the passing of a man who knew how to speak to the hearts of all.

Pope Paul VI The new pope, Giovanni Battista Montini (mōn tē′nē), was elected on June 21, 1963. He took the name Paul VI. He also announced that the Second Vatican Council would go on. Under Pope Paul's guidance the council completed its work in 1965.

During three years of debate and discussion, the pope and the council published sixteen documents. All of them were important. Some caused great change in the Church. The document on the Church gave a new understanding to the Church as "the People of God." A document dealing with the Church's responsibility to the world pointed out that the Church is to serve humankind by its mission to teach the gospel. In a document on the liturgy, the council called for the use of modern languages in the Mass and sacraments. Priests were allowed to concelebrate the Mass. That means they were able to offer Mass as a group. During the Mass, people were allowed to receive the cup as well as the Host in Holy Communion.

> **WORDS TO LIVE BY**
>
> ". . . Christ teaches us that the best use of freedom is the love which finds its fulfillment in self-giving and service."
>
> POPE JOHN PAUL II, ENCYCLICAL LETTER *REDEMPTOR HOMINIS (THE REDEEMER OF THE HUMAN RACE)*

One of the most important documents coming from the council was that on religious freedom. As early as 1885, Pope Leo XIII had said that "no one should be forced to embrace the Catholic faith against his will." The Second Vatican Council declared that every human person has a right to religious freedom. No one should ever be forced to hold a religious faith contrary to his or her beliefs. The council noted with sadness that the Church had not always practiced that principle in the past. It had acted "in ways which were less in accord with the spirit of the gospel. . . ."

Pope of the Third World During the fifteen years of his rule, Pope Paul VI carried out many of the ideas of John XXIII. He also placed his own mark on the world, especially in his concern for justice and peace. In his encyclical letter ***Populorum progressu***, (pōp′ ü lôr′üm prō′gres′sü), *The Progress of Peoples* (1966), Paul VI spoke of the great problem of poverty, especially in the countries of the *Third World*. Those are the nonindustrialized, underdeveloped countries of Africa, Asia, and South America. Paul pointed out the Church's duty to work for the development of people everywhere. That meant not only attacking the problems of poverty and disease but also "building a human community where liberty is not an idle word. . . ." The pope stressed the need for the world's wealthy nations to help poor nations and also to correct an economic system that caused poverty. The heart of the pope's message was that economic and social development is the new name for peace.

Paul VI not only wrote about the many needs in the Third World, he also visited Third World countries. In 1964 he went to India. There he made a special effort to be with the poor. He visited Bogotá in Colombia, South America, and told poor farmers that he would continue to speak out against unjust economic differences between rich and poor. Pope Paul promised that he would work for a more just distribution of the world's goods. In Uganda, Africa, in 1969, Pope Paul told the African peoples

they were now "missionaries to themselves." The African peoples, said the pope, had to bring the Catholic Church the "precious and original contribution of 'blackness.'"

Paul VI died on August 6, 1978. He was a modern pope who traveled to all parts of the world. But he especially reached out to the poor and the exploited peoples of the world. He spoke for social justice and for peace among nations.

A Year of Three Popes Albino Luciani (lü chē än′nē), the smiling and friendly archbishop of Venice, was elected pope on August 26, 1978. He took the name John Paul I. Thirty-three days later Pope John Paul I was dead. On October 16, 1978, the

Third World missionaries must fight poverty and disease. Sister Lorraine, a Catholic nurse, teaches women in India about health problems.

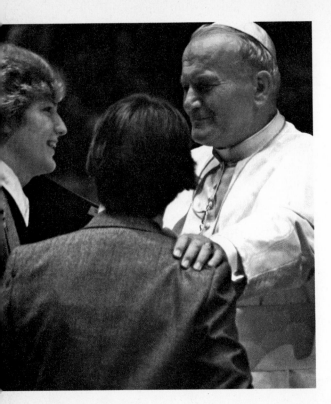

In 1979, Pope John Paul II told young people in Madison Square Garden that "the purpose of Catholic education is to communicate Christ to you."

who must face the problems of today. But we must do more than face them. As members of Christ's Church we must preach with our lives that all problems have their answer in Christ.

In the next and final chapter, we shall see how the Church has been part of the history of our own country. The Church in the United States has many challenges and is carrying out its mission in new and different ways.

Recall and Reflect

1. What changes in Church practice were introduced by Pope Pius XII?

2. Why can we say that the Second Vatican Council was a pastoral council?

3. How did Pope Paul VI show his special concern for the people of the Third World?

4. Pope John Paul II has told the youth of today that "the Church wants to communicate Christ." Since you are a part of the Church, what is the most important thing about Christ that you want to communicate to the world? How will you do that?

cardinals elected Cardinal Karol Wojtyla (voi tē′wə), archbishop of Kraków, Poland. He took the name John Paul II and became the first non-Italian pope since the election of Pope Adrian VI in 1522.

Strong, vigorous, and athletic, Pope John Paul II has put his own stamp on the papacy. In his first full year as pope, he visited Poland and the United States. Pope John Paul II also promised to carry forward the ideas of John XXIII and Paul VI as he leads the Church.

The history of the Church is far more than the history of popes, bishops, or saints. It is the history of a people, a pilgrim people, the "People of God." We are the Church today. Together in Christ, under the leadership of the pope, we are the ones

REVIEW AND CELEBRATE

Doctrinal Summary

"[The Church] has no fiercer desire than that . . . she may
be able to develop herself freely under any kind of
government which grants recognition to the basic rights of
person and family and to the demands of the common good"
Vatican Council II, *Pastoral Constitution on the Church in the Modern World*, 42.

Religious Vocabulary

encyclicals	social justice	liturgical movement	*Pacem in terris*
Rerum novarum	Vatican Archives	ecumenical movement	*Populorum progressu*
Mater et magistra	Lateran Treaty	World Council of Churches	

Review Questions

Answer the following questions on a separate sheet of paper.

1. Why is it important for the Catholic Church to change and adapt its teaching methods according to the needs of the times?

2. What were some of the problems that the industrial revolution caused for working people?

3. Why did the Church react strongly against Mussolini and Hitler?

4. What changes were made in the missionary activity of the Church between the two world wars?

5. How has the Catholic Church contributed to the ecumenical movement today?

Prayer Celebration

Leader: God our Father, open our hearts to Your holy word as we listen to a reading from the Gospel of Luke, Chapter 16, verses 19 to 31.

Reader: "Once there was a rich man who dressed in purple and linen and feasted splendidly every day. At his gate lay a beggar named Lazarus who was covered with sores. Lazarus longed to eat the scraps that fell from the rich man's table. The dogs even came and licked his sores. Eventually the beggar died. He was carried by the angels to the bosom of Abraham. The rich man likewise died and was buried. From the abode of the dead where he was in torment, he raised his eyes and saw Abraham afar off, and Lazarus resting in his bosom.

"He called out, 'Father Abraham, have pity on me. Send Lazarus to dip the tip of his finger in water to refresh my tongue, for I am tortured in these flames.' 'My child,' replied Abraham, 'remember that you were well off in your lifetime, while Lazarus was in misery. Now he has found consolation here but you have found torment. And that is not all. Between you and us there is fixed a great abyss, so that those who might wish to cross from here to you cannot do so, nor can anyone cross from your side to us.'"

Leader: Teach us to bear one another's burdens. We ask this through the power of Jesus, Your Son and our Savior.
All: Amen.

*On October 7, the last day of his visit to the United States in 1979,
Pope John Paul II celebrated Mass on the Mall in Washington, D.C.*

17

The Church in the United States

In 1539 a Franciscan missionary, Marcos de Niza (mär′kos ͰHā nē′sä) (1495–1558), headed northward from Mexico into the present-day states of New Mexico and Arizona. He was called Fray (Spanish for "friar") Marcos, and he had been chosen to lead an expedition into lands where no European had ever been. Fray Marcos had come to the New World in 1531. He had served as a missionary in South America and in Mexico. On this expedition, Fray Marcos was not only a missionary. He was also an explorer. He was to search for "seven cities of gold." From the Indians the Spaniards had heard many stories about golden cities. Fray Marcos wanted to find out if the stories were true.

Fray Marcos set out accompanied by a freed black slave named Esteban, or Stephen. Esteban had learned many Indian languages. Together with several Indian scouts, Fray Marcos and Esteban reached what is now the western part of New Mexico. Along the way they met Indian tribes who lived in villages of flat-roofed stone or adobe (mud-brick) houses. Sometimes the houses were several stories high. A Spanish word for "village" is *pueblo* (pweb′lō), and the Spanish explorers called those Indians "Pueblo Indians." When Esteban was killed by unfriendly Indians, Fray Marcos and his little band hurried back to Mexico. As he went back, Fray Marcos thought he could see one of the seven golden cities gleaming in the distance.

The following year, 1540, Fray Marcos went with a much larger expedition into what is now the southwestern part of the United States. Fray Marcos accompanied Francisco Vasquez de Coronado (väs′ kath ͰHā kō′rō nä′ͰHō) (1510–1554) in search of the seven cities "rich in gold." That time the Spaniards not only visited the area now called Arizona and New Mexico, but they also pushed farther into the Great Plains, reaching what is now Kansas. They found more pueblos and many Indian tribes. But they found no cities of gold.

Fray Marcos returned to Mexico City. There he took charge of the Franciscan missionaries. But he did not forget the Pueblo Indians he had met in New Mexico. Franciscan missionaries were soon working among them.

As this story reminds us, the history of the Catholic Church in the United States begins with Spanish missionaries who lived and worked among the Indians of the American Southwest. In fact, the Church came to the southwestern part of our country and to what is now Florida almost a hundred years before it arrived in the thirteen colonies that declared their independence from Great Britain in 1776.

In this chapter we shall learn about the work of the Spanish and French missionaries in North America. We shall also see how the Catholic Church grew from very small beginnings in thirteen English colonies into the largest Church in our country. Indeed, as we shall learn, the history of the American Church is closely tied to the history of the United States.

AMERICAN BEGINNINGS

Spanish Missionaries in the Southwest By the end of the 1500s, missionaries had already begun to work among Indian tribes of what is now New Mexico. Ten Franciscan friars had opened the Mission of San Juan (Saint John) in 1598. In 1605 the Spaniards founded the city of Santa Fe (Holy Faith), the oldest capital city in the United States.

A mission was like a little village. It had storehouses, workshops, and living quarters for the missionaries. And it had a church. The Indians who became Christians settled near the mission, where they received their religious instruction. They were given the means to farm and raise livestock. Near some of the missions were *presidios*, or forts, where soldiers lived. The soldiers were there to keep order and to protect the missionaries and the Indians. The missionaries tried to keep their Indian converts from too much contact with the soldiers in order to protect the morals of the converts.

The Spanish missionaries made many converts among the Indians of the Southwest. In 1680 an uprising of pagan Indians almost wiped out the Church in New Mexico. But twenty years later the Franciscans were again back at work.

SPANISH MISSIONS IN CALIFORNIA

Between 1769 and 1823 the Spanish Franciscans founded twenty-one missions in California.

San Diego de Alcalá (1769)

San Carlos Borromeo (Monterey-Carmel) (1770)

San Antonio de Padua; San Gabriel Arcángel (1771)

San Luís Obispo de Tolosa (1772)

San Francisco de Asís; San Juan Capistrano (1776)

Santa Clara de Asís (1777)

San Buenaventura (1782)

Santa Barbara (1786)

La Purísima Concepción (1787)

Santa Cruz; Nuestra Señora de la Soledad (1791)

San José de Guadalupe; San Juan Bautista; San Miguel Arcángel; San Fernando Rey de España (1797)

San Luís Rey de Francia (1798)

Santa Inés (1804)

San Rafael Arcángel (1817)

San Francisco de Solano (1823)

Fray Junípero Serra founded this Mission of San Carlos Borromeo at Carmel, California, in 1770. Fray Junípero died here and is buried in the church.

Fray Junípero Serra Perhaps the best-known of the Spanish missionaries in the Southwest was another Franciscan. He was Fray Junípero Serra (hü nē′pā rō ser′rä) (1713–1784). Born on the island of Majorca (mə jôr′kə), just off the east coast of Spain, he became a Franciscan at the age of sixteen. When he was thirty-six, he sailed to the New World to work in the missions. From 1769 to 1784, Fray Serra worked in what is now the state of California. He is remembered for starting the string of missions that were built in California—from Mission San Diego de Alcalá in the south (1769) to San Francisco de Solano in the north (1823). In all, the Franciscans started twenty-one missions.

Many of the early Spanish missions are now cities and towns in California. The Mission of San Francisco de Asís, founded in 1776, is now a great city. Besides starting the missions and presidios, the Spaniards also set up colonies for Spanish settlers. San Jose and Los Angeles, California, began as such settlements.

Fray Junípero Serra brought domestic animals and European methods of farming to California. For fifteen years he traveled from mission to mission, though in poor health. Fray Junípero Serra died August 28, 1784, at the Mission of San Carlos Borromeo at Carmel, California. He is buried in the mission church at Carmel.

In 1821, Mexico became independent of Spain. The American Southwest, with its rich Indian and Spanish cultures, became part of the new nation of Mexico. In 1846 war broke out between the United States and Mexico. The Treaty of Guadalupe Hidalgo ended the war in 1848. Mexico gave up all claims to what is now Texas, Arizona, New Mexico, Utah, Colorado, Nevada, California, and a part of Wyoming. The Spanish, Mexican, and Indian peoples who lived in those territories now became American citizens.

Sad to say, some English-speaking Americans have looked down upon the Spanish-speaking and Indian populations of these lands. They also have looked down upon the Catholic faith. All too often the Indians were treated unjustly. Still the Church survived because of the strong faith of the people. The Indian and Spanish cultures not only have survived but have continued to grow.

Florida also was explored and settled by the Spaniards. As early as 1526, several Dominican friars tried to make a settlement. It failed, as did later attempts. In 1565 the Spaniards began a military expedition against a French settlement in Florida. This led to the founding of St. Augustine. There the first parish in the American Southeast was set up. Spanish missionaries also tried to work in what is now South Carolina and Georgia. They were stopped by attacks of English settlers in those territories.

French Missionaries The Church was brought to the northeastern part of North America through the work of French missionaries and explorers—explorers for souls as well as for land. Jacques Marquette (1637–1675) is a typical example. Father Marquette, a Jesuit missionary, was born in France in the city of Laon, just north of Paris. He came to the colony of New France, in what is now Quebec, Canada, in 1666. Father Marquette worked among the Indians on the western shore of Lake Superior and in what is now the state of Illinois. He knew six different Indian languages.

In 1673, Father Marquette set out with the Canadian-born French explorer Louis Jolliet (1645–1700) to explore the Mississippi River. With five companions, the two men went down the Mississippi to the point where it is joined by the Arkansas River. Father Marquette kept careful records of the location of Indian tribes so that he might return to preach the gospel. On his return, Father Marquette went back to his mission in Illinois. In 1675 he became ill. While returning to Quebec, Father Marquette died near the present town of Ludington, Michigan, on May 18.

The North American Martyrs French Jesuits worked among the Indian tribes in the northeastern part of North America in what is now upper New York State and the southern portion of the Province of Ontario in Canada. Between 1642 and 1648, eight Jesuit missionaries were martyred for their faith. In 1930 they were declared saints under the title of "The North American Martyrs." Six of the martyrs were priests and two were lay assistants called *donnés* (dô nāz′). Although donnés took no vows, they worked for the missionaries without pay. The feast of the North American Martyrs is celebrated on September 26.

The French Jesuits founded many missions among the Indians of the northeastern and middle western parts of our country. Benedictines, Franciscans, and many other religious orders, as well as Jesuit priests and brothers, continue to work among the Indian people of the United States and Canada. Indians who were converted to the Church have been very strong in their faith. They have often traveled great distances to beg for priests to live and work among them.

Kateri, or Catherine, Tekakwitha is an example of the strong faith among Chris-

THE NORTH AMERICAN MARTYRS

Father Isaac Jogues, S.J.   October 18, 1646

Father Antoine Daniel, S.J.   July 4, 1648

Father Jean de Brébeuf, S.J.   March 16, 1649

Father Gabriel Lalemant, S.J.   March 17, 1649

Father Charles Garnier, S.J.   December 7, 1649

Father Noël Chabanel, S.J.   December 8, 1649

René Goupil   September 29, 1642

Jean de la Lande   October 19, 1646

The first North American Martyr, the donné René Goupil, was put to death in 1642. Father Isaac Jogues and the donné Jean de la Lande were put to death by the Mohawk Indians in 1646 (near what is now the town of Auriesville in central New York State). The other Jesuit martyrs—Fathers Jean de Brébeuf, Antoine Daniel, Gabriel Lalemant, Charles Garnier, and Noël Chabanel —were put to death in Ontario, Canada, during 1648 and 1649.

Most of the settlers in all the English colonies were members of Protestant Churches. These people saw the French and Spanish Catholics as enemies. In fact, the practice of the Roman Catholic religion was against the law in all but two of the English colonies—Maryland and Pennsylvania—just as it was in England.

Maryland was settled by Protestants and Catholics. The colony belonged to George Calvert, the first Lord Baltimore, a convert to the Catholic faith. After his death in 1632, his son, Cecil, the second Lord Baltimore, also a Catholic, insisted upon religious freedom in Maryland. Catholic settlers arrived in Maryland's Chesapeake Bay in 1634. Mass was offered by one of the two Jesuits who came with them. The work of those first Jesuits in Maryland was very

Kateri Tekakwitha was baptized on Easter, April 5, 1676, at the age of twenty. She died four years later. On June 22, 1980, Kateri was beatified in Rome.

tian Indians. She was baptized in 1676. When she became a Catholic, Kateri was forced to leave her village because of persecution. She found a home among Christian Indians who lived along the St. Lawrence River. Among them she lived a short life of intense prayer and good works. She died in 1680 at the age of twenty-four. Today the process has begun that may make Kateri Tekakwitha a saint.

Catholics in English Colonies Between 1609 and 1733, the English founded thirteen colonies along the Atlantic Coast. They stretched from the Massachusetts Bay Colony in the north to Georgia in the south.

On November 22, 1633, the first Catholic settlers left England for Maryland.
Mass was offered for the first time in the colony on March 25, 1634.

important for the Church. Their teaching planted the seeds that would lead to the growth of an American clergy.

Even though the Calverts had promised religious freedom, Catholics were persecuted in Maryland. A large number of Puritans had also found refuge and religious freedom in the colony. They gained the upper hand in Maryland, and in 1654 began to attack Catholics. Not until 1707 could Catholics legally practice their religion and then only in the privacy of their homes.

Some Catholic settlers in Maryland became wealthy landowners. Such families were able to build chapels in their large homes. They supported priests who said Mass and taught catechism on their estates.

Those rich families were also able to send their sons to Europe to be educated in Catholic schools.

Pennsylvania was founded in 1682 by William Penn, an English Quaker. *Quaker* is a popular name for a member of the Religious Society of Friends, which was founded in England in the 1600s. Quakers reject all war and violence. They worship by gathering together and praying in silence. William Penn gave his colony a constitution that protected the religious liberty of all citizens. Many German Catholics and some English Catholics from Maryland settled in Pennsylvania. Jesuit priests came to minister to those Catholics. By 1734 a Catholic chapel had been opened in Philadelphia, the capital of Pennsylvania.

Recall and Reflect

1. Briefly describe the kind of mission that was set up by Spanish missionaries in the southwestern part of our country.

2. What were some of Fray Junípero Serra's contributions to the missionary work of the Church in what is now California?

3. Why did many German and English Catholics settle in the English colony of Pennsylvania?

4. An interesting point in the history of our country is that many of the first settlers were seeking religious freedom. But many of those settlers denied religious freedom to others. Can you think of a time when you asked for understanding from someone—parent, teacher, friend? Have you ever been willing to show understanding? What can we learn from such experiences?

THE CHURCH IN THE UNITED STATES (1776–1860)

An Independent Country The thirteen English colonies declared their freedom from Great Britain in 1776. At that time there were about twenty-five thousand Catholics in the colonies out of a total population of some two and a half million. Most of the Catholics—about fifteen thousand—lived in Maryland. In all the colonies, even Maryland, Catholics were barred from public office, and prejudice against them was very strong. The resentment was voiced openly in newspapers, sermons, and speeches. In 1774, when Great Britain granted religious freedom to the French Catholics in Canada, Protestant colonists in America had objected strongly.

Yet Catholics in large measure backed the Declaration of Independence and the revolt against Great Britain. Charles Carroll, a rich Catholic landowner in Maryland, signed the Declaration of Independence on July 4, 1776. Carroll, a delegate from Maryland to the Continental Congress, was the only Catholic to sign. In 1776, Charles Carroll was thirty-nine years old. He died in 1832 at the age of ninety-five, the last of the signers of the Declaration.

Catholic patriots fought bravely in the War of Independence (1775–1783). After the United States became a free country, they sought to take part in its public life. Charles Carroll was one of two Catholics who took part in the Constitutional Convention in 1787. The other was Thomas FitzSimons (1741–1811) of Pennsylvania, who like Carroll was very active in public life. He had been a member of the Continental Congress from Pennsylvania.

The American Constitution was approved in 1789. It put forth the idea of the complete separation of Church and state: "Congress shall make no law respecting an establishment of religion or prohibiting the free exercise thereof." In South and Central America, Europeans had brought only one Church—the Roman Catholic. In the United States, many religions existed in the one country. This is known as **religious pluralism**. It has always been a fact of American life. Freedom of religion has also allowed the Catholic Church in the United States to grow enormously. It has become the largest Church in our country.

First American Bishop English Catholics in the thirteen colonies had never had their own bishop. But in 1789 the pope appointed John Carroll (1735–1815) to be the first bishop in the United States. John Carroll was a cousin of Charles Carroll. As a young man, he had been sent to France to be educated. While in France, John Carroll entered the Jesuit order and became a priest. When Pope Clement XIV suppressed the Jesuits in 1773, John Carroll returned to Maryland.

In America, Father Carroll joined the small number of Catholic priests who were working in the colonies. Like himself, many of those priests had been Jesuits. John Carroll soon became a leader among them. When the pope chose him to be bishop, John Carroll said he would not accept unless his fellow priests elected him. Twenty-four of the twenty-six American priests voted for John Carroll to be bishop. They also chose Baltimore, Maryland, to be the first American diocese. John Carroll was ordained the first bishop of Baltimore on August 15, 1790, in the chapel of Lulworth Castle in England.

When John Carroll became bishop, the diocese of Baltimore included the whole United States. Then President Thomas

John Carroll, the first Catholic bishop of the United States, was a good organizer. In 1791 he called the first national synod of the American Church.

Jefferson purchased the Louisiana Territory from France in 1803. The size of the country—and Bishop Carroll's diocese—more than doubled.

Bishop John Carroll was a good administrator. In 1791 he called the first national synod of the American Catholic Church. Rules were drawn up for giving and receiving the sacraments and for Catholic worship throughout his huge diocese. As the number of American Catholics grew, Rome set up new dioceses. Four were added in 1808. Boston, Massachusetts; Philadelphia, Pennsylvania; New York, New York; and Bardstown, Kentucky, became the seats of the new dioceses. John Carroll now became the first Archbishop of Baltimore. From 1808 to 1846, Baltimore was the only archdiocese in the country, and the seat of the only **Church province**. If you look at the map of the Church in the United States, pages 262–263, you will see that there are now thirty-one Church provinces in today's fifty states. The number of American Catholics has also grown from a mere three hundredths (.03) of the total population to 22 percent today.

An American-Born Saint During John Carroll's time as bishop and archbishop, the Catholic Church in the United States grew not only in numbers but in spirit. One example of spiritual growth can be seen in the life of Elizabeth Bayley Seton. As a woman, wife, mother, and religious sister, Elizabeth Seton lived a life of genuine holiness.

Elizabeth Seton was born Elizabeth Bayley in 1774, two years before the Declaration of Independence was written. Elizabeth was raised an Episcopalian, or Anglican. Her father, a medical doctor, was related to the leading families of colonial New York. He supported Great Britain in the Revolutionary War. Elizabeth's mother was the daughter of an Anglican clergyman. She died when Elizabeth was only three. Her father married again and had seven children by his second wife.

In 1794, Elizabeth married a wealthy New Yorker named William Seton. They had five children. William Seton became very ill with tuberculosis. In 1803 the Setons went to Pisa, Italy, in hope of a cure. William died in Pisa. Elizabeth and her children stayed in Italy for a year, living with a kind Italian family. In Italy, Elizabeth Seton became convinced of the truth of the Roman Catholic religion. But she did not enter the Church until after her return to the United States. Despite the strong opposition of family and friends, Elizabeth Seton became a Catholic on May 14, 1805.

By birth and marriage Elizabeth Seton belonged to the upper class of New York City. Almost all Catholics in New York were poor, illiterate immigrants from Ireland and Germany. Becoming a Catholic, Elizabeth found herself cut off from the world that she knew so well. When her sister-in-law also became a Catholic, her friends and family rejected them both. Through the kindness of Bishop John Carroll and Father John Cheverus, later the first bishop of Boston, Elizabeth Seton found aid and support. Her husband had lost his fortune, and Elizabeth was very poor. She tried to support herself and her five children by opening a school.

In 1808, at the urging of Bishop Carroll, Elizabeth Seton moved to Baltimore. There she opened a school for girls. Attracted by her work, several other young women joined her. In 1809, Elizabeth and her little group moved to the town of Emmitsburg, Maryland. With Bishop Carroll's permission Elizabeth founded a religious community of nuns. Thus began the **Sisters**

Mother Elizabeth Seton, founder of the American Sisters of Charity, is also credited with beginning the American parochial school system.

of Charity, the first religious order founded in the United States. Elizabeth Seton took her vows as a nun and thereafter was known as Mother Elizabeth Seton.

Mother Seton and her community opened the first American parish school in Emmitsburg. Later they set up the first American Catholic orphanage in Philadelphia. Mother Seton also became ill with tuberculosis. She died of that disease in Emmitsburg on January 4, 1821. She was forty-seven. In 1975, Pope Paul VI declared Mother Seton to be a saint. We celebrate her feast on January 4.

Saint Elizabeth Seton was a member of the first generation of American Catholics after the creation of the United States. In her life of service, she proved that Catholicism was not opposed to American values and that American Catholics could grow in genuine, heroic holiness.

The Church on the Frontier Among those who helped Mother Elizabeth Seton and her little community were two French priests. One was Father Benedict Joseph Flaget (flä zhā'), who would become the first bishop of Bardstown, Kentucky. The other was Father Simon Bruté (brü tā'), the first bishop of Vincennes, Indiana.

Benedict Joseph Flaget was born in France in 1763. After his ordination in 1788, he joined the **Sulpicians**, a group of secular priests who dedicated themselves to the education of priests. In 1792, Father Flaget came to the United States to teach at St. Mary's Seminary in Baltimore. St. Mary's, the oldest seminary in the United States, was founded by Bishop Carroll.

Because of the great need for priests on the frontier west of the Alleghenies, Bishop Carroll sent Father Flaget to a French settlement at Fort Vincennes in what would later become the state of Indiana. Father Flaget remained at Fort Vincennes for two years. Returning to Maryland he taught at Georgetown College—the future Georgetown University—and then worked for a short time in Cuba. Upon his return to Baltimore in 1801, Father Flaget was chosen to be the first bishop west of the Allegheny Mountains. He was ordained by Archbishop Carroll in 1810 as the first bishop of Bardstown, Kentucky.

Many Catholic families from Maryland had settled in Kentucky around Bardstown. However, Bishop Flaget's diocese included not only Kentucky but also what are now the states of Tennessee, Ohio, Indiana, Michigan, Missouri, and Wisconsin. Life was difficult for priests and lay people on the frontier. Settlements were few and far apart. Bishop Flaget and his priests spent much of their time on horseback. Many Catholic families saw a priest only a few times a year.

St. Joseph's Cathedral, Bardstown, Kentucky, was begun in 1808 and consecrated in 1819. It was the first Catholic cathedral west of the Alleghenies.

Bishop Flaget was a remarkable man who attracted people by his saintly and kindly manner. He was a bishop for forty years and managed his huge diocese very well. In 1841 the seat of the diocese was moved from Bardstown to Louisville, Kentucky, where it is now. Bishop Flaget died in Louisville in 1850. He was eighty-seven.

An Immigrant Church With the Louisiana Purchase large numbers of Catholics, both French and Spanish, became United States citizens. But the remarkable growth in the size of the Catholic Church in the United States was chiefly due to immigration from Europe. During the nineteenth century and through the first quarter of the twentieth century, the population of the United States increased rapidly. Much of the increase came from immigrants from Catholic countries of Europe. Between 1830 and 1870, over 2,720,000 Catholics entered the United States as immigrants. Over a million and a half were from Ireland. Over half a million were from Germany. Over a hundred thousand were French. In the five years between 1905 and 1910, there were 5,988,809 immigrants admitted. Most of those later immigrants came from Southern and Eastern Europe. Again, great numbers were Roman Catholic.

In the 1800s, most of the immigrants were Irish. This gave the Irish and those of Irish descent a great influence in the Church in America. By midcentury, the greater number of priests and bishops were Irish. That Irish domination was not entirely welcomed by Catholic immigrants from Germany or the other countries of Europe. Rivalry between the Irish and German groups, especially, grew up in the United States during the nineteenth century. Irish Catholics were most numerous in the cities of the Eastern Seaboard. German Catholics were found in great numbers in the towns and farms of the Midwest. At the same time, other Catholic immigrants — Italians and Poles, for example—often felt they were being shut out or ignored by German and Irish bishops.

Anti-Catholic Bigotry The large number of Catholic immigrants made trouble within the Church. It also awakened **religious bigotry** among Protestant Americans. Bigotry is a stubborn attachment to one's own opinions and an unwillingness to respect the beliefs of others.

The people of the thirteen colonies, except for the black slaves, had been mostly English and Scottish. A few were from Holland, Germany, and Sweden. Both the English and the non-English, however, had been Protestant. Whether on the frontier or in the city churches of New York or Philadelphia, the Protestant tradition was part of American religious background.

It was not surprising that many Protestant Americans became alarmed at the growing number of immigrants who did not share their own background. Thousands came from Ireland, Germany, and other countries. And they continued to come year after year. Many Protestants feared that Catholics would soon be in the majority. What would then happen to freedom of religion? What influence would the pope have on the country? The Protestant Americans who built the United States saw themselves overwhelmed by waves of Catholics whose religion they felt was based on superstition.

The result of such Protestant alarm was fear. The fear led to resentment and opposition to Catholic immigration. Ministers began to speak on the dangers of "popery" at their services. Popery is a belittling way of speaking about the Roman Catholic Church. Newspapers spread false stories about Catholics. There was rioting in some American cities. Catholic churches were burned down. Some priests were tarred and feathered. Some Catholics were even killed.

In August of 1834, for example, a mob attacked a convent and school for girls run by nuns in Charlestown, Massachusetts.

False stories had been told that some of the nuns were kept within the convent against their will. A crowd of over a thousand gathered at the convent. The nuns and their students—many of whom were Protestants—were able to escape unhurt, but the convent-school was burned down.

This anti-Catholic bigotry became a political movement in the 1840s and 1850s. Several anti-Catholic parties appeared. The most important was the American Party, formed in 1854. The people who founded the party were bitterly anti-Catholic. They belonged to a secret society, and when questioned, always answered "I know nothing." Their party quickly became known as the "Know-Nothing Party." It was successful in many local elections but never in a national one.

Anti-Catholic feeling began to die down at the time of the Civil War. But it has never entirely disappeared from the United States. Along with other religious and racial prejudices, anti-Catholicism can still be found. Religious bigotry is often linked with other kinds. After the Civil War another secret society, the Ku Klux Klan (kü´ kluks´ klan´), was formed in the South of the United States. The Klan was violently antiblack, anti-Jewish, and anti-Catholic. In one form or another, the Ku Klux Klan still exists in many parts of our country today.

The Slavery Question The question of slavery divided the American people in the 1800s. Slaves were important to the economy in Southern states. Many Americans believed slavery was evil. Some Americans, known as abolitionists, were outspokenly against it. Protestant ministers who were abolitionists helped slaves to escape from the slaveholding states of the South. The escape route was known as the Underground Railroad. By the 1850s, the issue of slavery had divided not only families and communities but many Protestant Churches as well.

Catholics in the United States were also divided in their attitude toward slavery. In Maryland, Kentucky, and Louisiana, black as well as white Catholics were numerous. In those states, some Catholics were slaveholders. There, even priests and religious communities had slaves. Catholic slaveholders were told to baptize and teach their slaves and to protect family life. In some cases, perhaps, that was done. But historians will have to check the evidence a little more carefully before concluding that slaves were better off under Catholic slaveholders than under Protestant ones.

In general, Catholics were not abolitionists. Many Catholics were opposed to the abolitionists. Slavery has existed since ancient times in Western society. Saint Paul, for example, looked upon slavery as a fact of life. Some Catholic theologians even seemed to say that slavery was allowed under certain conditions.

By the 1800s most Catholic theologians believed that any conditions that would allow the keeping of slaves were no longer valid. Certainly, no one could say it was just, or fair, to seize black Africans and sell them as slaves in the United States. Many popes had pointed out that it was not just for people to make slaves of other human beings. In 1839, Pope Gregory XVI condemned the African slave trade as evil.

American Catholics, however, tended to share the attitudes of other Americans about black slaves. That was true of many bishops and priests as well as of laypeople. One Southern Catholic bishop publicly wrote that the condemnation of the slave trade by Pope Gregory XVI did not concern slaves in America.

First Plenary Council of Baltimore From the time of John Carroll, the bishops of Baltimore had called general meetings of the United States clergy. When Baltimore became an archdiocese, the meetings, now called provincial councils, continued. By 1850, there were three church provinces and twenty-nine dioceses in the United States. A general meeting of all the dioceses in the country had been planned for 1850 but did not take place until 1852. A meeting that takes in the whole country is called a **plenary** (plē′nə rē) **council**. There have been three in the United States. They were held in Baltimore in 1852, 1866, and 1884. Since the third, the American archbishops and bishops have usually met every year, but no more plenary councils have been called.

Six United States archbishops and twenty-seven bishops were at the **First Plenary Council of Baltimore** in 1852. Even though the fight over black slaves was growing, the bishops did not speak out on slavery. They felt that it was a political question. But political questions very often are also moral questions. It is hard to understand the bishops' thinking. Perhaps they feared the anti-Catholic bigotry in the country. Slavery was a question that no one could talk about without making enemies. The bishops did not want to stir up more Protestant anger. In addition, there were more bishops from the Northern states. The Northern bishops spoke for the poor Catholic immigrants—mostly white—who lived in the Northern cities of the United States. The bishops from the South, on the other hand, felt

Begun in 1806 by Bishop John Carroll, Baltimore's Cathedral of the Assumption was the site of many sessions of the three plenary councils.

that they had to take into account the feelings of Southern Catholics who were slave-holders. Some bishops urged better treatment for the slaves, but they could not bring themselves to oppose slavery.

Most American Catholics on the eve of the Civil War lived in the large cities of the North. The poor Catholic immigrants in New York, Philadelphia, and Boston were often exploited. They worked in factories for little money. A number of free blacks also lived in those cities, but few of them were Catholic. Blacks, too, were victims of oppression and racism in Northern cities. But no one spoke for them. Blacks and poor Catholics often competed for the same low-paying jobs. As a result, relationships between Catholics and free blacks were often strained, and marred by violence.

Although it is important to remember that individual Catholics did try to help the slaves before the Civil War, the American Church did not speak out. After the war, it was Rome that showed the greatest concern for the welfare of the freed slaves. Rome insisted that the American Church develop a religious program for the black population of the United States.

Recall and Reflect

1. How did the few Catholics living in the English colonies help the cause of the American Revolution?

2. What led Mother Elizabeth Seton to found the Sisters of Charity?

3. Why was there rivalry between Irish and German Catholics in the United States during the 1800s?

4. List some of the reasons why slavery was not discussed at the First Plenary Council.

5. We find many reasons not to talk about things that are difficult for us—disagreements with friends, parents, etc. Why is that harmful?

THE CHURCH IN THE UNITED STATES (1860 TO PRESENT)

The Second Plenary Council In October 1866, American bishops again met in Baltimore. Their meeting, known as the **Second Plenary Council,** was the largest meeting of the Church in this country up to that time.

The bishops had many problems to face after the Civil War (1861–1865). In the South, Church property had been destroyed. Growing numbers of immigrants continued to arrive in the United States. Immigration, in fact, would keep increasing until the First World War. The Second Plenary Council covered the whole range of the Church's activity in the United States. Decrees were passed on divine worship, the administration of the sacraments, religious teaching, and Church discipline.

One of the major problems facing the Church was what kind of religious care and teaching would be offered to the four million freed slaves. The archbishop of Baltimore, Martin John Spalding, pointed out that now there was a "golden opportunity" for the Church to work among the blacks of the United States. That was also the desire of the pope in Rome. A whole chapter, or session, of the council was devoted to the freed slaves. But no united efforts were made by the bishops to convert blacks. In many places bishops and priests had little interest in their black population. In some places there was even racial hostility on the part of Catholics.

The Second Plenary Council also asked the pope to send priests to the United States to work among black Americans. Pope Pius IX asked an English priest, Herbert Vaughn (vôn) (1832–1903), later cardinal archbishop of Westminster, in England, to send members of his newly formed missionary congregation, The

Saint Joseph's Society for the Foreign Missions to the United States. These missionary priests are popularly known as the **Mill Hill Missionaries**, after the location of their seminary in England.

Four Mill Hill Missionaries arrived in Baltimore in 1871 and began to work among American blacks. They set up black parishes, opened schools, and finally opened a seminary in 1887. In 1893 an American community, The Saint Joseph's Society of the Sacred Heart, was set up. Popularly called the **Josephite Fathers,** priests and brothers of that community have continued to work among American blacks.

From Slave to Priest Augustine Tolton was the first publicly acknowledged black priest in the United States. His parents were slaves, and he himself was born a slave on April 1, 1854, in Missouri. He was the second of four children. His family was Catholic. During the Civil War, his father escaped to the North and fought in the Union Army. He was killed. After his father's death, Augustine's mother also escaped with her four children. They fled across the Mississippi River to Quincy, Illinois.

In Quincy, Mrs. Tolton and her children found freedom but also much hardship. The family was very poor. Because Augustine had to work, he missed much school. The family also met a great deal of opposition from some of the white Catholics of Quincy.

From the time he was a young boy, Augustine Tolton had the desire to become a priest. He was helped by Franciscan friars. They gave him private lessons in Latin and Greek. Efforts were made to get Augustine into a seminary in the United States. But that was not possible because of

Father Augustine Tolton, born in slavery, became the first publicly acknowledged black priest in the United States. He was ordained in Rome in 1886.

racial prejudice. Yet Augustine did not give up. Finally, through the efforts of the superior general of the Franciscans, young Tolton was sent to study in Rome. He was to be trained for the missions in Africa.

Augustine Tolton was ordained a priest in Rome in 1886. Cardinal Simeoni, who

SIDELIGHTS ON CHURCH HISTORY

A Black Woman of Great Faith

The country of Haiti is located in the western part of the Caribbean island that Columbus called Hispaniola. The Dominican Republic now occupies the rest of the island. At the beginning of the nineteenth century, however, the whole island was a French colony. In 1804 almost half a million slaves and freed blacks defeated the French and won independence for Haiti. The Spanish Dominicans reconquered the eastern part of the island for Spain. Many French and black Haitians fled the country to escape the war and violence. Among them were the parents of Elizabeth Lange. They fled to Cuba, where Elizabeth was born. The date of her birth is unknown.

In 1817, Elizabeth Lange came to the United States. The young woman went to Baltimore where many other refugees from Haiti had already settled. In Baltimore the French-speaking black refugees worshiped in the basement chapel of St. Mary's Seminary. Their priest was Father Jacques Joubert, a French Sulpician, who had also fled the Haitian revolution.

Elizabeth and another black woman from Haiti, Marie Balas, began to teach young black children in Baltimore. At that time there was no public education for black children in the United States. Father Joubert wanted to provide Catholic schools for black children. He decided to found a religious order for this purpose. Under his guidance Elizabeth, Marie, and two other black women took vows and formed a religious community. They called their community the Oblate Sisters of Providence. Father Joubert gave them a rule. They rented a house in Baltimore. Elizabeth Lange became superior.

The Oblate Sisters of Providence was the first congregation of black sisters in the country. In 1829, Archbishop James Whitfield (1770–1836), the fourth archbishop of Baltimore, approved the community's rule. In 1831, Pope Gregory XVI gave his approval to the new congregation.

Archbishop Whitfield, who gave the sisters strong support, died in 1834. The new archbishop, James Eccleston, was not very favorable to a community of black sisters. Some white Catholics—priests and others—also were opposed. The sisters were not even given their own chaplain. The sisters supported themselves, their students, and the orphans for whom they cared, by taking in laundry and acting as cooks for the seminary.

Father Joubert died in 1843. Father John Neumann, the superior of the Redemptorist Fathers (later the archbishop of Philadelphia and now a saint in the Church), took an interest in the Sisters of Providence. He sent a young Redemptorist priest, Father Thaddeus Anwander, to be their spiritual director and chaplain. Father Anwander was able to get Archbishop Eccleston's approval for the community to continue. Mother Elizabeth and her sisters were able to extend their work to Philadelphia and other cities. By 1900 they had schools and orphanages for blacks in many states in both the South and the North.

Mother Elizabeth Lange died in 1889. Victims of racial prejudice and neglect within the Church, Mother Elizabeth bore witness—and her sisters continue to bear witness—to American Catholics that the Church is universal, embracing all peoples and races.

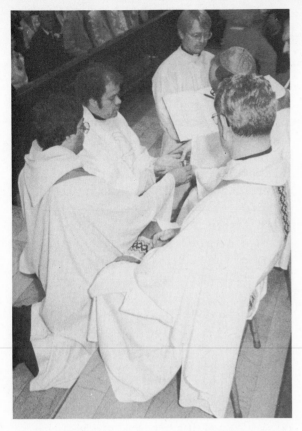

The bishop anoints the hands of the newly ordained Josephite, Father Lowell D. Case. Josephites help to meet the spiritual needs of American blacks.

was in charge of all mission territory, decided that Father Tolton would not go to Africa. He would serve as a priest in the United States. "America has been called the most enlightened nation," said the cardinal. "We will see if it deserves that honor. If America has never seen a black priest, it has to see one now."

Father Tolton became pastor of a black parish in Quincy. Although he soon earned a national reputation as a speaker, his life as a pastor was hard. He was opposed by one of the leading priests in the city. Difficulties became so great that Father Tolton got permission to work in the archdiocese of Chicago, Illinois. In 1889 he became pastor of St. Monica's Parish in Chicago's black community. A pastor only eight years, Father Tolton died suddenly in 1897, at the age of forty-three. He was buried in Quincy, Illinois.

Augustine Tolton was, in more ways than one, a pioneer. Other black priests followed in his footsteps. Many experienced the same difficulties that he had met. Today there are only three hundred black priests in a black Catholic population of almost a million. Even that modest number owes much to the work of Father Tolton, a man born in slavery, who refused to give up his dream of becoming a priest.

The Church and Labor At the end of the 1800s, the vast majority of American Catholics belonged to the working class. As immigrants, they were at the bottom of the social scale in the large industrial cities of the United States. As factory workers, they suffered the same indignities as European workers. They had long hours of work, little job security, no safety laws.

As in European countries, labor unions were formed in the United States to fight for the rights of the workers. Most American factory owners, however, were able to keep unions from organizing in their factories. Workers' strikes for higher pay and better working conditions often became bloody battles. Factory owners brought in other workers, or strikebreakers, and sometimes called upon police to help break up the strikes.

Because workers who joined unions were often forced out of their jobs, the first labor unions were secret organizations. The Knights of Labor, founded in 1869, was one such secret union. In 1879, Terence Powderly, a Catholic layperson, became the head of the Knights of Labor. The Knights, which later dropped its oath of secrecy, worked for greater safety in the factories, an eight-hour workday, and equal pay for men and women for equal work. In 1886, the Knights had 700,000 members.

Many American bishops wanted the pope to condemn the Knights of Labor and not let Catholic workers join it. But the archbishop of Baltimore, Cardinal James Gibbons (1834–1921), a leader among the American bishops, understood the sufferings of the American working people. Cardinal Gibbons knew Terence Powderly and was sure that nothing in the program of the Knights should be condemned by Rome. On the other hand, Gibbons knew that a condemnation would be a terrible blow to the Catholic workers of the United States. Through the efforts of the cardinal, the Knights of Labor was not condemned in the United States.

As archbishop of Baltimore, Cardinal Gibbons was one of the principal leaders of the American Church. He helped solve many of the problems it faced.

Catholic American thinkers have continued to defend the rights of workers in the United States. Their ideas have counteracted Socialist and Communist ideas among American workers. Perhaps the most important Catholic social thinker in the United States was Father John Augustine Ryan (1869–1945). In his book *A Living Wage: Its Ethical and Economic Aspects* (1906) he spelled out a Catholic theology of work. Through his writing and teaching, Father Ryan did more than any other person to teach Americans about social justice. When he died in 1945, the *Washington Post* said: "Most of the reforms of Doctor Ryan have now been accomplished. . . . The most radical of them, the principle of minimum wages, has been incorporated into law. All in all, he was one of the most effective as well as the most energetic champions of labor ever to arise in the United States."

Bishops like Cardinal Gibbons and priests like Father Ryan who aided the workers in the United States kept the working classes from leaving the Church as they did in many of the countries of Europe. It is part of the glory of the Church in the United States that it upheld the principles of social justice and defended the rights of working people and the poor.

The Third Plenary Council By the 1880s the Church in the United States was gaining many thousands of members every year, chiefly because of immigration. In 1883 the American archbishops were called to Rome to plan for a plenary council. The **Third Plenary Council** met in Baltimore in November 1884 under the presidency of Archbishop James Gibbons. (He was made cardinal in 1886.) Seventy-two bishops attended. The council renewed the laws of earlier councils and again asked that schools be set up in all parishes. A committee began to work on what became the **Baltimore Catechism.** The book would be used by three generations of Catholic students.

During the 1800s the Church in the United States owed much to the generosity of Europe's Catholics, who gave to the missions through the **Society for the Propagation of the Faith**. That society is now the official organization of the Church for gathering and giving out all money for the missions. It was founded by a young Frenchwoman, Pauline Jaricot (1799–1862), in Lyon, France, in 1822. That same year, the Society made its first gift—$4,582 to the American Church. Between 1822 and 1861 it gave $7,020,974 for the support and spread of the Church in the United States. The Third Plenary Council in 1884 ordered that a branch of the Society should be set up in the United States. It was finally organized in this country in 1896.

The Church in the Twentieth Century Until the year 1908, the United States was officially considered a mission country. The American Church was under the control of the Congregation for the Propagation of the Faith. As we learned in Chapter 14, the Congregation for the Propagation of the Faith was set up in Rome in 1622. It has since guided all the Church's missionary activity in places where the Church was not firmly established. It was certainly clear by 1908 that the Church was well established in the United States.

From the First World War to the Second World War the Church grew in membership. The number of dioceses also continued to grow. Schools, churches, and hospitals were built. Colleges and universities were opened. American Catholics were faithful in receiving the sacraments and going to Mass, and they were loyal to the

All three plenary councils of Baltimore urged that schools be set up in every parish. Parochial schools continue to be a vital part of the American Church.

pope. Vocations to the religious life and to the priesthood flourished in the United States. Catholics did more than their share in serving in the country's armed forces during the two world wars.

There was still much anti-Catholic feeling among Protestant Americans. Religious bigotry flared up when a Catholic, Alfred E. Smith, ran for President of the United States in 1928. Religious feelings played a large role in Smith's defeat. In 1960, John F. Kennedy, a Catholic, became the thirty-fifth President. His election showed that America as a country no longer thought of Catholics as threats to the American way of life.

261

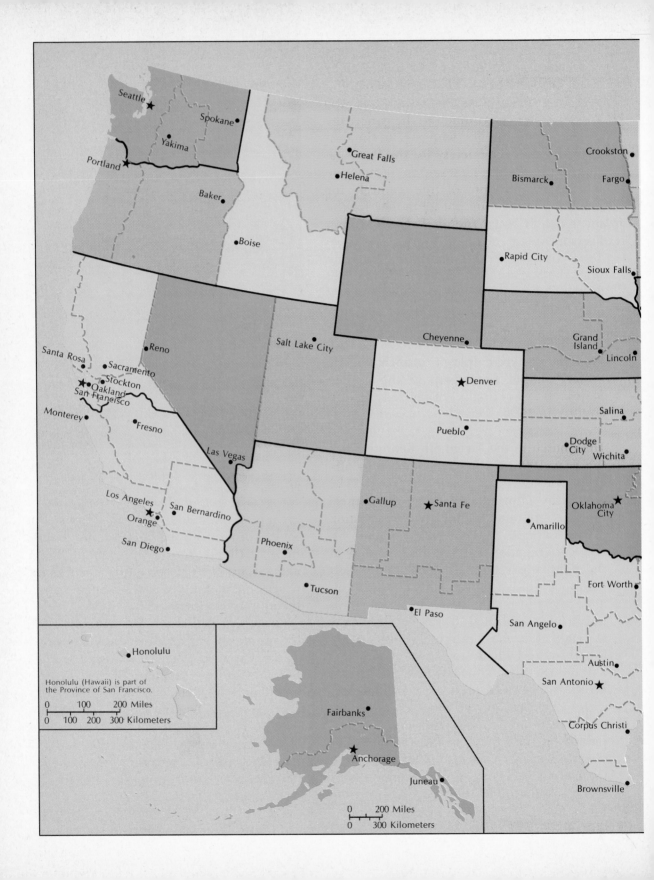

Seattle ★
Spokane ●
Yakima ●
Portland ★
Baker ●
Boise ●

Great Falls ●
Helena ●

Crookston ●
Bismarck ●
Fargo ●

Rapid City ●
Sioux Falls ●

Reno ●
Santa Rosa ●
Sacramento ●
Stockton ●
Oakland ●
San Francisco ★
Monterey ●
Fresno ●

Salt Lake City ●

Cheyenne ●

Grand Island ●
Lincoln ●

Denver ★

Salina ●

Pueblo ●

Dodge City ●
Wichita ●

Las Vegas ●

Los Angeles ★
Orange ●
San Bernardino ●
San Diego ●

Gallup ●
Santa Fe ★
Amarillo ●

Oklahoma City ★

Phoenix ●

Tucson ●

El Paso ●

Fort Worth ●

San Angelo ●

Austin ●

San Antonio ★

Corpus Christi ●

Brownsville ●

Honolulu ●
Honolulu (Hawaii) is part of
the Province of San Francisco.
0   100   200 Miles
0   100   200   300 Kilometers

Fairbanks ●

Anchorage ★

Juneau ●

0   200 Miles
0   300 Kilometers

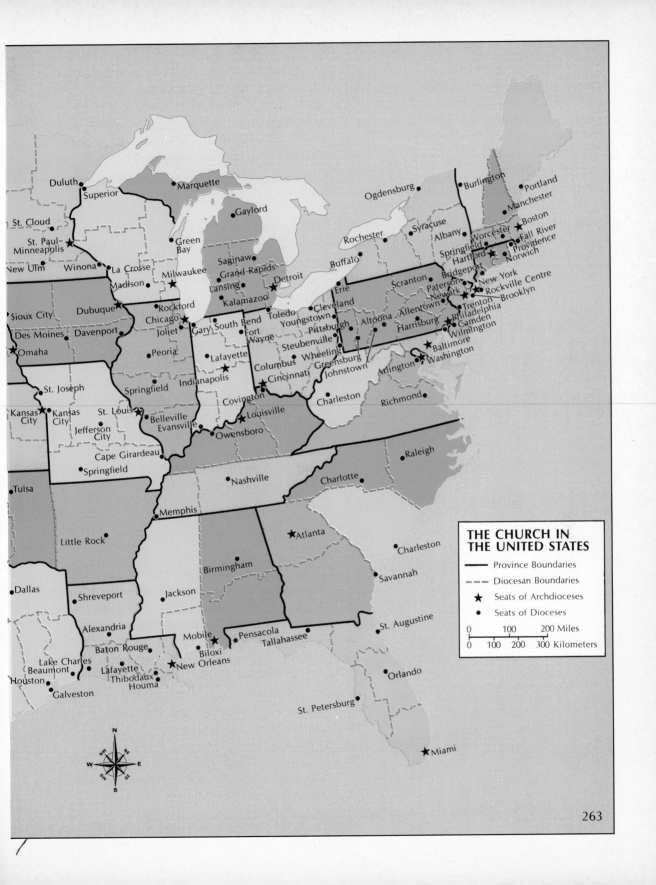

THE CHURCH IN THE UNITED STATES

— Province Boundaries

--- Diocesan Boundaries

★ Seats of Archdioceses

• Seats of Dioceses

0   100   200 Miles

0   100   200   300 Kilometers

Duluth
Superior
Marquette
Gaylord
St. Cloud
Green Bay
St. Paul-Minneapolis
Saginaw
New Ulm
Winona
La Crosse
Milwaukee
Grand Rapids
Madison
Lansing
Detroit
Sioux City
Dubuque
Rockford
Chicago
Kalamazoo
Des Moines
Davenport
Joliet
Gary
South Bend
Fort Wayne
Toledo
Cleveland
Erie
Omaha
Peoria
Lafayette
Columbus
Youngstown
Pittsburgh
Steubenville
Wheeling
Greensburg
Johnstown
St. Joseph
Springfield
Indianapolis
Cincinnati
Covington
Charleston
Kansas City
Kansas City
St. Louis
Belleville
Evansville
Louisville
Owensboro
Jefferson City
Richmond
Cape Girardeau
Springfield
Nashville
Raleigh
Tulsa
Charlotte
Memphis
Little Rock
Charleston
Atlanta
Savannah
Dallas
Birmingham
Shreveport
Jackson
Alexandria
Mobile
Pensacola
Tallahassee
St. Augustine
Lake Charles
Baton Rouge
Biloxi
Beaumont
Lafayette
New Orleans
Houston
Thibodaux
Houma
Galveston
Orlando
St. Petersburg
Miami
Ogdensburg
Burlington
Portland
Rochester
Syracuse
Albany
Manchester
Boston
Worcester
Fall River
Springfield
Hartford
Providence
Norwich
Buffalo
Scranton
Bridgeport
New York
Paterson
Newark
Rockville Centre
Brooklyn
Allentown
Trenton
Harrisburg
Philadelphia
Camden
Wilmington
Altoona
Baltimore
Arlington
Washington

N
NW NE
W E
SW SE
S

263

Many of the movements that developed in the Church in Europe during the nineteenth and twentieth centuries were also found in this country. The liturgical movement was begun in this country by Virgil Michel (1890–1938). He was a Benedictine Monk of St. John's Abbey in Collegeville, Minnesota. He had studied in Europe and knew Lambert Beauduin and his Belgian monks. St. John's Abbey became the center of the liturgical movement in the United States.

During the years of the Great Depression (1929–1938), Dorothy Day, a former Communist, was converted to the Church. She opened a center to help the poor and unemployed in New York City. Her movement, known as the **Catholic Worker Movement**, still helps people. "Houses of Hospitality," as the centers are called, are found in New York and other American cities.

Dorothy Day, founder of the Catholic Worker Movement continued to write for the Catholic Worker *until her death on November 29, 1980.*

Dorothy Day began a newspaper, the *Catholic Worker*, to spread Catholic social teachings. Volunteer workers, many of them college students, help staff the centers of the Catholic Worker organization. Dorothy Day always worked for social justice. As a Catholic pacifist, she also worked to end all war.

The American Church Today In their yearly meetings the bishops of the United States continue to speak out on moral questions. They have reminded us of the rights of working people. They have championed the civil rights of blacks and other minorities. One recent example is the bishops' 1979 letter against racism, called "Brothers and Sisters to Us."

In 1919 the bishops set up the **National Catholic Welfare Conference** in Washington D.C. That group, now called the **United States Catholic Conference**, helps to bring together the efforts of the bishops and of American Catholics to carry out the social teachings of the Church in our country.

With great enthusiasm, the American Church took part in the Second Vatican Council (1962–1965). Two American Jesuit theologians presented many important ideas to the council and the Church. Father Gustav Weigel (1906–1964) wrote clearly and deeply about how important the ecumenical movement is to the Church. Father John Courtney Murray (1904–1964) defended the American example of religious liberty. Although Father Murray's ideas were questioned by some Church authorities, he helped draft the council's *Declaration on Religious Liberty.*

Three things have greatly changed the Catholic Church in the United States. The Second Vatican Council has made American Catholics more aware of the Church's

Young American Catholics know that the gospel command to love requires them to practice the spiritual and corporal works of mercy.

need to respond to the social problems of our country. And American Catholics have responded with energy to the council's suggestions. In doing so, they have given new directions to the Church's work in this country. Before the Second Vatican Council, the American Church had been chiefly taken up with its own internal problems and growth. Now the Church in the United States has begun to reach out to other churches and to work with all Americans of good will in seeking to correct social evils in our country.

The second change has been the way in which Catholics have acted upon the desires of blacks for racial justice. Priests, nuns, and laypeople have taken part in civil-rights marches and demonstrations. Catholics have spoken out against racial prejudice in ways they have never done before.

The third change that has deeply affected the Church in the United States has been

the Vietnam War (1961–1975). The American Catholic response to this war has been a divided one. Many Catholic people became convinced that the United States presence in Vietnam was not just. They took part in demonstrations and even in acts of civil disobedience against the war.

In the autumn of 1979, Pope John Paul II visited the United States. The press and television coverage of the pope's visit gave the whole world a picture of the American Church. It is a Church that numbers almost fifty million people, a Church that includes many races and ethnic groups. Just as the United States has been called "a nation of nations," the American Church is made up of Catholics from many countries and peoples, from Ireland to Vietnam. Today, American Catholics are found in all economic and social classes. They are found in the inner cities, in the suburbs, and on the farms.

care of His Church through the centuries—despite conflicts and changes, obstacles and uncertainties. The history of the Church is our history also, for we are part of the Church. This history is not yet over. We, too, have a part to play. The saints and holy people mentioned in this book remind us of that fact. What we do for Christ depends on how well we follow their example, just as they followed Christ's. The last chapter of the Church's history will only be written when Christ comes again in glory!

Wherever they are, American Catholics, like all members of Christ's Church, have the duty of living out the Gospel and following Jesus. They must see Christ in their neighbor and in the poor and suffering, not only in the United States but throughout the world. American Catholics, who have been blessed in so many ways and who enjoy full religious liberty, must work everywhere for the justice and peace of Christ.

There is an old proverb that says, "God writes straight with crooked lines." No one can study the history of the Catholic Church without becoming aware of God's loving

Recall and Reflect

1. What were some of the topics handled by decrees of the Second Plenary Council in Baltimore?

2. Why did the Mill Hill Missionaries come to the United States?

3. Who was the first publicly acknowledged black priest in the United States?

4. In what two ways did the Third Plenary Council affect the education of Catholic schoolchildren?

5. We have learned that the history of the Church is our history, too, because we are a part of the Church. How can you spread the teaching of Christ? How have your friends helped you to live the gospel?

REVIEW AND CELEBRATE

Doctrinal Summary

In the Christian view, all human history leads to or away
from a central event in time, the Incarnation. The history of
the Church also begins with Christ's birth. But at the same
time, the Church is leading to another event—Christ's coming
again at the end of time. We do not know how or when this
will happen. We do know that as Christians we are called
upon to work in our own time to bring all peoples to Christ.

Religious Vocabulary

religious pluralism
Church province
Sisters of Charity
Sulpicians
religious bigotry
plenary council

First Plenary Council
  of Baltimore
Second Plenary Council
  of Baltimore
Mill Hill Missionaries
Josephite Fathers

Third Plenary Council
Baltimore Catechism
Society for the Propagation of the Faith
Catholic Worker Movement
National Catholic Welfare Conference
United States Catholic Conference

Review Questions

Answer the following questions on a separate sheet of paper.

1. Who is responsible for the beginnings of the Church in what is now the United States?
2. Why has the Church in the United States been called an "immigrant Church"?
3. What were some of the reasons for the rise of anti-Catholic bigotry in the United States?
4. How did the Church help working people in the United States?
5. What three things have caused major changes in the Church in the United States today?

Prayer Celebration

Leader: Let us pray together in the words of
"America, the Beautiful" by Katharine
Lee Bates.
All: O beautiful for spacious skies,
    For amber waves of grain,
    For purple mountain majesties
    Above the fruited plain.
    America! America!
    God shed his grace on thee,
    And crown thy good with brotherhood
    From sea to shining sea.
    O beautiful for pilgrim feet,

    Whose stern, impassioned stress
    A thoroughfare for freedom beat
    Across the wilderness.
    America! America!
    God mend thine every flaw,
    Confirm they soul in self-control,
    Thy liberty in law!
Leader: Lord God and Father of all, we thank
You for the blessings You pour out on us and
our country. Help us to be generous with
what we have been given through the power
of Jesus Christ.
All: Amen.

UNIT FIVE SUMMARY

The Revolution that began in France in 1789 destroyed the old way of life, the old regime, in France and in most of Europe. From 1792 until the fall of Napoleon, the Church suffered much. Under Pope Pius VII the Church began learning how to do its work of teaching Christ's gospel within the new order brought about by the Revolution. Pope Pius IX and the popes who came after him continued that task. In many ways, the Church after the French Revolution was stronger and more spiritual than it was in the 1700s.

Pope Leo XIII asked scholars to return to the thought and method of Saint Thomas Aquinas as they tried to solve the problems of the times. In 1891, Pope Leo wrote *Rerum novarum*. In that letter the pope stressed the rights and dignity of working people in the industrial society.

Pope Leo XIII and the popes of this century have always reminded us that the Church is for all peoples and races. In 1919, Pope Benedict XV gave new guidelines for the Church's missions in the whole world. Pope Pius XII condemned the Nazis in Germany. And in two terrible wars, the Church stood firm for the oneness of all peoples. After 1945 much of Eastern Europe came under the power of Communist Russia. That made the Church's work more difficult in that part of the world.

In 1958, John XXIII was chosen pope. His greatest work was the calling of the Second Vatican Council. It began in 1962. The council stated once again that the Church is the People of God, made one in Baptism and fortified by the other sacraments and by Christian teachings.

In 1776 there were only about 25,000 Catholics in the English colonies. Through the nineteenth century and into the twentieth century, hundreds of thousands of Catholic immigrants entered the United States, most of them poor working people. By great sacrifice and effort, the Church helped them to keep their faith and to become good citizens of their adopted country. The American Church today is made up of people from many countries and ethnic groups.

1600s	Spanish and French missionaries work in the Southwest and Northeast of what is now the United States
1634	Catholic settlers arrive in Maryland
1642–1649	Deaths of the North American Martyrs
1680	Death of Kateri Tekakwitha
1769	Fray Junípero Serra begins to work in California
1773	Pope Clement XIV suppresses the Jesuits
1789	Crisis of the French Revolution
1790	John Carroll is first bishop of Baltimore
1810	Diocese of Bardstown, Kentucky, set up
1821	Death of Saint Elizabeth Seton
1850s	Issue of slavery divides American Catholics
1866	Second Plenary Council of Baltimore
1870	First Vatican Council
1870s	Almost three million Catholic immigrants have arrived in the United States
1884	Third Plenary Council of Baltimore
1891	Pope Leo III writes *Rerum novarum*
1910	Liturgical movement begins in Church
1919	Pope Benedict XV issues new guidelines for missions
1933	Dorothy Day founds Catholic Worker Movement
1948	World Council of Churches created by Protestant ecumenical movement
1958	John XXIII becomes pope
1962	Second Vatican Council begins
1969	Pope Paul VI visits Africa
1978	John Paul II becomes pope

WHAT IT MEANS TO BE A ROMAN CATHOLIC

In *The Church: A Living Heritage* we have studied the history of the Roman Catholic Church—from its beginnings almost 2,000 years ago to the worldwide community it is today. In every age, the mission of the Church has been the same. It is to proclaim the good news of Jesus and to bring all peoples to God through His Son. As Saint Paul points out, there is "one Lord, one faith, one baptism (Ephesians 4:5).

Christians believe that God has revealed Himself to us in and through His Son Jesus. It is God's plan to "bring all things in the heavens . . . into one under Christ's headship" (Ephesians 1:10). The mission of the Church, then, is the mission of Jesus Himself. And Jesus, living in His Church, works through all those who believe Him. Jesus called Himself the "light of the world" (John 8:12). But for many people, the light that is Christ can only be seen in the lives of those who call themselves Christians.

What does it mean to be a Roman Catholic? To be a Roman Catholic and a member of Christ's Church means many things.

- We are called by God to be holy.
- We are members of the body of Christ, which is the Church.
- We are a sign of Christ's presence in the world, and we make visible to all peoples Christ's love for the world.
- We share in the priesthood of Christ, and through that priesthood we worship God the Father in the liturgy of the Roman Catholic Church, especially the Eucharist.
- We are witnesses by word and action to the gospel of Jesus.
- We seek to offer love and support to those in need, and we exclude no one from our love.
- We seek to foster peace and reconciliation in the world.
- We believe that Jesus entrusted his followers to Peter and the apostles.
- We believe that the pope is the successor to Peter and is the supreme ruler and teacher of the Church.
- We believe that the bishops are the successors

of the apostles and are also authentic teachers in the Church.
- We believe those teachings of the pope and bishops that are put forth as belonging to our Catholic faith.
- We take seriously and respect the teachings of the pope and bishops on contemporary problems.
- We realize that the gospel message of Jesus develops through the tradition of the Church, which is guided by the Holy Spirit.
- We join the pope and the bishops of the Roman Catholic Church in appreciating the presence of God in all men and women of faith.
- We believe in the presence of Jesus in all denominations of His divided Church, and we pray for the Church to be one as Jesus wishes.
- We appreciate the fullness of Jesus' sacramental presence in the Roman Catholic Church.
- We are proud to express the faith of the Roman Catholic Church in dialogue with other Christians.
- We respect the beliefs of other Churches.
- We believe in the real presence of Jesus in the Holy Eucharist.
- We believe that reconciliation is a true sacrament of the forgiveness of sins.
- We believe in the dignity of all human life.
- We are specially devoted to Mary, who brought the Word of God into the world.
- We see Mary as the symbol of human dignity.

The above statements only partially describe what it means to be a Roman Catholic. They point out some of the things we believe as Roman Catholics, and how those beliefs affect our lives.

What does it mean to be a Roman Catholic? To be a Roman Catholic means to give ourselves to Jesus entirely—in mind, heart, will, emotion. Our response must be personal and total. As Pope John Paul II has reminded us, we "are called to proclaim, by the conduct of [our] daily lives, that [we] really do believe that Jesus Christ is Lord!" With all members of Christ's Church, we have the duty of living out the gospel and following Jesus.

INDEX

CREDITS

Cover: An original stained-glass work created for Silver Burdett by Andrea Vuocolo

Illustrations: Martin Boelen/Craven Graphics

Maps: R. R. Donnelley Cartographic Services

Time lines: John Lind

Chapter 1 2: Biblioteca Medicea Laurenziana, Florence. 4: The Bettmann Archive. 7: Silver Burdett. 8: Culver Pictures. 9: Shostal Associates. 10: Collegio S. Clemente, Rome.
Chapter 2 14: Bibliothèque Nationale, Paris. 16: Silver Burdett. 19: Courtesy of the Dumbarton Oaks Collection, Washington, D.C. 20: Culver Pictures. 23: Accademia Carrara di Belle Arti, Bergamo. 25: By Courtesy of the Vatican Museums. 26: V. Lefteroff/Shostal Associates.
Chapter 3 28: Joe Barnell/Shostal Associates. 32: Historical Pictures Service. 33: © 1978, The Benedictine Foundation of the State of Vermont, Inc. 34: Abbey of Gethsemani, Kentucky. 35: Margaret McCarthy/Peter Arnold, Inc. 37: Donald Siebert. 38: The Bettmann Archive.
Chapter 4 40, 42: Editorial Photocolor Archives. 44: Fabian/Sygma. 47: Imagery. 48: © Louis Goldman/Photo Researchers, Inc. 49: © Louis Goldman/Photo Researchers, Inc. 50: Ray Manley/Shostal Associates.
Chapter 5 54: Hugh Rogers/Monkmeyer Press. 59: Culver Pictures. 60: Stadtbibliothek, Trier. 61: The Granger Collection. 63: The Bettmann Archive. 64: Niedersachsische Staats und Universitatsbibliothek, Göttingen, W. Germany.
Chapter 6 66: Louvre/Giraudon, Paris. 69: Musée Condé/Giraudon, Paris. 71: *The Normans,* © Macdonald Educational Limited. 73: The Pierpont Morgan Library, New York. M.399, F. 5v. 74: Courtesy Delbarton School. 76: The Bettmann Archive. 77: James Karales/Peter Arnold, Inc.
Chapter 7 80: Fransen, G.: Les Collections Canoniques. Turnhout, Edition Brepols, 1973. (Typologie des Sources du Moyen Age Occidental. Fasc. 10.) 82: Bayerische Staatsbibliothek Munchen, EC 7406. 83: Ann-Victoria Phillips. 84, 85: Giraudon, Paris. 86: Burgerbibliothek, Bern. 88: Wide World Photos. 90: Alain Keler/Sygma. 92: Culver Pictures.
Chapter 8 94: © Peter Larsen/Photo Researchers, Inc. 97: Brown Brothers. 98: Editorial Photocolor Archives. 99: © Mehmet Biber/Photo Researchers, Inc. 101: Culver Pictures. 103: Leon V. Kofod. 104: Giraudon, Paris.
Chapter 9 110: W.B. Finch/Stock, Boston. 112: Brown Brothers. 113: John Oller. 115: The Bettmann Archive. 117: Donald Siebert. 119: Brown Brothers. 123: © Tom Hollyman/Photo Researchers, Inc. 124: Reproduced by permission of The British Library: Ms. 5102 f. 32.
Chapter 10 126: © Berretty/Photo Researchers, Inc. 130: Silver Burdett. 130: Copyright The Frick Collection, New York. 131: J.E. Bulloz. 133: Donald Siebert. 134: Brown Brothers. 137: Scala/Editorial Photocolor Archives. 139: Culver Pictures. 140, 142: Editorial Photocolor Archives. 144: Historical Pictures Service.
Chapter 11 146: Editorial Photocolor Archives. 148: The Bettmann Archive. 149: Eric Carle/Shostal Associates. 151: Historical Pictures Service. 152: Basilica Caterinaiana Di S. Domenico, Siena. 155: Keler/Marcelli/Sygma. 157: The Bettmann Archive.
Chapter 12 162: The Mansell Collection Limited, London. 165: Scala/Editorial Photocolor Archives. 167: © Leonard von Matt/Photo Researchers, Inc. 168, 171: Scala/Editorial Photocolor Archives. 173: Culver Pictures. 174: © Björn Bölstad/Photo Researchers, Inc. 176: Culver Pictures. 177: Ralph F. Kresge/Shostal Associates. 178: © Photo Researchers, Inc.
Chapter 13 182, 185: Culver Pictures. 187: The Granger Collection. 189: Musée du Louvre. 190: Leon V. Kofod. 194: The Bettmann Archive.
Chapter 14 196: Leon V. Kofod. 198: Missionhurst. 200: The Bettmann Archive. 201: Leon V. Kofod. 202: No credit. 204: Museo De América, Madrid.
Chapter 15 208: Musée Victor-Hugo/Giraudon, Paris. 211: The Bettmann Archive. 213, 214: The Granger Collection. 217: Musée du Louvre. 218: The Bettmann Archive. 220: Monumenti Musei E Gallerie Pontificie.
Chapter 16 222: Sygma. 225: Ann-Victoria Phillips. 226: Silver Burdett. 228: The Bettmann Archive. 230: Maryknoll. 231: Courtesy St. Meinrad Archabbey. 232: Leon V. Kofod. 234: Brown Brothers. 237: United Press International. 239: Leon V. Kofod. 240: Michael O'Brien/Black Star.
Chapter 17 242: © 1979 Dilip Mehta/Contact. 245: Ellis Sawyer/Shostal Associates. 247: United Press International. 248: Maryland Historical Society. 250: Culver Pictures. 251: Courtesy of the Daughters of Charity, St. Joseph's Provincial House, Emmitsburg, Maryland. 252: Department of Public Information, Kentucky Department of Tourism. 255: Kathleen/Graham/Baltimore Catholic Review. 257: National Catholic News Service. 259: Rev. Earle A. Newman, S.S.J. 260: Brown Brothers. 261: National Catholic News Service. 264: Bob Fitch. 265: Silver Burdett.